Other books by the author

Japan (1961)
Kafu the Scribbler (1965)
Gendai Sakkaron (1965)
Genji Days (1977)
This Country, Japan (1979)
Low City, High City (1983)
Tokyo Rising (1990)
Very Few People Come This Way (1994)

Translations

Some Prefer Nettles (1955) (*Tade Kuu Mushi,* by Tanizaki Junichiro)
The Makioka Sisters (1957) (*Sasameyuki,* by Tanizaki Junichiro)
Snow Country (1956) (*Yukiguni* by Kawabata Yasunari)
Thousand Cranes (1959) (*Sembazuru,* by Kawabata Yasunari)
House of the Sleeping Beauties (1969) (*Nemureru Bijo,* by Kawabata Yasunari)
The Sound of the Mountain (1970) (*Yama no Oto,* by Kawabata Yasunari)
The Master of Go (1972) (*Meijin,* by Kawabata Yasunari)
The Decay of the Angel (1974) (*Tennin Gosui,* by Mishima Yukio)
The Mother of Michitsuna (1955) (*Kagero Nikki,* by Mishima Yukio)
Revised as *The Gossamer Years* (1964)
The Tale of Genji (1976) (*Genji Monogatari,* by Murasaki Shikibu)

TOKYO CENTRAL

A MEMOIR

EDWARD SEIDENSTICKER

A McLellan Book

University of Washington Press
Seattle and London

This book is published with the assistance of a grant from the McLellan Endowed Series Fund, established through the generosity of Mary McCleary McLellan and Mary McLellan Williams.

Printed in the United States of America
Designed by Sigrid Albert

Library of Congress Cataloging-in-Publication Data

Seidensticker, Edward, 1921–
Tokyo Central : a memoir / Edward Seidensticker.
p. cm.
"A McLellan book."
Includes index.
ISBN 0-295-98134-2 (alk. paper)
1. Seidensticker, Edward, 1921– 2. Critics—United States—Biography. 3. Translators—United States—Biography. 4. Japanese language—Translating into English. 5. Japanese literature—History and criticism. I. Title.
PL713 .S45 2002
895.609—dc21
[B] 2001044283

The paper used in this publication is acid-free and recycled from 10 percent post-consumer and at least 50 percent pre-consumer waste. It meets the minimum requirements of American National Standard for Information Sciences-Permanence of Paper for Printed Library Materials, ANSI Z39.48-1984.

CONTENTS

TOKYO CENTRAL

A MEMOIR

ONE

COLORADO YEARS

I WAS BORN ON FEBRUARY 11, 1921, in an isolated ranch house high up on the north slope of the Arkansas Divide, about half the distance between Denver and Colorado Springs. February 11 marks the anniversary of the founding of Japan. The day is held, on very insecure historical grounds, to be that on which the first ruler of Japan set up court. It used to be called *Kigensetsu,* which means something like "Anniversary of the Beginning." Now it is called *Kenkoku Kinen no Hi,* which means "Anniversary of the Founding of the Land." The earlier name, current when I was born, had been sullied by the excessive nationalism of the war years and the years just before.

Many a Japanese has told me that my birthday indicates a bond from a former life. Though not a believer in the doctrine of reincarnation, I am willing to admit the possibility of my having had earlier lives. I find it hard to imagine the same for Japan. Be that as it may, my birthday is one which Japanese remember. This was more fun back in the days when I was a good toper than it is now. We need not worry about the fact that by the hour of my birth, in late morning, Japan was already several hours into the next day, once known as Lincoln's Birthday. When I am in Japan, I celebrate my birthday on the Anniversary of the Founding of the Land.

Though I rarely if ever felt lonely, my early years may be described as solitary ones. There were not, most of the time, many people around. There were my mother and father, my sister and brother, a shifting assortment of hired hands, increasing and diminishing with the seasons, and an elderly German lady whom, for convenience, we called the housekeeper, but who was really like a member of the family. She was with my father and grandfather before my father was married. Several attempts to live with relatives in Denver ended in failure, and she would come back to us. I think that she was the only person to die in the house, even as I was the only one to be born there. She did not much like me, thinking me a precocious brat, but that was all right. I was devastated each time she departed for a new go at Denver.

The house was then a very new one. My father put it up to welcome his bride. Two other dwelling places stood on the premises. One, in which I can only remember chickens dwelling, was the original claim shanty, already a half-century old when I was born. It was a place we children preferred to stay away from after dark, for it was the site of the great family mystery. Many pioneer families had stories of violence, and this was ours. On a night in 1880 my grandfather's brother Adolph came home on horseback from the village, put his horse up outside the shanty, and was never seen again. People have told me that the whole county joined in the search for him. No trace was ever found. He must have been buried or carted some distance away. Otherwise turkey buzzards would have led to the body the next day.

Years later, my sister Mary Hier took it upon herself to go through correspondence in the basement of "the big house." She learned interesting things.

Here is a part of my diary entry for April 27, 1968. "Adolph . . . seems to have been the entrepreneur of the family. He invested widely in breweries and in mines, and, as my sister remarked, the land seems to have been a sort of sideline, and the other brothers like hired men, while he was around. And who knows, she remarked further, the world might now be drinking Seidensticker beer and not Coors had he survived.

"Our grandfather early decided, to judge from notes for letters back to Germany, that Colorado was not suited for agriculture. He was, in the 1880s, looking around for something else, and meant to move on. And if he had, of course, none of us would have been born. And then what would reality be? Sometimes Buddhism seems to make rather better sense than Christianity.

"In the matter of Adolph's disappearance, all sorts of interesting complications emerge. The land, or most of it, was leased out in 1880, at a time when there seems to have been another lease, not yet expired; and very shortly after Adolph's disappearance, William [my grandfather's other brother] was summoned down from Silver Cliff [in the mountains west of Pueblo, then the second largest city in Colorado], where he was running a brewery, to help cope with the complications, their nature unspecified, on the place. It all sounds very much like an inside job. Grandfather seems to have been in Germany at the time, fetching his mother, and so he at least would seem to be in the clear.

"What lugubrious documents the letters from Germany are, full of illnesses and scoldings and bad weather. Complaining would seem to have been nothing new with us."

The other dwelling place, my grandfather's house before my father married, was a log house covered over with clapboard. In my childhood it was "the bunk house," in which the hired men lived spartan lives. They had neither running water nor an indoor toilet. Then there were barns, corrals, a windmill, and a cistern. The water supply was precarious. A brook called Willow Creek flowed northwards a few yards to the east, except that often it did not flow. In the summer it was often dry. Then it would flood from thunder storms higher up on the divide. It never did us much harm, but occasionally it would help ravage Denver. A few miles to the north it flowed into a larger stream called Cherry Creek. Denver was built at the confluence of Cherry Creek and the South Platte River. Both of these would occasionally overflow their banks and carry off a large part of Denver. We were rather proud to be able to ravage Denver. A Denver flood was almost the only thing that got Douglas County into the newspapers. The upper part of Douglas County, the southern boundary of which was almost at the divide, was famous lightning country. I early learned to reject the notion that lightning never strikes twice in the same place. Certain trees and eminences were constantly being struck.

Though now it has many more people than when I was a child, Douglas County is still the smallest of the piedmont counties, the tier along the east foot of the Rockies in which most Coloradans dwell. The Continental Divide, the ultimate fringe of the Mississippi basin, lies less than a hundred miles to the west. Douglas County was divided between the English, to the west, and the Germans. As should be quite apparent from the name, my father's side of the family was German. Although the Spanish were in the southern part of the state much earlier and there had been French trappers in the northern part, permanent northern-European settlement really got started with the "Pikes Peak gold rush" of 1859.

The center of mining activity was actually in the mountains west of Denver, and Pikes Peak is not far from a hundred miles to the south. It was probably because of the rush that Denver got the lead on Colorado Springs which it has maintained ever since. I have always, myself, preferred Colorado Springs ("The Springs" it is, to us, even as Pikes Peak is "The Peak"). It is a beautifully situated city, at the foot of The Peak, and it has held on to its past as Denver has not. The old north side, the wealthy part of the city, is still back in the Willa Cather days, as I like to call them. Because Denver was nearer and downhill all the way, we did not often go to The Springs.

My mother's maternal grandfather, George Ratcliff, an English immigrant, was a Fifty-Niner. We continue to be very proud of this fact. Having missed out on all the gold, however, he homesteaded land near the mountains and the Platte, on West Plum Creek.

In *A Lady's Life in the Rocky Mountains,* Isabella Bird describes a journey from Denver to Colorado Springs in the 1870s. It took her through the English part of Douglas County, and must have taken her past my great grandfather's house. She went up West Plum Creek and across the divide at a beautiful outcropping of red rock called Perry Park, and down into Colorado Springs. My great grandfather's house lay near the creek. She said that the most conspicuous quality of the English settlers was their greed. This rings true. The pioneer spirit has been much romanticized, and no doubt the pioneers were brave and industrious people, but a conspicuous element in their character was an urge to grab everything in sight.

West Plum Creek probably at the time seemed the natural north-south route across the county. Then the railroad age discovered that gentler gradients lay along harsher and less sheltered East Plum Creek. So that is where the railroads, two of them, went, and it is where such things as interstate highways go.

To West Plum Creek came my grandfather, William Dillon, the son of an Irish political refugee, John Blake Dillon, who lived for a time in New York and then was allowed to return to Ireland. My grandfather was born in New York in 1850, the earliest of my ancestors to be born in America. John Blake Dillon was a leader of the Young Ireland movement, which advocated repeal of the Act of Union with Great Britain. His son and my grandfather's younger brother, John Dillon, was enough of an eminence in Irish politics to merit a photograph and sixty-five lines in the *Britannica.* (He is on the same page as John Dillinger; Joe DiMaggio is on the facing page with a photograph and only half as many lines.) "Through the 1880s he was perhaps the most important ally of the greatest 19th-century Irish Nationalist, Charles Stewart Parnell; but after Parnell's involvement in a divorce case, Dillon repudiated him for reasons of political prudence." An advocate of Home Rule for Ireland, he was more than once imprisoned, and was a member of the British House of Commons from 1880 to 1918, with a gap of two years. His party was thoroughly discredited by the Easter Rising of 1916. Though he made a "passionate speech" (*Britannica*) in Commons defending the rebels, he lost to de Valera in 1918 and retired from politics.

My grandfather came to Colorado for his health. The high, dry air was held to be good for respiratory ailments. He behaved as did The Shining Genji, the hero of the finest Japanese work of fiction, which I was to translate. Here is perhaps further evidence of a bond from a former life. Genji found a most lovable girl not yet of nubile age and waited for her to grow up, that he might marry her. So did my grandfather. My grandmother was a daughter of the Fifty-Niner, earliest of my ancestors to arrive in Colorado.

My grandfather set up a law practice in Castle Rock, the county seat, on East Plum Creek. The first two of his and my grandmother's ten children were born in Castle Rock and died in infancy. The family then removed to Chicago, where the other eight, including of course my mother, were born. The family moved back to Castle Rock during the First World War, and my mother and father met.

The cluster of fences and edifices on Willow Creek was surrounded by hills and out of view of any other building, though the lights of a village far down Cherry Creek could be detected at night. Part of my father's property, just over a hill to the west, was in the Plum Creek valley. Castle Rock lay some five miles away, to the north and west. The population of Castle Rock in the 1930 census was under five hundred. With greatly improved highways and vastly increased use of the automobile, people now commute to Denver. No one would have thought of doing so in my childhood. An expedition to Denver was always allotted a full day.

Castle Rock was tiny and isolated, but it did not seem so, largely because of family. The town was full of aunts of cousins of whom I was fond. I loved blizzards, which were not the dangerous events that they are farther out on the plains, in the Willa Cather country. A blizzard meant, if we were in the village when it started, that the school bus would not venture to Cherry Creek valley. So we would stay with one of the aunts (my mother's sisters-in-law and aunts). My father was an only child. His only Colorado relative, Uncle Wenzel, was a reclusive and somewhat eccentric man of whom we saw little. Until his death he was famous for his chain-drive automobile. I have little notion what a chain drive might be, but I do know that even in those days it belonged to an earlier age. Uncle Wenzel and his chain drive were famous. Children would cheer as he passed.

I did not know either of my German grandparents. My grandfather died when I was a very small child; my grandmother, when my father was a very small child. Had my grandfather lived a few years more, I would probably have learned to speak German. It is a matter of great regret that I did not, though I did presently learn to read it, after a fashion. It was said that my brother, William, who did know my grandfather, initially spoke English with a German accent.

My father always told us what his father had told him, that our German ancestors were Bavarian, from Augsburg. Years later, after my father's death, my sister's scrutiny of surviving letters from Germany persuaded her that, though they may have had origins in the south, they (or my grandfather and two brothers, and presently their mother) came to America from farther north, probably Hesse. I doubt that my father fibbed to us, but his father may have fibbed to him. Maybe Bavaria sounded better than Hesse.

The last years of my grandfather's life were not good ones for Germans and German culture. To be German was bad enough, but to be Hessian was far worse. German was the obvious second language of the county, but it ceased to be taught during the First World War. Spanish instead became the second language, though its only speakers were a score or two of Mexican railway workers.

Prejudice there may have been, but, except for the Mexicans, who definitely were treated as outcasts, it was gentle, unassertive prejudice. The English felt somewhat superior and the Germans somewhat inferior, and that was all. Often people from the two elements were close to and fond of each other. In 1965 my sister received a most wonderful Christmas present from our cousin Mary Clarke, daughter of our redoubtable Aunt Lucy. It was a twenty-dollar gold piece, dated 1888, the year Mary's father, known to us all as Uncle Dick, and a very sweet old man, arrived in Colorado from Devonshire. He was a member of a family with an entry in Burke's Landed Gentry, and so, genealogically, was without question the most eminent person in Douglas County.

The gold piece was given to Uncle Dick by my German grandfather in payment for a head of livestock. Uncle Dick, according to Mary, said he would borrow money before he would let the piece go. He never needed to. The Clarkes were affluent people, and we all wondered why. Aunt Lucy used to say that Uncle Dick never did anything more strenuous than poison prairie dogs after he sold his ranch on West Plum Creek, around the turn of the century, and moved into Castle Rock. Prairie dogs, rather sweet little rodents, had the unfortunate habit of forming large, burrow-digging colonies, and were considered a pest. Probably the Clarke money came from prudent investments of the money from the sale of the land.

I vaguely remember my English grandmother, on her deathbed, beside a window looking up towards the basalt outcropping that gave the town its name. Among my grandparents, my Irish grandfather was the only considerable presence. A cousin in Ireland recently sent me copies of letters from my grandfather to hers. They inform us that his earliest Colorado years, before the Chicago years, were financially troubled. I knew him only as a prosperous lawyer with money to spare for rental properties and such good works as sending my brother and me to Los Angeles for the 1932 Olympics. It was the first time either of us had set foot out of Colorado. My grandfather was a benign presence, an old-world intellectual, very good for a boy who grew up in an isolated, somewhat frontier-like place where there were scarcely any intellectuals at all.

The hills immediately around the house were brown through most of the year. In winter they were often white and in late spring and early summer they were briefly green, and the oak scrub turned russet in the autumn; but for the most part the hills were straw brown. They were not the rich golden brown of California hills in the summer, and yet I came to see them as beautiful, and this for two reasons.

The first was subtle changes in the hills themselves. The untrained eye saw a uniformly insipid brown, but it was not the same brown in August as in March. It was dotted and occasionally carpeted with wild flowers, a parade of them, from April, when plum, pasque flower, and witch hazel came out, to September, when frost got the last holdouts, wild asters and the like. I especially loved the columbines of early summer and the Indian paintbrushes of full summer. The Rocky Mountain columbine blooms on the plains as well as in the mountains. On the plains it finds a hollow no more than three or four feet deep to shelter it from the harsh summer winds, and blooms, a miracle of delicate purple and white (the colors, and they cannot have been accidental, of Douglas County High School). The paintbrushes are bolder, both in color and in choice of habitat. They let the winds tear at them, and would carpet a hillside here and there, not just every hillside, with a brilliant vermilion. The columbines seemed of the mountains and the paintbrushes of the plains, and it was here that the two came together.

Not every element in those hills was benevolent. I remember standing on a high one with my sister, who frequently went walking with me (my brother, always being about business of his own, never did). "I wonder how many rattlesnakes there are down there," said she, with a sweeping gesture that included most of the three hundred sixty degrees. How many indeed. I had no notion then and have none now, though the count must have been considerable. I sometimes encountered them and was not afraid of them. No one I knew had ever been bitten by one, though there were stories of pioneers who had. James Michener, in his book about Colorado, has a tall tale in that regard. To me, they seemed shy, rather polite creatures. They gave warning of their presence and speedily got out of the way. My acceptance of them has something a touch Japanese about it (such numbers of bonds from former lives). Nagai Kafū, one of my favorite modern writers, includes unfriendly elements, such as mosquitoes, in his poetic evocations of summer, and it is as if summer without them would be a damaged, incomplete summer.

Then there was the distant view. From the second floor of our house we could see the summit of The Peak. We always gathered there on New Year's Eve to watch the fireworks set off on The Peak by some band of madmen. We could see no other fragment of the Rockies. From the hills to the east they were spread out grandly, a hundred miles or so of them, from The Peak on the left to Long's Peak, beyond Denver, on the right.

It has often enough been pointed out that the Rockies in themselves are not all that much. The plains have already risen some seven thousand feet before the mountains take over and add another seven thousand and a bit more. This is true. Yet the sudden wall of mountains after all the hundreds of miles of flatness must have been salvation for the pioneers. It was something like that for me, too. As a boy, despite my fondness for the brown hills, I felt protected by the mountains on the west and exposed to the plains on the east. Standing on a hill to the east of the house and gazing at the mountains in the sunset, I think I sometimes had what may be described as a mystic experience. I felt a divine flow. Sometimes when

I went back down to the house my mother would ask why I had been so utterly still up there for so long a time. I did not try to explain. Often it was very cold up there, the best times being in winter, when the twilight would turn a hundred miles of snow, Pikes Peak to Long's Peak, to a deep rose.

Many years later, almost a half century after I had left Colorado, I read, in George Kennan's *Sketches from a Life* (Pantheon 1989), an account of his visit to the Air Force Academy, a few miles north of Colorado Springs, in the land of my early years, where the plains and the mountains meet. He found the academy "a stark and forbidding place," and as for the setting, "one wonders why they chose it, unless it be that there is endless room around it for airports."

Several thoughts came to me almost simultaneously. Nearly everyone in Colorado assumed that the site had been selected because Mamie Eisenhower was from Denver. Moreover, we all considered it a beautiful site. I wondered if Kennan was aware that Katharine Lee Bates wrote "America the Beautiful" in the Antlers Hotel in Colorado Springs, after an ascent of Pikes Peak.

And I thought: the casual visitor does not see very much. It is a thought that came to me repeatedly during the fifties, the golden age of the "progressive" intellectuals in Japan. They were always coming back from a week or a fortnight in The New China and telling us of the paradise they had seen. How little they can really have seen, I thought.

There was no Air Force Academy there at the edge of the plains during my boyhood in the 1920s and 30s. Indeed there was no Air Force.

The Catholic Church of my boyhood was built from money donated by one of my Irish uncles, of a part of the family that stayed in Dublin. A quarter of a century or so ago a new church was built, high on a hill east of the town, with a splendid view, beyond the windows beyond the altar, of Pikes Peak. At first I thought that the view must be exactly as the pioneers first saw it. This is no longer true. The hills leading up to the divide are now dotted with houses. Of the old church I have a little to say in a diary entry from the summer of 1976, the bicentennial summer for the nation and the centennial one for Colorado, the Centennial State. "The old Catholic Church, down in the creek bottom, has become a restaurant. I would feel very strange going in and having a hamburger there where rested all the family coffins; but no one else in the family seems to be bothered in the least."

All three of us went through elementary school and high school in Castle Rock. Douglas County was not, at the time, big enough to have a junior high school, though it has several now. Elementary school was cozy, like the town itself. Douglas County had only one high school, and uncouth elements from the outer reaches of the county came to it. I had no trouble communicating with my teachers in elementary school. High-school teachers sometimes seemed next to incomprehensible. The worst was the physics teacher during my third year in high school. He picked up a junked automobile somewhere and brought it to school and told us to get it running. That would be the course. I did not know where to begin and never found out, and I still know scarcely anything about physics. It was the only time in my life when I seriously considered quitting school. The teacher told my mother that I certainly did hate to get my hands dirty. That was not the point at all.

Adolescence is doubtless a difficult time for many people, but it is especially difficult for a youngster who cannot do the things that command the respect of his peers. I was no good at baseball or basketball or yet again at football. I was a dreadful dancer. I was a complete failure at getting pieces of junk to cough and turn over. And although Douglas County was in those days very much horse country, I was no good at horses. I kept falling off and being ordered back on again, lest I give up horses permanently. I got good grades, which were if anything a handicap. Good Colorado boys did not get good grades. Even the physics teacher gave me an A.

My maternal grandfather, the lawyer, died while I was in high school. His office, down near the courthouse, stood unused. I had a key, and after a fashion I took over. Tired of being the last person chosen for noon-hour games of basketball, I would have my lunch and slip away to his office, where I would read. He had a good if somewhat eccentric library. The office was unheated, freezing cold through most of the Colorado winter, but I did not mind. A cold never killed anyone, I told myself. I knew as well then as I know now that this is not true. I do not know how precocious I was in general, but my reading was precocious. While he was alive my grandfather kept pressing Scott on me. After he was dead I turned to better authors, Dickens, Thackeray, Twain, and (yes) Tolstoy. I do not dissemble when I say that I liked Tolstoy the best of them, and Mark Twain the least.

The village people were most of them good people. There was, to be sure, the Ku Klux Klan, which burned a cross outside my grandfather's house on the night in 1928 when one of my uncles was elected to the state legislature. As the fright wore off, the cross-burning came to seem far less important than my uncle's election to the legislature.

Another Klan incident, still more frightening, had to do with Aunt Lucy. At a church gathering, the possibility was brought up of accepting a contribution from the Klan for some building project. Aunt Lucy got up and said that if the church accepted such a contribution she was taking her own contribution back. She had her way, but some men insisted on seeing her home, lest she be assaulted.

Aunt Lucy was a remarkable woman, an ecologist long before the word was invented. I wondered even as a boy why she allowed Uncle Dick to go poisoning prairie dogs. (Maybe it was to keep him out of the house. Once, when he returned from a trip to England, she said to us: "You know in some ways I'm kind of glad Dick's back.") She fiercely defended the bats that had taken up residence over the ceiling of her sun porch. Leave them alone, she said. They do no harm and they are there for a reason. Insecticides were thought a blessing because they destroyed the swarms of grasshoppers that otherwise destroyed the crops. Aunt Lucy was against their use. They may kill grasshoppers, said she, but they kill bees too. Everyone in Castle Rock kept chickens in those days. Now no one does. Castle Rock is now suburban Denver, and chickens offend suburban sensibilities. For most households it was a disaster when the coyotes captured a chicken. Aunt Lucy took a different view. She raised half her chickens for herself, she said, and half for the coyotes.

I did not come to know until much later how very good the people of the village could be. I did not know in what straits our family was during the depression, and the two are related. The facts were kept from us children. I do not remember that my mother and father ever spoke of money in our presence. Much later, when things were better, my father would say that the very worst time was during the years of the agrarian depression of the 1920s, which preceded the great depression.

My brother was no help to my sister and me when we cleaned out the house. He was usually off pursuing idiosyncracies. He was an intelligent and eccentrically gifted person, but he was very badly organized. (I use the past tense because he died a few months short of his eightieth birthday.) Once in a high-school basketball game he scored a basket for the opposing team. Exactly the sort of thing you would expect him to do, we all said, smiling, though without great amusement. He started medical school at the University of Colorado, left after his first year, and thereafter did not do much of anything. He never held a job for any length of time. It was good that the family fortunes improved sufficiently, after the great depression, that my brother did not have to work.

He had a remarkable feeling for rocks, and what seemed to me an uncanny ability to spot a rock that was not where it should be. He would pick up a rock on a rocky slope and say: "An Indian thing. See? Here is where the fingers went." And I would see. Until then it had been merely another rock on a rocky slope. I used to say myself that something could be done with the talent, but I could not think of anything, and he never thought of anything for himself. The only other member of the family who noticed and cared was my Yokohama uncle, who was not around very much, and of whom more will be said later.

After the war, when my mother died and my sister and I were clearing out the house preparatory to renting it, I went snooping through my father's hugely accumulated correspondence. He seems not to have thrown away the smallest and most worthless scrap of paper. All the bills from the agrarian depression were there. They showed how very good the merchants of the village had been to us. Grocery bills, for instance, accumulated to what were in those days astronomical proportions. I came upon no suggestion from the grocer that even fragmentary payment might be called for. Doubtless he knew that it would come when it was possible, and he could manage until then. People did not much worry about inflation in those days.

Nor was I aware what a dirt-poor place Douglas County, on the whole, was. A professor at the University of Colorado remarked one day that if we wanted to see real poverty we should explore the hills south of Denver. I was startled. This had to be my own Douglas County. I looked at it more carefully, and saw that he was essentially right. Some of my elementary-school fellows lived little better than the French trappers.

The urge to run away from it all lasted only through that physics class. When the time came to leave Castle Rock and Douglas County, I did not show huge courage and enterprise. I wanted to go East to school, but my father did not have enough money, and I was not up to venturing forth on my own. I made do with the University of Colorado, at Boulder, about as far north of Denver as Castle Rock is south. I grumbled about going there, but went all the same, and took with me a certain sense of privilege. My brother and I were the only ones in the graduating class at Douglas County High School to go to college at all.

The University of Colorado was better by a good deal than Douglas County High School had been, but I did not really like it. Quite a few years after I graduated, a letter from the university soliciting a donation caught me in a surly mood. I wrote back that it owed me money for having failed to do better by the most impressionable years of my life. This was not a pleasant way to put the matter, though requests for donations did not cease to flow in. Nevertheless it sums up a problem I have trouble putting into words at all, the reasons for my discontent with Boulder and its university. I suppose the basic trouble was that "the East" was still there. I had no immediate knowledge of this entity, having never been east of Chicago, but there it was, and it was better.

My grandfather and several of my uncles were lawyers, and it seemed to be assumed by everyone, including myself, that I would be a lawyer too. Towards this end I chose a most inappropriate major, economics, and for this choice I must blame family, and not the university. Even we on the remote edge of the Mississippi basin could see that war was coming, from one direction or the other, and quite possibly from both. So I decided to enjoy myself through the last year before I would go out to fight for my country. I changed my major to English. I made noises as of going on to graduate school, largely to placate my parents, who saw no future in English.

I was not aware, either in Castle Rock or in Boulder, of something that was wanting in both places. I had made no fixed friends. I continue to go back to Colorado to visit relatives. I still have no real friends there. With one or two isolated exceptions, my oldest friends are from the war years. I may not have been very fond of Boulder, but I was and am fond of Douglas County. Perhaps it is one of those phenomena that must be set down to chance. Or perhaps the point is that when I went away from Colorado, I went away with some firmness and finality, knowing that I would not live there again.

The attack on Pearl Harbor came a few months before I was due to graduate from the university. I had until then not the slightest interest in Japan or other places out in that direction. An aunt and uncle lived in Yokohama for a half dozen years just before the war, and what they told me of it aroused neither interest nor affection. It was a bad time, and for them, as for most of us, Japan was a bad place. My aunt said that throughout her first three years in Yokohama, she was lonely; throughout the second three, she was frightened.

Nor was I attracted by what small amount I read about the place. Geisha, with their massive, unwashable heaps of black hair, were ugly, unclean creatures. Fuji was an uninteresting pimple of a mountain. And Japanese gardens were dark, murky places. Imagine it, they had no flowers. My aunt and uncle came home as war loomed near. My aunt said that a huge and spontaneous cheer swept over the ship as it pulled away from the Yokohama docks. The Japanese below shouted something back, but she did not understand it. One cannot believe that it was friendly. So things were in those days.

Boulder provided devices for getting through the war in reasonable safety and comfort. I had not the smallest notion, when I went into the university, that this would happen. I am grateful. I am very sure, though I cannot be absolutely certain, that a life of Japanese was more interesting than a life of English would have been.

TWO

WAR YEARS

IT IS SAID THAT EVERYONE WHO is old enough to remember the Kennedy assassination remembers exactly where he or she was when the news came. I think the same is probably true of the smaller band that remembers Pearl Harbor.

I went to Mass that Sunday morning at Mount St. Gertrude's, a Catholic girls' academy up the hill from my fraternity house. Though I was not really much of a Greek, as they were called, to contrast them with the barbarians, who were all the others, I did belong to a fraternity and lived in a fraternity house. I had came back from Mass and was sitting down to morning coffee and the heap of comic strips and ads known as the *Denver Post* when I heard the news. It was no surprise. Seeking to give legitimacy to the horrid things "they" were doing in China, they were bound to attack us some Sunday (when we were all innocently at Mass).

So how, then, did I become interested in Japan? I fear I am not one of those who experienced an epiphany that started it all. One hears of this person for whom it was a Japanese cherry tree in full bloom, or that person for whom it was a copy of *The Tale of Genji* come upon for almost nothing in a used-book store. Whatever it was, it brought a conviction, an illumination. The person must learn Japanese. I regret to say that I am always reminded of Senator Joseph McCarthy, whose afflatus came, I believe, as he was looking into the sunset over the Arizona desert. He suddenly knew what he must do. He must root out evil Communism. From my own experiences with Colorado sunsets I can believe that such things occur, even though I find it hard to imagine divine grace coming over the loutish countenance of the senator. So it is too with accounts of beautiful beginnings of beautiful engagements with Japan and the Japanese. They may have happened, but I wonder.

Certainly nothing of the sort happened to me. I have said that I had no interest in Japan and the Japanese before Pearl Harbor. Pearl Harbor did not suddenly bring it. The attack seemed a crime, and not the sort of crime that arouses fascination, as serial murders might, with the character of the perpetrators. For me there was only the big question: How was I to get through the war?

In terms of the military, I occupied an unfortunate in-between position. I have always had perfectly sound though imperfectly shaped eyes. I was probably born with them. Ever since I began school, I have worn glasses to correct myopia and astigmatism. This meant that I could not hope for the better things, one of the elite (or so they seemed) services or a commission. Yet I remained eligible for the draft. I by no means wanted to go into the infantry as an enlisted man. My parents were not ideally supportive. They probably thought me a bit of a coward, not a proper heir to the pioneer spirit, and they were probably right. For my father there was an added complication. He was on the draft board in Douglas County and wanted nothing to do with my problem. So he had my case transferred to Boulder. In these circumstances, staying on in Boulder, after I graduated in June of 1942, made sense.

I got a job in the university library, the temporary and poorly paid kind which the Japanese call *arubaito,* and hoped that something would come along. During those peaceful summer months, for summer is the loveliest season in Boulder, as it is not in Castle Rock, I had my first taste of war. I was summoned by the Boulder draft board for an examination of some sort. I sent regrets, for I had a prior engagement. A man called and gave me the first real dressing down I had ever had. I would be present at the hour specified, he said, and no ifs or buts would be tolerated. So I was. Unfortunately I passed the test. I hoped ever more fervently that something would come along. I was obsessed with my problem all through that summer. A kind professor at the university invited me to attend, with all fees waived, a writers' conference of which he was in charge. I declined. Would my life have been different had I accepted? I shall always wonder.

Something did come along. Even as I fretted, the president of the university seems to have fretted on a much larger scale about getting a sadly depleted university through the war. One of the devices he hit upon was to invite the Navy Japanese Language School to Boulder. The invitation was accepted, and that summer the school came, leaving the University of California. It could not stay there because most of the teachers were either Japanese or Americans of Japanese ancestry. Even though they were doing valuable work for the United States, they had to leave the West Coast, the extremely unfortunate business of relocation having been decided upon. So all of them, students and faculty, picked up and came across the mountains, and their arrival in Boulder made a huge difference in my life.

Among the students was Donald Keene, to become a good friend in Japan and a colleague at Columbia. I read the first chapter of his memoirs, *On Familiar Terms,* with much astonishment. This event of such major importance to me seems to have meant nothing at all to him. The language school is in the memoirs, but the move to Boulder is not, and neither Boulder nor Colorado is in the index.

Because my work in the library was at the circulation desk, I got to know several students in the language school. Some of them, of course, I liked better than others. Some of them seemed a touch supercilious.

Here, in any event, was a very good thing. The navy was prepared to grant waivers for people deemed admissible to the language school. I could get a waiver for my dysfunctional eyes and presently a commission. Here, in a word, was the solution to my problem.

I screwed up courage to ask for an interview with the navy captain in charge of administering the school, seeing that all the boys (there were no girls until later) got fed, and that sort of thing. He was discouraging. I came to suspect, presently, that he did not know what he was talking about. Then I went for an interview with the lady in charge of instruction, Florence Waln, from the University of California, now long in her grave. A plump, bouncy lady, she was not encouraging exactly, but she was friendly, and gave me a good notion of what was to be done.

Admissions to the school were managed in Washington, D.C. Since the eminences there did not propose coming to Boulder in the foreseeable future, I must go to them. The next group of students, a small group, was to begin its studies in October. The one after that would not be coming until December. I was almost certain that by December the Boulder draft board would have me. So I borrowed money from my father, who was by then able to pay the grocery bill, and went to Washington. He was better off because of the war, which in 1942 was having its effect on the

American economy. It is an ill wind, the Japanese saying has it, from which the cooper does not profit.

I have said that I had never before been east of Chicago. I was frightened about going to Washington, but if I did not go I would almost certainly end up in the least desirable of the armed forces. I rather enjoyed the trip. I happened to have an uncle there, the uncle who had lived in Yokohama. He saw that my trousers were pressed for the interview with the eminence, and presently put me on the train for New York, which, being so close, I was determined to have a look at.

The eminence was a kindly gentleman of middle years and the interview proved to be not much of anything at all. His name was Glenn Shaw. Having read no Japanese literature at the time, I did not know that he was an eminence in another regard. He was a pioneer translator of modern Japanese literature, and his name was known to everyone whose ignorance was less complete. We had a pleasant chat for ten minutes or so, much of it about Colorado, for he too was a Coloradan. I suppose he looked me over and concluded that I had the proper count of limbs and would not be a disgrace to the navy. He had been in college with my Yokohama aunt and uncle (talk of Castle Rock, which, improbably, he knew, brought the fact out), and that helped. No word was spoken about my linguistic accomplishments and capabilities. After I got to know a little about Japan, I might have called it a Japanese sort of interview, touching on nothing genuinely relevant, but giving a certain feeling for things. When the ten minutes had passed, he told me to go back to Colorado and get ready for language school.

I did, but I spent a week or so in New York. My first impression has proved perdurable, that New York is a frightening but glorious place. The time of my visit lay on the border between summer and autumn, not a part of the New York Season. Still I thought it grand. Being afraid of the subway, I explored by bus and on foot, Fort Tryon to the Battery. I even took the Staten Island Ferry. Staten Island, or Richmond, was the only one of the outer boroughs on which I set foot. It seemed not so different from suburban Denver, except that there were no mountains on the western horizon.

As I look back over all my years, I find a continuity between the language school and what followed. There is very little except family between it and the years that preceded. I count, or counted until they died, perhaps a dozen people I met at language school among my friends.

There are few from my undergraduate years and before: a handful of aged and aging people from pioneer Douglas County families, Bret Kelly and his wife, who live in Pueblo, in southern Colorado, then the second largest city in the state, and Bonnie Larkin Nims—and no one else that I can think of. I am in touch with no one at all from my grade-school and high-school graduating classes, and only Bret and Bonnie from my college years. I would call Bret a friend, though we have met only once since our Boulder days.

Bonnie Nims, née Larkin, wife of the poet John Frederic Nims, was not really of Boulder. She went to summer school there in I think it must have been 1940. She and another girl from St. Mary's College in South Bend, where they were students, lived in my fraternity house. Also in summer school, I waited table. I quite fell in love with her, and then when summer school was over she went away. I had known no young woman in Boulder half so amusing.

On the afternoon before I returned to Boulder, to go thence with my new classmates to the navy recruiting office in Denver and become, myopia and all, a yeomen second class in the navy, I went on a lone walk through the hills. It was a beautiful walk. The hills were dotted with purple flowers of autumn. I knew that during the year ahead I could go on other similar walks, but the expedition to Denver and the recruiting office seemed to mark an end to my Colorado years. I think if I had been told that evening that I could spend the rest of my life at home doing not one thing but walk through the hills, I would have accepted.

The expedition was rather fun, as it turned out. The recruiting staff kept coming upon discoveries that made it laugh its heads off (for we were a band that needed a lot of waivers). The most remarkable was that among my classmates was a fellow who had only one testicle. I never asked him, though we became rather good friends, what happened to the other, and he never told me.

The Navy Language School was a very good school. Students always grouse about their teachers and classes, and we groused. I still think we should have been taught a little grammar. Because we were taught none, I go on having trouble with verbs, especially in remembering which are transitive and which are not. This does not keep me from being understood, but I am quite aware that I must sometimes sound a bit peculiar. Every course of instruction can be improved upon, and the important point is that this one taught us a remarkable amount of Japanese in fourteen months (it was only a year when Keene went through it). The theory behind the absence of grammar was that we should learn the language as an infant does, by using it. We were immediately plunged into speaking the language and reading the remarkably complicated, some might say ridiculously complicated, system of writing. The theory ignores the inconvenient fact that infants and young adults are not the same creatures.

I still hear things about the language school that are not true. I hear, for instance, that we were not permitted to use English. It was Japanese all through the day and into the night. Miss Waln was much too sensible a person for anything of the sort. She probably knew that we were a rather neurotic lot from the outset, and that any such regimen would have pushed us over the border into madness. Still it was a crash course, and perhaps a revolutionary one.

Accepted truth before the war was that no person without an epicanthic fold (the slanted eyelid) could learn any of the Oriental languages. That the school dismissed this as nonsense was an important breakthrough. By the end of the fourteen months we could read a newspaper. We may not have read it with ease, but the fact that we could do so at all was, by prewar standards, scarcely believable.

Another important thing about the school was that, though we yeoman second class were required to march in formation for an hour or so a week, we might as well not have been in the navy, for all the difference military things made in our lives. The Navy Japanese Language School was better, in my view, than the Army Japanese Language School in Ann Arbor. High on the list of explanations must be the fact that they were required to be more military than we.

The band that began studying Japanese in October, 1942, and went on doing so until December, 1943, was known as the fall group. Those who came in December were known as the winter group, and then all seasonal designations ceased, because the flow of new students was strong and steady. We were the smallest group in the school, under thirty in number, and as such, we had had a certain esprit. We were most of us about the same age, and most of us recent college graduates.

There were among us objects of awe, yeomen who had learned spoken Japanese as children in Japan. These were the BIJs, our aristocrats, "born in Japan." They had a discouraging effect. We suffered from a social disability we could never overcome, having been born in the wrong place. It was impossible to think that we could ever know as much Japanese as they.

Some of us did manage, after a fashion. A BIJ colleague at the University of Michigan once remarked that the BIJs presently got overtaken, and the important scholars of later decades were not among their numbers. He is a generous, self-effacing sort of fellow, and what he said was not entirely true; but there is an element of truth in it. BIJs are scarce among the most conspicuously productive scholars of their generation.

There were a couple of men who were even more aristocratic, perhaps, than the BIJs. They had been taken by the Japanese in China, one, I believe, in Hong Kong and the other in Shanghai, and they had been brought home by the device known as the *Gripsholm* exchanges. Japanese internees were taken from the United States to Mozambique, the Portuguese colony in southern Africa, and there exchanged for American internees who had been brought to Mozambique by the Japanese. The *Gripsholm* was the Swedish ship that negotiated the western half of the journey. An air of wild adventure hung over these two. One of them had actually tried to escape from Japanese internment and had been recaptured.

There were people who, though not born in Japan, had lived there and picked up an amount of the language. (My Yokohama aunt and uncle picked up not the smallest bit of it—but they were business people, and business people tended not to associate much with Japanese.) These were people from universities where Japanese was taught, as it was not at the University of Colorado. Most of them had taken advantage of this fact to get a small start.

And then there were those, a minority, who had no start at all. I need scarcely say that I was one of them. These facts considered, I am not at all ashamed of my performance at language school. We marched into the graduation ceremony in the order of our scholastic record. I do not remember precisely my number, but I was among the top half dozen.

The year at language school was the best of my five Boulder years. The reason is by no means difficult to define. The fall group, man for man, were more interesting than my fellow undergraduates. But for them, I would not have come to love Bach and Mozart as I do, which fact is of little importance to the greater world, but of much importance to me. Though the members of the fall group are not all of them still living, I am in correspondence with a high percentage of those who are. This is not because we were, some of us, to face boot camp and presently bullets together but because they were interesting. Most of them were educated on one of the two coasts, and this fact is not without significance.

I perhaps aroused suspicions of having suicidal tendencies when the time came for us to become officers. We had our choice between the navy and the Marine Corps. About a quarter of the class chose the latter, and we were together through the rest of the war. I think that among the half dozen of us I had the poorest qualifications for becoming a good leatherneck.

I think boyish romanticism best explains why I chose the marines. A heavy air of the romantic, Montezuma and Tripoli and all that, hung over the corps. And possibly I wanted to convince my parents that I was not a coward. I did not, in the process, wholly convince myself.

So, just two years after the momentous attack, graduation came, and farewell to Colorado. I sensed that it was a conclusive sort of farewell. I have gone back, many times, even for whole summers. I would not live there again, however.

Colorado still means a great deal to me. I see more and more that my solitary boyhood was also a beautiful boyhood, and those high, dry hills (along with my grandfather's library) are what made it so. I feel, in an elusive way, that being from Colorado is somehow distinguished. In an obvious way it is, because the count of people from Colorado is such a small one. Colorado has the highest average elevation above sea level among the states, and so can look down on the others. The name is a beautiful one, much more so than those of the neighboring states, except possibly Wyoming. I was presently to learn that a great many Japanese know of Colorado because of moonlight on it. The nature of "it" was for a time somewhat troublesome. I would try to explain to Japanese that Colorado and *the* Colorado are not the same, but I soon gave up. The distinction is not possible in their language. I tried initially to point out the silliness of the song. A person bathed, with his or her beloved, in moonlight on the Colorado has to be stranded in the middle of the night in very harsh desert. In this regard too I soon decided to leave well enough alone.

We of the marine contingent headed for the East Coast, each by his own devices. I chose to go via St. Louis, chiefly because I wanted a look at Kansas and Missouri. The standard route from Denver to Chicago went farther north, along the Platte and across Iowa. Western Kansas was much like eastern Colorado, harsh plains repellent to most people but not to me. I was much surprised to see that eastern Kansas was rather pretty.

So was Missouri. Most of the hired men of my boyhood had been from Missouri. They had not prepared me for anything so gentle. St. Joseph was the starting point for the Oregon Trail, early stages of which were also a major route to Denver and Colorado. I looked eagerly for St. Joseph but did not find it. I think probably it lay a bit farther north. I kept thinking how poorly the gentle lushness of Missouri must have prepared the pioneers for the high plains and the desert.

My second sojourn on the East Coast was by no means as pleasant as my first. My bourne, and that of the others from Boulder, was the coast of North Carolina. It was not the fault of North Carolina that I had such a bad time there. It was the fault of boot camp, which was genuinely dreadful. Being for officers, it was doubtless less demanding and more tolerant than the camp for enlisted men. Still it was dreadful, enough to make one wonder what sort of hell the Marine Corps could have contrived for enlisted men.

The gentility of the South may have lain across the pine barrens somewhere, but it was no part of our lives. For us there were sand and snow driven by nor'easters and a regimen of obstacle courses (which inevitably brought immersion in freezing water), and forced marches (which inevitably brought frostbite and blisters). The corps seemed diabolically resourceful at devising a more unpleasant day to succeed an unpleasant one; and this was a training school for commissioned persons who outranked most of their instructors.

There was one touch of Southern gentility, a trip a friend and I took by automobile to Charleston. Here were beauty and grace. Since Charleston is reported to have escaped progress and development in large measure, it is probably as pleasant a place now as it was then. I would not at all mind going back to Charleston, and have not the smallest desire to return to Wilmington, North Carolina.

It was winter when we left North Carolina, and full spring when we reached Camp Pendleton, across the continent, between Los Angeles and San Diego. More than a continent stood between the coast of North Carolina and the coast of California, and more than a change of seasons. The journey westward was like an escape from hell. The dry, open landscape was like home, though the colors were richer, all gold and purple into the distance. North Carolina was all black and white, pine trees and snow. And California had hills. There was not the smallest mound along the coast of North Carolina.

I have since come to prefer the north of California, but in my youth I liked the south. Los Angeles was a beautiful, medium-size city when first I saw it in 1932. I especially loved the way the golden hills would emerge, late each morning, from the coastal fogs. It was still a beautiful city during the war, and the bus ride from Camp Pendleton to Los Angeles, through the orange groves that then carpeted Orange County, was uncommonly beautiful.

At Pendleton we were in training for we knew not what, though it turned out to be Iwo Jima. The training was more military than at Boulder and less so than in North Carolina. We went on long marches, free of sand, wind, and snow, and we maneuvered inflatable boats through the surf. We climbed up and down landing nets, and we learned how to make our way out of hopeless situations. One of the Boulder contingent failed to return one evening from a practical exercise in the hopeless. When finally he did come straggling in, he said that things had gone from bad to worse after he took an azimuth on a cloud. One of our generals broke a leg in a landing net and was unable to go to Iwo. How we did laugh. I have rather pleasant memories of it all. Not a good leatherneck, I received more than one dressing down, for superior officers had a way of attributing mischief and malice to what was merely ineptitude; but memory softens the pain and resentment of such experiences.

It was during the Pendleton months that I first encountered prisoners of war. Japanese soldiers captured in the Solomon Islands and Micronesia were being held in a camp in northern California, a short distance inland from San Francisco Bay. We were sent to practice our Japanese on them. With regard to these unfortunates, I have long wanted to say a thing or two. It is not easy, in the middle of a battle, to take a prisoner, even one who wishes to surrender, and the Japanese tended strongly not to. Arrangements must be made for sending the prisoner back to headquarters, and meanwhile the battle rages. It is far more expeditious to shoot him.

We spent quite a number of hours, especially in the Hawaiian Islands, lecturing enlisted leathernecks on the importance of prisoners and the procedures for taking and enrolling them. Our audiences listened quietly but with little show of interest. Probably not a few were deciding that they would do the expeditious thing. I hate to think how many of the young men listening to our sermons died on Iwo.

Another thing is that we were good to our prisoners of war, and it may be said with some confidence that the Japanese were not good to theirs. I have used the word "camp" to designate the place where they were interned by the bay, but it was not an encampment at all. It was a pleasantly seedy, hot-spring hotel whose good days seem to have been around the turn of the century. Probably the worst thing about the prisoners' life was the boredom, and not much could be done about that.

They themselves did their own tiny bit towards alleviating it, as we learned through our arrangements, probably illegal under international law, for eavesdropping on them. They had great fun imitating us. We could tell which of us they were imitating, for some of them were rather good mimics. They never imitated our two BIJs. It would have been like self-imitation, which is not easy. Occasionally I identified myself. I doubt that anyone would enjoy such an experience. Certainly I did not. Yet, though chagrined, I could not be angry with them. They seemed like perfectly good boys who had had bad luck. What they might have done had they had San Francisco to rape, as they had Nanking and Manila, is another matter. In any event, I acquired a distaste for interrogation that never left me.

We arrived at Pendleton early in 1944, and we departed it late in 1944 for the Hawaiian Islands. Our camp was beyond the highest if not the biggest of the mountains, Mauna Kea, from Hilo, on the "Big Island," Hawaii. It was called Tarawa, after the atoll captured in the bloodiest battle thus far in the central Pacific. It was situated on the Parker Ranch, on a very dry and dusty tract, with, such being the spottiness of the island climate, rain forest an easy walk away. Volcanic dust would get into the most tightly locked and taped trunk.

When I am asked to relate my most horrid experience all through the war, an honest answer must be a somewhat disappointing one. It had to do with the pistol that was, after all, loaded. I was cleaning mine, and it went off. The bullet went through the side of the tent and on into the tent across the way, and who knows what beyond that. I sat petrified, pistol in lap, waiting for the police to come. They did not, and presently I put the pistol away. That is the end of the story. Miraculously, the bullet had struck nothing of significance. I never even received an inquiry about the holes in the two tents and perhaps others. That this should have been the worst of my wartime experiences demonstrates that for me the war was not replete with horror. It embarrasses me to have to admit that on the whole I rather enjoyed it. The weeks in North Carolina were worse than the weeks on Iwo.

We language officers were presently sent to Pearl Harbor, to keep ourselves at work on the language. We were on the staff of the translation and interpretation section of CINCPAC-CINCPOA. In charge of the wondrous acronym was the highly respected Admiral Nimitz, whom we thought of as keeping General MacArthur out of our hair. I would pass him on a street occasionally, out for a stroll, and would salute him and get saluted back. He reminded me of the kindly gentleman of the interview in Washington.

The general, not at all popular in the corps, was the butt of many a joke and many a jingle in those days, and in Occupation days as well. I sometimes thought that the Marine Corps, in those days, hated the army more than it hated the Japanese. One quatrain of doggerel remains with me. It was sung to the tune of "Bless 'em All."

> We asked for the Army to come to Tulagi
> But Douglas MacArthur said no.
> He gave as his reason it wasn't the season.
> Besides, there was no U.S.O.

Tulagi is in the Solomon Islands, and the fighting in the Solomons was the turning point in the South Pacific. The Japanese advanced no farther towards Australia and would presently have been in retreat had there been anywhere to retreat to. The U.S.O. is probably better remembered. It stands for United Service Organizations, which offered genteel and innocent female companionship to lonely boys in uniform.

Our routine in Pearl Harbor was to alternate weeks of translation of captured documents with weeks of interrogation. The documents were chiefly conspicuous for their dullness, though an occasional flash of unintentional humor was to be detected. I especially liked, though it presently got to be a bore, a standard paragraph in battle orders: "We will fight to the last man on the beach. Then we will withdraw and fight to the last man at the airstrip." The impression that the Japanese are sometimes not very rational has never completely left me.

In a hallway lay a big heap of documents through which we could rummage in search of something that might perhaps be ever so slightly interesting. The heap was constantly being sorted into boxes by subject and importance. One box bore the label: "Pure crap. Send to Washington."

The objects of the interrogation were Japanese prisoners. There was a camp full of them, and this really was a camp, at Iroquois Point. I hated interrogation. At Iroquois Point it came to seem utterly without meaning. I was sure that it would do nothing to improve my spoken Japanese.

I had come to think of myself as more a reader than a speaker. I still do, which is a pity, since speaking makes good money.

It was moreover quite unlikely that any new information would emerge from the interrogations. The prisoners seemed completely bored with it, and they had every right to be. They had been interrogated to the teeth. Since some of them were fairly literate, it seemed strange that they did not make things up for us to take back to the harbor and use for brownie points.

I had fairly friendly feelings towards the prisoners in California, no feelings of any sort towards those in Hawaii. I have often wondered why. It may have been, partly at least, because in California we had the prisoners to ourselves. In Hawaii, the navy was always messing around.

In any event, the prisoners did not emerge as individuals. It would be good to be able to say that I formed lasting friendships, but it would not be true. In the years since the war I have occasionally come across a Japanese who had been at Iroquois Point. I got to know a journalist or two fairly well, and for a time I went to an ear doctor who had been there. But I have never come upon a face that called up memories of the point and its camp.

So one day I asked the captain if I could be excused from interrogation. I did not think for a moment that I would be, but I was. The captain was the highest ranking officer among us from Camp Tarawa, and the navy on the whole let him do what he wished with us. Maybe I caught him in a good mood. Maybe he agreed, unflattering thought, that I would never make it at the speaking thing. At any rate, he said that I need do no further interrogating. I was sorry that I had not made the request earlier—except that I might have caught him in a bad mood. I immediately moved on to the next problem, my schedule as a translator. I had a choice between the day shift and the night shift. I proposed to the commander in charge of the translation section that I work only the night shift. He too was agreeable.

So, lovely arrangement in a lovely place, I had my days to myself. I spent them sitting on beaches and exploring the town and the island. The former process caused my skin to grow darker and darker, and skin cancers, though never of a highly virulent kind, were presently to be a result. People would ask why I wished to be so dark. I would answer that I did not especially wish it, but thought tropical beaches among God's most deliciously sensual creations, and could not get enough of them.

I still think so, more than a half century later. There are people who hold palm trees to be scraggly, wimpy things. I think them, and the coconut kind in particular, to be majestic, especially in their constant bouts with the caressing winds that come in from the ocean.

I quite fell in love with the town. In those days the old parts, around the harbor, were still the most important parts, and Waikiki did not look gigantically down on everything else. There were still open lands and duck ponds between the harbor and the beach hotels, which were about three in number. I sometimes ask myself why I did not, like Melville, jump boat and stay in Honolulu, which we passed through on our way home to be discharged. Remarkably, the thought did not occur to me. Jumping boat would have been a touch too adventuresome.

Honolulu did not have high-rise buildings. At its most ostentatious it did not go above three and four storeys. The Big Five had their headquarters down near the harbor in modestly pleasing buildings that seemed ineffably tropical. The Big Five dominated the plantation economy. The New Dealers among us, and I must be counted one of their number, thought it dreadful that a mere five companies should run everything. We did not consider, I think, what a small place Hawaii is, and, since the tourist economy did not yet exist, we had no way of knowing how superior to it the agrarian economy was.

The rich parts of town were elegant, but I liked the scruffier parts better. Beretania Street was no longer the moneyed place it had been when Robert Louis Stevenson wrote his flaming defense of Father Damien. Nor yet was it the nondescript mercantile quarter it has since become.

I do not know whether I should number Chinatown among the scruffier quarters, but there was little evidence of the wealth for which the Chinese are famous almost everywhere. I loved the noises and the voices and the smells and the green clapboard fronts. I had not explored the New York Chinatown on my hurried visit in 1942. We had none in Denver. The Honolulu Chinatown spoke to me alluringly of new worlds for the young person from the far rim of the Mississippi basin.

But I liked Hotel Street and River Street best, and they were most definitely scruffy. They were where the whores hung out. Many of them were said to be Gypsies, and they may well have been. Certainly they had wild, wild black hair and wild, wild black eyes. Timidity kept me from venturing inside. I but walked the streets and had an occasional outlandish dish in what would today be called an ethnic restaurant. (The only decent bars in Honolulu in those days were in the officers' clubs.)

In February 1945, training ended and we were taken by truck and train to Hilo, there to board ships bound for the beaches of Iwo. The ride on flatcars to Hilo from the rail head up the Hamakua Coast was marvelous. That is the only word for it.

Troop ships were among the vilest weapons of war, always carrying too many people, always dirty and smelly. The latrines, or loos, or jakes, or whatever, were especially horrible. Water sloshed back and forth as the ship rolled, and disgusting objects sloshed with it.

The night before we arrived on Iwo was, I think, my worst night all during the war. I probably did sleep a little, for one rarely goes through a completely sleepless night, but my conviction that morning was that I had slept not a wink. I had been too frightened. I have not been back to Iwo since. People tell me that it is now rather a lush island. That morning it was brown as a slag heap. Bombardment had destroyed the last shred of greenery. That the season was winter had little to do with the matter. The island, being subtropical, would doubtless have been green but for the bombs and guns.

As we stood on deck that morning, waiting for the first waves of men to board their landing craft, Mount Suribachi, soon to become famous, was on our left. A neck joined it to the rest of the island, which was a low mound, the more level portions occupied by the air strip in the defense of which, presumably, every last man was to die. Quite a number failed to die, for the worst fighting was to the north of the air strip, on the right as we observed from our ships.

The Fifth Division was to land on the southernmost beaches, or the ones farthest to our left. They looked quiet enough, but the lay of the land was very threatening, with the mountain glowering down on it. In fact, the northernmost of the sectors with its high cliffs proved to be the bloodiest. The Fifth was to cross the neck and, having split, to advance on the mountain and up the west coast. It got an unlooked-for bounty, the most famous news photograph to emerge from the Pacific War.

I would like to say that I was in one of the first waves, but I was not. The captain made all the decisions in that regard, and he probably knew full well that I was not the most reliable leatherneck around. Presently I did land, and I struggled up the beach, loaded down with dictionaries, to the air strip.

There was by that time no gunfire. The Japanese had withdrawn to the north, where presently they would fight and die almost to a man. I had no trouble finding my colleagues in D-2, as it was called, the first element signifying "division" and the second, after some old and mysterious tradition, intelligence. They were exactly where I expected them to be, just below the far side of the strip. There I spent the rest of the battle, except for hikes through the mine fields to bathe in the ocean.

I was told not to stand there like the fool I unquestionably was but to get to work on a foxhole. I did, and only when I was almost finished did I take notice of a conspicuous and macabre object only a few feet away. I was not about to dig another foxhole and so I lived with it until the burial detachments came to take it away. It was a bare Japanese arm, raised from a heap of litter as if in some last gesture of exhortation and defiance. The rest of the corpse was under the heap.

I did not venture to climb Suribachi until after the island had been declared "secure" and just before we were to leave. The famous picture of the raising of the flag has been the object of many theories, most of them holding that it was posed. I may confess that when first I saw it, I thought it too good to be true. Whether faked or not, the picture is certainly a stunner. I have no notion what I was doing as the flag was going up. Probably wearing my eyes out over some useless captured document.

The battle, for me, was not at all what it should have been. Those weeks of early spring should have been ones of gore and terror. My chief recollections are of grime and boredom. I suppose I was in danger from time to time, but I was not aware of it and was not frightened. Division headquarters and corps headquarters (which exercised control over all the divisions) were subjected to repeated mortar fire. The Japanese obviously knew where they were. There is no reason why the translation section and my foxhole should not have been hit as easily and with as much probability as anywhere else there along the airstrip. They were not. I have no recollection of ever being afraid they would be hit.

We took very few prisoners on Iwo. I have had an occasional report on what happened to one and another of the prisoners, some of whom would have preferred suicide to going home and facing the shame. There have been no reports that such fears were justified. My diary entry for July 26, 1964, records my favorite piece of information about our prisoners: "A fascinating series in the *Asahi* by Toita Yasuji . . . on the strolling Kabuki troupes. One of our prisoners on Iwo, it seems, has been playing all these years for old ladies in the western provinces. So that is the sort of thing the lives so precariously saved have been dissipated on. It all seems very sad, and very beautiful."

There were suicide charges towards the end of the battle. The Japanese, having been indoctrinated in a cult of death which seemed demented to most of us Americans, would rush forth in the middle of the night, seeking to bring it upon themselves if it would not come of its own volition. One night, one did pass only some tens of yards to the north of our headquarters. Had it veered only a little to its left, it would have gotten all of us. I learned of it only the next morning and was not greatly startled. I spent none of the nights remaining before our departure in anything approaching the stark terror of that night before the landing.

One day in early April we went back down to the east beaches, many fewer of us than had crossed the beaches in the opposite direction, and got into amphibian craft, clambering up embarking nets and heading eastward across the Pacific. Our destination was Hilo. We were aboard ship some days out of Hilo when news came of Roosevelt's death. Groans filled the air. Good God (or something stronger), now we have Truman, was the near-universal reaction. I am very glad that I found the courage to disagree articulately, because I would have been hard put to defend myself against all the pokes in an eye, a nose, and elsewhere with which I was threatened. Give the man a chance, I said. Dear old Harry was to live up to the trust I reposed in him.

As we made our way up the coast from Hilo, the welcome from the island people was even more moving than the departure had been. They must have had among the most efficient of grapevines, for once again they all knew what was about to happen. I have often regretted that I did not try harder to make friends with a few of them; but we Boulder people were off in Pearl Harbor much of the time, and there were not many of "them" around Camp Tarawa.

Before the wounds had healed, we were back in training, though none of us language officers had been so much as nicked. Our count of Purple Hearts was as dismal as could have been possible. Some of us, I may say, had been very brave in the endeavor to root out Japanese from the caves that were everywhere in the northern part of Iwo and on the mountain as well. I do not count myself among their number. Though the island was "secured" before our departure, there were Japanese holdouts long after.

More of us knew where our next landing would be than had known about Iwo. The other three of the marine divisions having landed on

Okinawa later in the spring, it was our turn again. In the fall, we would be landing in the southernmost part of Japan proper. Iwo and Okinawa, though parts of that entity in theory, were not quite proper.

We language officers again went off to Pearl Harbor. I do not remember why we were back in Tarawa in August, but I remember vividly where I was when news of the bomb came. It was the second big occasion during those last weeks of war on which I disagreed with everyone around, certainly everyone who spoke out on the subject. I did not speak out, as I had a few months earlier when Harry was being so roundly condemned. I did not even take the opportunity to ask how they now felt about Harry.

The general mood was joyous. The war would soon be over, and, be it ever so humble, home awaited. I had nothing to say in that regard; I did not disapprove of Truman's dropping the bomb, but was frightened by it. It was good, certainly, that we would not have to go ashore again and face probably even fiercer resistance. We had already invaded outposts of Great Japan. Now we would be invading the heartland.

But news of the bomb had a deeply unsettling effect on me, as the prospect of the invasion did not. I have never been among those who hold that the bomb should not have been dropped. I have never felt the smallest urge to go off to Hiroshima for purposes of setting down my apology in the visitors' book. I think that, had I been at Harry's desk, I would have made the decision he made. The important things were to get the war over with and to save lives; and that more lives, American and Japanese, were saved by the bombing than were destroyed by it seems the next thing to certain. I did not become aware until later that there might have been another motive, to keep the Russians in their place. I would have endorsed this motive too, had I known about it. Certainly it does not seem sinful to me, as apparently it does to large parts of the Japanese Left as well as a number of Americans. But we had that day entered a new world, and it was a world fraught with dangers about which we knew almost nothing.

In September we went over to Hilo and down to the ships once more. It was my last ride on that glorious railroad, and I cannot hope for another. We arrived in Sasebo a bit over a month after General MacArthur put down in suburban Tokyo.

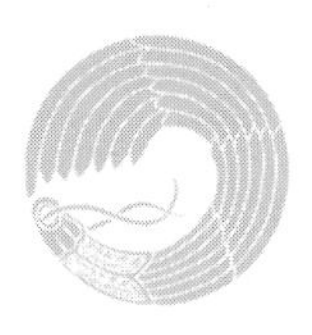

THREE

THE AFTERMATH

SASEBO IN SEPTEMBER 1945 was a devastated city. Its heart had been bombed and burned away. The most conspicuous building along the harbor front was a Catholic church. It seemed strange beyond description, a thing of medieval Europe rising starkly over wastelands half the world away. On a Sunday soon after, I went to Mass there. It, too, seemed more Japanese than Roman. The Latin was unlike any I had heard before. More curious yet was the fact that one had to take off one's shoes. People tried hard not to notice me, but without complete success.

The navy yard too was a curious place, remarkably small. My idea of a navy yard appropriate to a country about to fight a major war was San Diego or Pearl Harbor. This, by comparison, was a little toy of a navy yard. What could have possessed the military of that country to go to war against such odds? I suspected that the answer was sheer insanity, and I may have been right.

When I last saw the Sasebo navy yard in 1996, surprisingly little had changed from those post-war years. I suppose that anything so nakedly military in a country so belligerently pacifist has no chance at all of being named an Important Cultural Object under the protection of the government, but with so little else surviving from its day, the Sasebo navy yard should have strong claims.

I saw Nagasaki several times during my Sasebo months, which lasted until early 1946. I thought Sasebo much the more pitiable of the two cities. It had been nothing until the navy yard came to it, and the navy yard would no longer be performing the old functions. What future did it have? That it yet survives and even seems to prosper is tribute to the human spirit, and more particularly, to the famous Japanese spirit.

Nagasaki is a hilly city, and its center was in large measure spared from the bomb's devastation. Not much survives from the years of isolation, the seventeenth through the first half of the nineteenth century, when it was the only Japanese window on the world. But much survives from the Meiji Period, when things were opened up.

I have been to both Sasebo and Nagasaki several times since. Japanese ask me what place in Japan I like best. First, I give the honest answer, Tokyo. But I know that it is not the sort of answer that is expected, and so I have others at hand. Sasebo and Nagasaki are among them. I have an especially soft spot for Sasebo, which refused to die.

Japan in general refused to die. Those Sasebo months completely changed my view of the Japanese and of their language, about which I had never been really serious. Language had been a device for getting through the war, and during the war I was not interested in knowing more than I had to. When an immediate need had passed, I would forget what I had learned. I went on, with some difficulty, reading newspapers, but I did not acquire the vocabulary necessary, and especially the count of Chinese characters necessary, for reading serious literature.

During the war I had read Arthur Waley's translation of *The Tale of Genji,* the eleventh-century work which is often called, I think with justice, the first great novel in the literature of the world. I thought it a wonderful thing, but I was not for several years to read it in the original. The literary work I first read in the original was *The Setting Sun* by Dazai Osamu in 1948, when almost everybody was reading it. In that same 1948, Dazai drowned with a lady friend in a canal in the western part of Tokyo. Whether he killed himself or was pushed in by the friend we will never know. Perhaps he himself did not know. He was a dissolute, addictive sort. Two Dazai stories were my first published translations of modern Japanese fiction. I must have liked them at the time, but I do not much like them now. They are confessional, not my favorite strain (a reason, incidentally, for not wanting these memoirs to be very confessional). Contemporary Japanese fiction is much given to it, I might say excessively so. When I was choosing longer works to translate, I avoided it.

It was being among the Japanese that changed me. Their comportment in those first years after the war may be characterized as beautiful.

I was occasionally sent down to assist on a ship bringing Japanese soldiers back from China. The most striking thing was how cheerful they all were—and this must have been a terrible time for them. Saeki Shōichi, later to become an eminent literary critic and good friend, was also down there working the repatriation ships. Neither of us can remember whether we met, but it seems not at all improbable. He is a specialist in American literature, but his critical writings range widely. His most recent book is on letters, in the sense of epistles, mostly by English and American notables. High among his merits as a critic must be put the fact that he is never doctrinaire.

It was not only the men about to be demobilized and left to fend for themselves in a comfortless world. It was the people of Sasebo and Nagasaki, especially the former, since I saw much more of them. Having shaken off the shock of the surrender, they looked about them. Military expansion had not had the results they had hoped it would have. So they had to try something else. With that, they all set to work, cleaning away rubble, rebuilding, making and selling things. I did not immediately foresee an economic miracle and a gigantically productive machine; but I did see that studying these people and their language would not be a waste of time.

In those days, it was often said, by way of justifying the fact that the emperor was not held accountable for his part in the fiasco, that Japan needed a royal family to keep it from going to pieces. I did not believe it then and I do not believe it now. Foreigners, mostly Americans, said it. Citizens of the great republic seemed to have pronounced monarchical tastes. The Japanese had sufficient inner strength to see their way through, royal institution or none. That the emperor was neither forced to abdicate nor taken to court as a war criminal was owing to General MacArthur's vanity. He loved having an emperor under him—and great was his disappointment when he found that he did not have an American president under him as well. The day may not come soon when the palace grounds in Tokyo are a huge central park, the royal family having been sent on its way. But it would be nice.

Our principal assignment was to disarm the Japanese. I do not think that we did it very competently, and certainly I do not give myself high marks. Finding and boring holes in guns to render them useless was easy, but then there were all the munitions and supplies. Absolutely monstrous inventories landed on my desk. Maybe the captain was telling me that the time had come to demonstrate what I had learned at Pearl Harbor when

I was not interrogating prisoners. Whatever his reason, I did not know where to begin. The first page was the obvious place, but I understood little on it, and there were hundreds and hundreds of pages. They were all neatly written. Someone, probably many people, had spent a great amount of time compiling them. We did not do much to verify them. We were vaguely aware at the time, and it has since been established beyond doubt, that huge quantities of munitions went into the black market, and that because of it, many a flattened Japanese company was able to pick itself up again. Far more harmful things could have happened. The beginnings of the great Akihabara electronics district, one of the marvels of Tokyo, seem to have been in matériel from Chiba Prefecture, east of Tokyo.

I was with the detachments sent to disarm Japanese forces on the Tsushima and Gotō offshore islands in late 1945. This was rather fun, and I saw interesting places I might not otherwise have seen. Korea is visible from Tsushima, which figures, most naturally, in early commerce with the mainland. The Gotō islands were a center of the Kakure Kirishitan, the "crypto-Christians" who held the faith during the centuries of isolation when it was prohibited. The Japanese detachments were very hospitable and dutifully led us to the guns we were to bore holes in. I have never been back to either group of islands.

Expeditions here and there to look into the black market were less fun. Whenever we had a complaint, we would send parties out to investigate. I argued from the outset that this was not our responsibility but that of the Japanese authorities. I think I was right. Certainly they were aware of the problem, and they were far more competent to deal with it than were we. We did not, so far as I can remember, uncover anything of significance. I did see a number of pretty places, such as Karatsu, an ancient potters' town that had black-market problems. Everything was rationed in those days, and rations were not enough to live on. The story of a judge who starved rather than patronize the black market had much currency in the media. There cannot have been a town in the land that did not have a black market. It was a little hard to know, therefore, why we were sent out to inquire into specific complaints.

During some of the Sasebo time we were in the city itself. We occupied Japanese officers' houses overlooking the navy yard. We did some rather dreadful things to our pretty little Japanese houses. From time to time there came a rumor that we would have yet another suicide charge, and we would do all we could to render the flimsy place secure. This meant driving numerous nails where they did not belong. There were, of course, no charges. I do not remember an occasion on which a Japanese laid a finger on an American. I do remember feeling constrained to lie to the police. Our houseboy was caught trying to get past the guard with a couple of cans of chocolate milk in his pockets. I felt very sorry for the poor fellow and said I had given them to him.

During the rest of the year (we left Japan early in 1946) we were at Ainoura, a small naval base on the coast north of the city. It is a beautiful coast, studded with islands, and, until the weather turned cold, the swimming was splendid. Nagasaki University now occupies the site. The smelly latrines are among my strongest sensual memories of those days. Those Occupation months were not unpleasant ones. They reinforced, at length, the idea that I must learn Japanese. In January of 1946 we returned to San Diego, and I was soon discharged. Most of that spring I spent gardening in Colorado. I had always been the family gardener, and in my absence the garden had returned to nature. I now think I should have left it there and not struggled to make it look again like a little corner of England. The best Colorado gardeners cut back grasses but otherwise leave the landscape alone.

By summer, I had resolved to go east and leave Colorado's grand prospects and its cultural narrowness behind for good. But where was I going, and what would I do?

I was determined not to become one of the dilettantes known as professors. Presently a glimmering of something concrete came over me. I would have a go at the Foreign Service. I applied for and was admitted to a cram school at George Washington University, whose purpose was to get people past the Foreign Service examination. I also applied and was admitted to a few Eastern graduate schools. I quickly decided that Columbia, at which I had glanced briefly during my one visit to New York, was the place for me. My chief reason was that it was in New York. So, an order of operations took shape for the year or so ahead. I would spend the summer in Washington and the academic year in New York.

I learned many things in Washington. The names of the several sultanates of Malaysia proved useful in the examination and were promptly forgotten. I took the written examination in New York in the fall, passed it, and was summoned down to Washington in the spring for an interview. All that remained before my induction into the service was confirmation by the senate.

A bit jumpy about delays in this, I went to see my senior senator, Ed Johnson. The name does not loom large in the history books, but he was a legendary figure in Colorado, successful in everything he undertook, up the ladder from legislator to lieutenant governor, to governor and senator, and back to governor again. Ed's (we all called him Ed) finest moment came when he served on the committee that censured Senator McCarthy. When I called on him he was obviously irritated at being confronted by a mere boy. He had expected to see my father, with whom he was acquainted and whose name and mine are the same. He contained himself, however, and said he would do what he could. This was obviously considerable, for the confirmation went through in a day or two.

At Columbia I took a master's degree in what was called public law and government, though it could as well have been called political science. Literature seemed irrelevant to the career I had chosen for myself. I took courses in Japanese subjects, but I have no degree in Japanese literature and no doctorate. Degrees are important, of course, but not supremely so.

In *On Familiar Terms,* Donald Keene indicates great affection for Ryūsaku Tsunoda, who was that year the whole of the Columbia establishment in Japanese literature, history, and thought. It is a feeling I share without reservation. For erudition, kindness, and gentleness, Tsunoda was in a class by himself. He was a gentleman and a gentle man. I saw something of Keene during that year, but always at a distance. I think that we first introduced ourselves the following year, at Yale or Harvard. I liked Columbia and loved New York, and, although I was a student there for only the one year, I came to think of Columbia as my alma mater.

Early in the summer of 1947, after I had taken the oaths and signed the papers for induction into the Foreign Service, I was told that someone in "the Department" wished to see me. It proved to be John Emmerson, a gifted and loyal public servant who would later fall afoul of McCarthy and never reach the eminence he deserved. A most unassuming man, he was pleasant and friendly. He wished to know whether I would be interested in becoming a Japanese language officer. If I accepted his proposal, he said apologetically, it would mean a year's delay in my returning to Japan. I was not as a matter of fact all that eager to return, even if to a more interesting place than Sasebo. His proposal was that, along with several other Foreign Service officers, I should spend a summer at Yale concentrating on the Japanese language, and then an academic year at Harvard doing pretty much what I and we wished to do, provided it was related to Japan. I happily accepted. And so my first post, a strange one for a new Foreign Service officer, was New Haven.

I am not sure that I learned much of anything at Yale, though the summer was a delightful one, much of it occupied with sailing, a pursuit quite outside the experience of a Colorado boy. We could sail most of the way to Long Island and back again. It was exhilarating. In my part of Colorado we had only puddles that dried up in the summer.

The arrangements at Harvard were as Emmerson had said they would be. We were expected to read and listen as time and energy permitted, and we would not be required to take examinations. We could sit in on whatever courses attracted us. In charge of us was a youngish professor, Edwin Reischauer, one day to become ambassador to Japan. He was tolerance itself. He would ask no questions of us, he said, but we might come to him with questions whenever we thought it necessary.

There were four of us from the State Department. My diplomatic career did not last long, and neither did that of the only one among us who at the time knew no Japanese. The other two, David Osborn and Owen Zurhellen, became ambassadors, but in neither case to an important country.

They were (neither of them is still living) among the most remarkable men I have known, and they should have had important embassies. The United States does not treat its career diplomats well. Important embassies, except, for some reason, those in eastern Europe, tend to go to political appointees. Other countries have different and I think better arrangements. England sometimes sends a political appointee to Washington. Ormsby-Gore was sent because he was a personal friend of John F. Kennedy. I cannot think of a recent instance when Japan has sent a political ambassador anywhere. Both countries are probably better served by their career appointees than is the United States by its political ones. Of American ambassadors in Tokyo, the best, in my view, have been career appointees. Tokyo does occasionally get a career ambassador. London and Paris, I believe, never do.

I may not have much further to say of my dear deceased friends, Osborn and Zurhellen. So, at a risk of being prolix and repetitious, I will emphasize my point. Both Osborn and Zurhellen were gifted linguists with sharply analytic minds and cool common sense. Both were dedicated public servants. Both, by the bye, were graduates of the Navy Japanese Language School, although they were earlier graduates than I, and I did not know them during my time in the school. Zurhellen and I were together in the

Fifth Marine Division. I first met Osborn in New Haven. They deserved grander assignments than Burma, Osborn's last, and Surinam, Zurhellen's. Like me, Osborn was from a remote place, the rural South. Zurhellen was one of those sharp city boys, a New Yorker. I think of another gifted career diplomat, Richard Sneider. Though his last assignment, Seoul, was more important than those of the other two, he once told me that the only place he wanted to go after Seoul was Tokyo, and since he could not, he proposed to retire. And he did.

The chairman of the department to which we were attached, now called that of East Asian Languages and Civilizations, was Serge Ellisséeff. A Russian émigré, he was, like Tsunoda, among the founders of Japanese studies in the United States. Finding him urbane and amusing, I liked him. Keene, who was also at Harvard through that academic year of 1947 and 1948, did not.

I liked Ellisséeff better outside the classroom than in it. He was not a good lecturer. He looked at his notes except when he wished laughter, when he would signal the wish by looking up at us. His English was not good. Neither was Tsunoda's, but with Tsunoda, one did not want to miss anything; with Ellisséeff, one was seldom sure that there was much to miss. Ellisséeff's mannerisms were initially amusing and presently tiresome. He had a fondness for plethoric locutions: "and etcetera," "vice and versa."

His survey of Japanese literature occupied an hour and a half twice a week. One day a French Jesuit sitting beside me moaned, in an English far more pleasantly accented than Ellisséeff's, "It is too long!" I was probably the only one who heard. I quite agreed.

The most eloquent comment on Ellisséeff the lecturer came from an eminent auditor, Joseph Grew, a career diplomat who was the last American ambassador in Tokyo before the war and who was on the board of visitors, or something of the sort, for the Harvard-Yenching Institute. Midway through Ellisséeff's lecture, Grew turned off his hearing aid. Again I was probably the only one to notice. He too was seated beside me. I smiled appreciatively. A coldly aristocratic type, he did not smile back.

I think I missed only one of Ellisséeff's tedious lectures all year, and of course people told me that it was the most interesting. It was on Nō drama and the withdrawn, restrained aesthetics of medieval Japan—the aesthetics commonly held to be most "Japanese," albeit the Japanese have all sorts of aesthetics. I felt deprived, of course, but in later years would get more than enough indoctrination in that sort of thing.

My favorite course was Benjamin Rowland's in Japanese art. It was held in the Fogg Museum at the sleepiest hour, the one after lunch, and it was held in darkness, that we might view illustrative slides. "May we have the first slide, please," Professor Rowland would say, in a hypnotically somnolent voice, and I would be asleep. Perhaps hypnosis did operate, for I remember more from that course than from any other. I still have my notes. I seem to have developed a knack for waking up briefly and making a pen sketch of the slide before us. The sketches are not at all bad. Some of the doodles I did in the Ellisséeff course, if I may return to it for a moment, seem almost worthy of Saul Steinberg.

Then there was "rice paddies." Rice paddies was a famous undergraduate course, a survey of Japanese and Chinese history and culture. It was taught by the other two Harvard eminences, Professors Reischauer and John King Fairbank, by no means as well known then as they were subsequently to become. Sometimes I liked rice paddies and sometimes I did not. I had greater misgivings about those two than about Ellisséeff, who did no harm, at any rate in my presence. I did not wholly trust either of them. I thought them, not always but from time to time, besotted, and besottedness is not a state in which calm reason prevails. They were both of them too fond of the objects of their inquiries.

I will give an instance of my fleeting, schoolboyish doubts in each case. I could give more, but my purpose is not to draw up a bill of indictment. Reischauer kept telling us that Japan had a venerable history of democracy, that what seemed to be happening before our eyes had not emerged out of nothing. I was not sure that what we seemed to see before our eyes was so very convincing, and as for a country whose experiments in democracy had been so feeble and had blown away upon the first huff without waiting for a puff—I did not think that such a country could be said to have strong roots in democracy.

Fairbank kept telling us what a peaceful country China had always been. It had no history of aggression and military expansion. We had before us maps of China as it was twenty-five hundred years ago and China as it may claim itself to be now, even without Taiwan. How did the little entity in the Yellow River valley grow into the gigantic one we now have? Did everyone come rushing in and demand to become Han Chinese? Such is not human nature, and the Chinese are among the most richly human of people. I was too timid to say so, but it is what I thought.

I did not like Harvard as well as I had liked Columbia. I thought it an unfriendly place. This may have been because I was not one of the boys. I did not live in a dormitory, as I had at Columbia. I would have my year there and would have no Harvard degree to display to the world. It is true that Harvard is rather generous in its definition of an alumnus. My single year made me eligible to belong to the most conveniently situated Harvard Club, which, during my years of membership, was in Tokyo. (In the early years, a fellow member of the Tokyo Harvard Club was a fellow diplomat named Cabot Coville. It was assumed that anyone with such a name had to be from Harvard, but in fact he was from Cornell.) Yet at department receptions in Phillips Brookes House and teas in the Fairbank house, very near Harvard Square, I felt subtly the outsider.

I did not, perhaps, like Boston as much as I had liked New York. It is not quite the cultural center that New York is. I liked it very much all the same. In one respect Boston was better. It had better Japanese art. This fact was not of major importance. My favorite Boston museum was not the Museum of Fine Arts, its glories snatched from under Japanese noses by shrewd Yankees. It was the Gardner, such a splendid clutter. It continues to be among my favorite museums the whole world over. I lived in a very beautiful part of the city, on Beacon Hill, just above Louisburg Square. It was a harsh winter. With easterly winds blowing down the hill, I sometimes had to crawl up it, literally on hands and knees.

Finally, the forsythia came into bloom and spring was at hand. When the academic year ended we four went back to Washington. We spent some weeks there learning about the diplomatic life and its elaborate procedures. One of the things I learned in Washington had little specific relationship to diplomacy. I learned that Reischauer had not given "the Department" a glowing report on my year at Harvard.

I do not hold this against him. It was not a malicious report, and it was about what I deserved. He thought me excessively given to quick and ill-considered enthusiasms. Sincere self-reflection (as the Japanese would put it) made me see that there was truth in the charge. I was still in what I now think of as my Tom Paine period. I was one of those who thought that he (or she) could persuade the world to see the light and correct its follies. This may seem to accord poorly with my essentially conservative suspicions of Reischauer and Fairbank; but, as has been remarked upon by persons far wiser than I, we are all of us bundles of contradictions.

Reischauer also said that I did not seem thoroughly committed to the diplomatic life and probably would not make it mine for long. The near future was to demonstrate how apt a perception this was.

Later that summer, as indoctrinated as ever we would be, we four headed westwards into the sunset, our destination Japan. There was no American embassy in Japan (no embassy of any country, for that matter), nor would there be until the San Francisco Treaty of 1952. So we were assigned to the occupying forces. Three of us were to go to what was called the Diplomatic Section of the Supreme Commander for the Allied Powers. The last half dozen words indicate General MacArthur. Only one of us, Zurhellen, chose a consular assignment in Yokohama. Osborn and I, the bachelors, chose to go by ship. The others went by air.

Osborn and I sailed from San Francisco on the *President Wilson,* one of the last scheduled passenger ships still in service. The *President Wilson* and its sister ship (if the expression is still permitted), the *President Cleveland,* made the round of Pacific ports in opposite directions, the former clockwise and the latter counterclockwise. The clockwise passage was a most excellent one. It took almost a month. In the course of it I started gaining weight for the first time in my adult life. Before arriving at Yokohama we put in at Honolulu, Manila, Hong Kong, and Shanghai.

The days in Shanghai and the passage up and down the two rivers to reach it are most vivid in memory. It was the only time I set foot on mainland China, apart from brief trips to Macao, Kowloon, and the New Territories of Hong Kong.

I would have had time for a quick trip to Peking while the *Wilson* was docked in Shanghai. I was to regret that I did not make it. There would be plenty of time later, I thought. The Chinese civil war was then held to be stalemated, but of course all of China except Taiwan was in Communist hands a year later. I have had no wish to go to Peking since it became the Communist capital (and I go on, futilely, calling it Peking, for what right have the Chinese to tell us what to call it in our own language, and is it at all likely that they say "Washington" as meekly as we say "Beijing?").

I remember the sounds and smells of the Oriental summer, which was stiflingly hot. "Smells" could with little distortion be changed to "stenches." The sounds were not an unmixed pleasure, either, but they were much better. Conspicuous among them was the shrilling of the cicadas, which I heard for the first time that summer and have heard every summer since. I was not sure at first that I liked it, for it disturbed my afternoon naps. It is so shrill a sound that when the greatest of haiku poets has it sinking into the very rocks the image does not seem strained. Shrilling cicadas have come in years since to seem so much a part of full summer that summer would be less full without them. Each year I look with foreboding to newspaper reports that the decibel count is falling. There always are such reports. Like so many creatures of the wild, cicadas do not take well to urban life. Each year I hope most earnestly that it is not true, and I tell myself that Japanese newspapers are unreliable.

The emergence of the cicadas from the earth is one of the more remarkable sights nature has to offer. It happens in the summer and is predictable, and so on nights when it is likely to occur we all go down to the park and wait until little pimples appear in the earth, and presently cicadas emerge and climb the trees, where they get rid of their shells, that they may use their wings.

Mostly I remember how unperturbed life seemed in this great city, and how peaceful the fields were along the river. One might not have known, though of course one did, that city and fields faced revolution. In the days after the San Francisco Treaty, which ended the Occupation, Japanese intellectuals back from whirlwind tours of China were always telling us what a peaceful, prosperous place it had become. I liked to retort, not that anyone really listened, that it had seemed even thus when I visited it back before "liberation." One does not learn much about a place from a whirlwind tour, I would say, and offer my impression of Shanghai on the verge of the great upheaval as an instance in point. I think that I was right, but I also think that I made no converts to my view. (By the time all the intellectuals were coming back from China, enraptured, my Tom Paine period was over.)

We arrived in Yokohama late in July. It too was stiflingly hot, and I had never before seen such a sky. My Sasebo months were in autumn and early winter, among the clearer of seasons. Perhaps Sasebo too has murky skies with no visibility even as the sun blazes above. As to that I could not say. The Yokohama miasmas could not be blamed on automobiles and such. The automobiles were most of them American, not that that mattered much, and there were not many. The miasmas were natural.

So we were driven to Tokyo and deposited at the Daiichi Hotel in Shimbashi, just west of the southernmost part of Ginza. The Daiichi, or Number One, was to be our billet. I would not have admitted it then, for the army was now the enemy, but the army was generous to us. The

Daiichi was for field officers, and here I was the most junior of Foreign Service officers.

The Daiichi was not much of a hotel. It was built for the 1940 Olympics, scheduled for Tokyo but cancelled because of the war, and it seems to have expected only diminutive guests. Everything was undersize. Osborn, a lanky fellow, complained that he was never able to get his knees wet in the bathtub.

My first Tokyo adventure resulted in a D.R., a delinquency report. I went out for a stroll from the Daiichi, intending to look at that other and far more famous Daiichi, the Daiichi Life Insurance Building, headquarters for General MacArthur. It seemed possible, for the hour was one when he might be making one of his famous passages from the insurance building to his billet in the American embassy, that I might even catch a glimpse of the great man.

At the Hibiya crossing, where the palace moat turns westwards at a right angle a few steps south of the Daiichi Building, there was a sudden blinding shower. The Hibiya crossing was famous for the two policemen who stood in the middle of it and directed the meager traffic of the day. They moved simultaneously, raising their arms to permit and restrain traffic. One was Japanese and one American. They only seemed to move simultaneously. The Japanese watched the American carefully, and moved a tiny fraction of a second after he did.

Unable to see in the rain, I started across but was shouted at by the American and given a D.R. I had moved in a direction forbidden by the two raised arms. So my Tokyo career and my overseas diplomatic career began with delinquency. Much more of that sort of thing, I was warned, and I would get kicked out. I was very careful thereafter when I saw an M.P., although when none was in sight I did many an illegal thing, such as use public transportation not specifically reserved for foreigners. Police officers of the Japanese sort were lenient towards us Americans. The reasons for the stickiness about public transportation were good ones. It was frightfully overcrowded. But doing the legal thing could be a great handicap for someone who wanted to learn all about the city.

My diplomatic career was from start to finish a peculiar one. My first two posts were New Haven and Cambridge. Then came Tokyo. It was a foreign place, to be sure, but we had no embassy, and our principal mission was to keep an eye on the army and report what we learned to the State Department. This was respectable enough work. The State Department, presumably, would one day be taking over, and the more it knew about what was going on, the better qualified it would be. Nonetheless, for a group of American diplomats to be spying on fellow Americans was not at all the usual thing. My diplomatic career was to be so short that I was never to get a taste of this last.

The State Department enclave in Tokyo had two names, Diplomatic Section (DipSec) and Office of the Political Adviser (Polad). To both of these was affixed the grandiose SCAP, Supreme Commander for the Allied Powers. The man who wore the two caps, as people said, was William Sebald, whom I had long admired. A naval officer before the war, he resigned his commission and became a lawyer so that he might marry a Eurasian woman, Edith DeBecker.

Our offices were in the main Mitsui building in Nihombashi, the mercantile and financial center of the pre-modern city. (Nihombashi may claim to be the financial center even today, for it houses the Bank of Japan, but there are bigger mercantile centers elsewhere.) Mitsui was the oldest and arguably the most powerful of the gigantic conglomerates. Across the street was the similarly gigantic Mitsukoshi Department Store, formerly the Mitsui Echigoya, at the beginning of Mitsui wealth and power. It should have been a good place for observing what the conglomerates were up to. I suppose that, in a vague, ill-informed way I did observe. My observations were largely negative. Mitsui certainly did not seem moribund.

Arriving for duty the same morning, Osborn and I flipped a coin. He went to the consular section, and I to the economic. I had half hoped it would be the other way. I was sure, though I presently became less so, that anyone could quickly learn the consular business, and despite my original undergraduate major, I knew precious little about economics. So off I went to report to the economic counselor. He was friendly, and asked which among the several possible economic concerns I would like to address myself to. I had very little idea, but I said deconcentration, which was the effort to break up the conglomerates, or cartels, by putting their stock up for public sale.

I think the Tom Paine thing had a great deal to do with the matter, both Tom Paine and deconcentration having populist and egalitarian tendencies. The fact that the task of deconcentration seemed so hopeless, and therefore should be easy to spy and report upon, may also have had something to do with the promptness with which I replied to the counselor. The people in deconcentration were almost excessively open and cooperative. I suspected that they felt under threat, for they were poor cousins in the huge Economic and Scientific Section. No one seemed to take their work very seriously, or to think that they had much chance of success.

I was of this last persuasion myself. I was given enormous balance sheets to show what had been accomplished and how bright the prospects were. In a way it was the demilitarization in Sasebo all over again, but with an important difference: having taken courses in accounting back in the undergraduate days when I had thought I would follow all those uncles and become a lawyer, I was able to make a dim and fumbling sense of the balance sheets, whereas I had been able to make virtually nothing out of the inventories down in Sasebo.

But mostly I relied on instinct for my conclusion that it was all doomed to fail. Those gnomes in the Mitsui Building were up to something, and they knew the workings of the highly involuted world of high finance and enterprise far better than any of us did. It should not be difficult for them to send a few sub-gnomes around to buy stock being sold to "the public" and thus retain control. Had I been aware of the fact that the presidents of all the companies bearing the name Mitsui were schoolmates, I would have been more confident of my position, which, in a wavering fashion, I did report back to Washington.

Nor did I foresee that a very Japanese thing would happen. Names would be "rectified" in accepted Confucian fashion and everything would go on much as it had before. The old *zaibatsu,* which word is rendered by the big Japanese-English dictionary as "a financial combine," would become *keiretsu,* rendered "systematization of enterprises," and what would the difference be? It is true that the old holding companies disappeared, but more informal gatherings, known as clubs or something of the sort, could be made to do quite as well. Then there was the little, notorious matter of intercompany holdings of stock.

I did not, certainly, predict all of this in precise detail, but these were my instinctive conclusions. Perusal of balance sheets contributed little to them. My reports to Washington, which I have not laid an eye on in almost a half century, were probably rather mealymouthed, but I cannot tax myself with having misled anyone in The Department.

My DipSec career lasted less than two years. Somewhere along the way there came a request for someone to go down to Taiwan. Osborn and I again flipped a coin. He won and chose Taiwan. It was a wise choice, for down there he could make a start at something more nearly resembling a diplomatic career. I was moved to his job in the consulate, the implication being strong that it was more important than mine in the Economic Section. I think it was, for it influenced people's lives, and my reporting on deconcentration can have had little influence on anyone or anything.

In both cases, the workday was the eight-to-five routine of the person the Japanese call "salaryman," although the expression does not, I believe, commonly cover the bureaucrat. It was not much to my liking, nor was the thought that thirty years and more of it were in prospect. In the consulate I had only one tiny office. In the Economic Section I had two, one in DipSec, of course, the other in Ginza among the deconcentration people, where I pored over balance sheets. Sometimes I would divide my day between the two; sometimes I would do them on alternate days.

Far more interesting was wandering about the enormous Economic and Scientific Section, of which deconcentration was a minor part. Its offices were by the palace moat, very near those of SCAP himself. There I formed lasting friendships, the most cherished one with Theodore Cohen. He had been in charge of the Labor Section, and then, being thought too radical when the Soviet Union emerged as an enemy, he was given an advisory position directly under the commanding E.S.S. general. He was a peppery little man, not to everyone's taste, but I was fond of him. He gave me a rich repertory of Jewish jokes, and wrote probably the best book on the Occupation.

Life in the consulate, although dull, was brightened by an occasional visa for a famous actor or athlete. Mostly it was notarials. The most interesting consular work of the day was the processing of war brides, and that was handled in Yokohama. There were amusing stories, the most amusing of them, probably, told to us by the vice-consul who did the necessary interviewing of prospective bride and groom. Going through the standard questionnaire, he asked the sergeant before him: "And have you seen your bride's *koseki tōhon?*" The last expression refers to the family register in which the important facts about every Japanese are entered. "Oh, no, sir," replied the sergeant. "We haven't done anything yet."

The time I could call my own, on the other hand, was fascinating. I explored the city. There was a warren of dubious little places, associated predominantly with the black market and prostitution, right across the street from the Daiichi Hotel. Like so much of the city, it was far more interesting then than it is now. It seemed to me that, for all the dubious nature of the commodities and services purveyed, it was remarkably unsleazy. There was something cheerful and healthy about it. I go on finding it altogether remarkable that the Japanese (and there were Chinese and Koreans as well) can do the most undignified things without losing dignity. Shimbashi was always beguiling the tedium of our days by catching fire. Firemen worked harder in those days than they do now. The flower of Edo (the premodern name of Tokyo), which is to say the conflagration, still flourished.

I loved the Tsukiji market, a walk of ten minutes or so from the hotel. We all called it the fish market, though it is officially the Tokyo Central Produce Market. No place in Tokyo excels it for sheer vigor, and the vigor soars to its greatest heights very early in the morning. On days when I did not have to bother with deconcentration and notarials, I would sometimes get up before sunrise to go have a look at it. I would breakfast on sushi, which was superb, but mostly I would just watch and admire, and think that a person could do worse than to become a fish vendor.

Tsukiji, which means "reclaimed land," is the site of the first Tokyo foreign settlement. The market was not there then. It was in Nihombashi, where it smelled up the offices and shops of people like the Mitsui. Stories went the rounds about the market too. My favorite is of the vendor upon whom the authorities sought to serve a warrant for some transgression. "Come back later," he said. "I'm too busy to bother with you now."

Presently I started touring the Yamanote, the loop line connecting a number of stations in the older part of the city. Not waiting for a car exclusively assigned to us alien ones, I would get on any car, wholly in defiance of regulations. I never got a D.R. after that first day. I often used the subway to go from Shimbashi to Nihombashi. That too was illegal. I lived dangerously.

I got off at famous stations and explored their environs. I think that Ueno, with its famous park and museums, including the National Museum, was the very first. Today it is a neat sort of park, though some of its denizens may be rather disreputable, but back then it was weedy and neglected. It contained one of two mortuary temples for the Tokugawa shoguns, and the graves of several shoguns, with the grave of many a lesser Tokugawa nearby. Among the good things about the neglect was that the fences had broken down. I did what would be quite impossible now. All by myself, I spent hours exploring the graves, and melancholy testimonial they were to the evanescence of glory. They were very beautiful, with the especial beauty of ruinous monuments.

One of my earlier expeditions must have been to Ikebukuro, one of the thriving new entertainment and commercial centers along the western arc of the Yamanote. It was not very thriving in those days, though it had a most excellent cluster of black-market stalls. One would see policemen having pleasant strolls up and down its alleys and doing nothing to enforce the law. It was hard to put down a suspicion that they recognized the worth of the black market, which kept many people alive, and did not wish to interfere.

My first visit to Ikebukuro was chiefly to have a look at Sugamo Prison, which is much nearer to Ikebukuro Station than Sugamo Station. When the prison was built Ikebukuro was nothing at all and Sugamo, a bit to the east, was already emergent suburbia. The reason for my visit was the "war criminals." So it must have been a fairly early visit. The big Class A ones, twenty-five of them, were then in the prison, and several were hanged late in 1949. I remember vividly a Christmas Eve party when my boss, William Sebald, appeared white and shaken after witnessing the hangings the night before.

In the matter of war criminals, I have wavered back and forth. I remember that on the day of my first look at Sugamo Prison, I felt rather sorry for them. My wavering has had to do in large measure with the emperor. The men on trial at the Tokyo International Tribunal had not been, as some of the Nazi war criminals had been, guilty personally of crimes against humanity, and if the concept of war crimes was to prevail at all in the Japanese instance, it should have been applied more thoroughly and consistently. It should have been applied to the reigning emperor.

The Shōwa emperor, as he is now called, might not have been able to stop the war in, say, the spring of 1945, thereby saving many thousands of lives and forestalling the bomb; but he should have tried. Or so I have often thought. There persists a strong suspicion that the emperor had his twinge of courage in August 1945 because he was afraid of losing his job, and he did not have it in April 1945 for the same reason.

Venturing away from the Yamanote, I ventured generally to the east, in search of red-light districts. As in Honolulu, I had no great desire to disport myself wantonly. I just wanted to look at them. The proudest of them was the Yoshiwara, to the east and somewhat to the north of Ueno. Almost as old as the city, it was once among the main centers of mercantile culture. It also had a rich history of conflagrations, and a tragic history of deaths in them. The former was inevitable because of the flimsy wood-and-paper architecture, and the latter because of moats across which the ladies could not escape. This was enough to give it, for me, a melancholy beauty, though it was in fact a cluster of what were called barracks, jerry-built shacks put up on the ashes of 1945. I got to be rather friendly with some of the elderly female touts. They would tell me where they were from and invite me to go home with them for the summer holidays. I was probably wise not to accept. It could have been embarrassing for a young diplomat. In 1958 prostitution was outlawed and there was another rectification of names. The houses became "Turkish baths." Eventually the Turks objected, so there came yet another. Now they are "soaplands."

It took me a while to venture east of the Sumida River. In that direction lay poverty and—people would say it in hollow, portentous tones—slums. I was timid about both of these things, but finally I set forth, again in search of famous red-light districts. The affection for the eastern flatlands which I formed then has never left me. They contain little that a person would go out of his way to see, but the street life was vibrant and the inhabitants had the warmth of an earlier day. Television now keeps people off the streets.

I did not find anything east of the river which I would have described as a slum. Tokyo may have genuine slums some day, when all the concrete starts falling apart, but it does not now and did not then. These people were poor, certainly, but seemed neither miserable nor embittered, and in an American city one expects slum dwellers to be these things. I would not at all have minded having a go at the kind of life I observed around me.

I do not propose a checklist of all the places I explored during my diplomatic career. Tokyo is a vast and varied city, and scarcely any part of it, save possibly the palace grounds, is empty. Two or three other places do, however, ask for mention.

Of the *sakariba,* the "thriving places," along the western arc of the Yamanote, I have already mentioned Ikebukuro. Among the three large ones, it was the slowest to start feeding at the trough of the economic miracle. It had the look of the frontier about it, and one of its charms is that it still retains a fading shadow of that look.

Shinjuku and Shibuya, which became parts of the city only in 1935, were already a little on the way to becoming the gigantic shopping and consuming centers they are today. Perhaps the liveliest part of the Shinjuku "West Mouth," now a mass of department stores and office buildings, was "Piss Alley," a place of tiny drinking establishments that warmed a person physically and spiritually. There is nothing like it now in Shinjuku. At the East Gate were a few neons dotting the dark residential districts to the east and north of the station. They looked rather lonely, and they were the beginning of Kabukichō, where today everything is to be had. The cold winter nights when we took sake and sushi at little shacks beside the station will not come again.

In general, change has been more rapid the farther south and west one goes from the old center of the city (Ginza and Nihombashi, we may say). When sudden change comes, it comes most strikingly to the south and west, and passes the north and east by. Shibuya was the place most changed by the Olympics. Its equivalent of Piss Alley was probably Koibumiyokochō, "Love Letter Alley," from the name of a popular novel in which it figures. Since then it has become a place of roaring youth who are indifferent to the past, indifferent, indeed, to most things except themselves. (Some of us liked it better the other way, when there were still earthy sounds, sights, and smells).

One evening in Shibuya a young man came up and addressed me. When he had practiced his English for a few minutes, he said: "I must go." And he went. The remark seemed a touch stilted until I saw him rush into a public lavatory, at which point it came to seem very idiomatic and colloquial.

Shibuya now has the hard crassness of a place through which too much money flows. I wonder if anyone would be as kind as the bar proprietress on the evening my pocket had been picked. I discovered it had happened only when I reached into my pocket for money to pay the bill. Although it was my first visit to the place and I was therefore an utter stranger, the lady said I could come back some day and pay it, and even lent me money for taxi fare home. Her attitude said that if I did not find it convenient to come back, the loss would not break her. I of course went back the next day, and many times thereafter, until the place went out of business, as most such places do in Shibuya, that there may be more department stores.

I may add in passing that I have had my pocket picked several times in law-abiding Tokyo. The Japanese reaction on hearing of these misfortunes, which I am not embarrassed to talk about, although the victim of a pickpocket is bound to look a trifle foolish, was ludicrously uniform: "Damned Koreans."

Tokyo was a battered city in those days, and almost everyone was poor. I would not wish to be understood as saying that the Japanese should remain forever poor; but long experience has persuaded me that they are better people when poor. It follows that, for me, Tokyo was a better city then. Reconstruction did not get underway until after my diplomatic career had ended. The start came largely from procurements for the Korean War. They did nothing sinful by profiting from troubled waters. Someone else would have done it if they had not, and they made better use of the windfall than most countries would have.

Most of my unoccupied evenings I spent in study. I had an ambition. I would be a scholar-diplomat. The scholar-diplomat is a scarce type in the American Foreign Service, but I had and have huge admiration for several such persons whom the British Foreign Service produced: Sir Ernest Satow, Sir Charles Eliot, Sir George Sansom. In a charming talk to the Royal Asiatic Society in London, Sir George described the species as extinct. It had thrived, he said, in a day when diplomats worked hard at their profession just before the monthly pouch went off, and the rest of the time devoted themselves to wandering about and making inquiry. The day had passed, and it could thrive no longer.

I had most evenings to myself. There were not many compulsory social events, in those days, though the fact that ours was such an eccentric sort of diplomatic life may have had something to do with the matter. So I would study and write.

It was not difficult in those days to find a sage willing to help you if you kept him in tobacco. I found one through a Japanese lady who worked in DipSec. He was a professor at a distinguished Tokyo university. He was a heavy smoker. Everything was in order. He would come to my Daiichi room two or three evenings a week, and we would read famous old prose.

Not being a very poetic type, I said that we would read prose from the Heian Period, the great day of Japanese courtly literature, almost a thousand years ago. I chose Heian because it was the age of the only considerable Japanese literary work that I had carefully perused, *The Tale of Genji.* I have already said that I thought it a rather marvelous work. I did not wish to read it in the original quite yet, however. I wished to read something that had not been translated.

We chose a tenth-century work called the *Kagerō Nikki.* Several years later the translation was to become my first book. It was published in 1953 by the Asiatic Society of Japan. Later yet, a revision called *The Gossamer Years* was published commercially. This is an attempt at translation of the original title, the first word of which has more than one meaning, among them "gossamer" in the original sense of spider threads that are scarcely seen at all as they drift through the air on a summer day.

The word "gossamer" perhaps conveys the nature of the work better than does the second word of the Japanese title. The latter signifies "diary," but it is not so much a diary as a set of reminiscences or memoirs. I did not really know what I was getting into when the professor and I started reading it. I was getting into something very good. It is to my mind the best of the works which the Japanese, for the most part misleadingly, call diaries, and it is a seminal work.

It is by a woman, and therefore was neglected down to modern times in favor of manly things in Chinese. Among womanish things, only *The Tale of Genji* and some poetry were much noticed. *Genji* was noticed for what seemed to many of us the wrong reasons. The cultural imperialism of the West, which has caused it to be seen for what it is, has not been an unmixed evil. I think that it was largely under the influence of the West that *Genji* ceased being read as a didactic work and came to be seen as a novel centered upon character. It was at least in part under our influence that the greatness of the modern novelist Tanizaki Jun-ichirō was recognized.

I decided early in 1950 that the Foreign Service was not for me and I was not for it. I have indicated that I never much liked the life of a salaryman. Unlike many salarymen, I was young enough and sufficiently without encumbrances to have a try at something else. My failure to be promoted in the spring of 1950 brought matters to a head. Zurhellen was on the promotion list that spring and Osborn had been promoted the previous spring. I would not wish to suggest that I was envious of two such good friends, but the evidence was clear. I was falling behind, and an early loss of momentum is not easy to overcome in the Foreign Service. There was time, and it was time, to try something else.

I was grateful to the Department for letting me know so soon and so clearly how things stood. When I told Sebald of my decision, he tried to talk me out of it. So did most of the other eminences in DipSec. The only exception was Cloyce Houston, Sebald's immediate deputy. He said that I was doing exactly the right thing and wished me good fortune. He was not everyone's favorite in DipSec, but at that moment he became mine.

Those were years of witch-hunting. Among the favored prey were bachelors. All manner of peculiar things were imagined about them, and when one of them left the service all manner of peculiar rumors were spread abroad. They spread, of course, when I resigned. I can only say that I was a virginal type and that I resigned entirely of my own volition. There was no pressure at all from The Department, unless, of course, those unsatisfactory promotion lists may be seen as subtle pressure.

I had cause to suspect that my room in the Daiichi was bugged. If someone had broken in during one of the long silences while the professor was in my room, he would have been embarrassed to find the two of us at the table, the professor smoking, and I doing a rough translation of a passage we had just read. It might have been amusing, although I am sure that I would have had to find another sage.

So, early in May of 1950, I put my Bach and Mozart and a few other things into crates and departed the Daiichi.

FOUR

COLD WARRIORS

IT WAS WITH DIREST FOREBODING that I headed north past the palace. I might find that I had made a dreadful mistake, and must pay for it. In fact I was heading into the most interesting years of my life.

We, crates and I, were in an American army truck with a Japanese driver. We drove through the central ward of the city, which contains the palace grounds, and into the ward immediately north, Bunkyō Ku. In it was to be my new abode, and in it I have, with very brief interruptions, maintained an abode through the almost half century since.

The wards, as they were then uniformly called, were reconstituted in 1947. Mostly, two and three wards in the old city were made into one. Two proud old ward names disappeared when Bunkyō Ku came into being. It is probably because they were both of them so proud that neither became the name of the new ward. Neither could abide the other. So the name it acquired was a bureaucratic monstrosity, probably the least lovely name among the twenty-three. It means something like "cultural capital." Bunkyō Ku contains two great cultural centers, the Kōrakuen baseball stadium and Tokyo University. For the most part, it is a pleasant place. That it has never become fashionable is for me a merit. It is not (with the possible exception of the baseball stadium and the amusement park surrounding it) an ostentatious place, and it changes, by Tokyo standards, slowly.

Tokyo University, which I had not yet learned to dislike, was to be my excuse for staying on in a city I did not wish to leave. That spring it became

Aunt Lucy (Lucy Ratcliff Clarke) on her wedding day, 1898. She disliked cameras and this is the only photograph I remember seeing of her. She had not changed much when last I saw her, fifty years later.

My maternal grandparents with three of their children, including my mother. The photograph was taken in Chicago around the turn of the century.

LEFT
My mother with my brother, on the right, and me. Denver, 1922 or 1923.

BELOW
A relic of pioneer days, a Christmas card that has been in the family for more than a century. It is said to represent the first Colorado dwelling of an uncle, Richard Clarke. If so, it must have been a dramatic change from the life of an English country gentleman. It stood on land later acquired by my German grandfather.

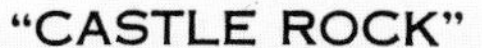

"CASTLE ROCK"

July 9th, 1925.

Mr. Henry Dillon,

Castle Rock, Colo.

Dear Sir:

It has come to our attention that you are indulging in a bit of kid-play by attempting to annoy the Women of the Ku Klux Klan during their meetings at Castle Rock.

Our organizations are not bothering you and our meetings are in all respects legal and are going to be held. We do not propose to put up with any annoyance from you. Any further such action on your part will only result in steps being taken to put a stop to such practices.

Yours very truly,

The Knights of The Ku Klux Klan.

How things were in my early childhood. Henry Dillon was one of my mother's many brothers. He would have been in his early twenties at the time. Klan meetings may have been legal, but it was disingenuous to say that they caused no trouble.

A westward view of the hills of home, mid 1960s. The southern outskirts of Castle Rock stretch out below me.

TOP
Fraternizing with the enemy, Tsushima, 1945. I am in left center, with hand raised.

BOTTOM
With Glenn Shaw, the kindly Coloradan who interviewed me for language school, and Howard Hibbett, of U.C.L.A. and later Harvard, probably early 1950s.

TOP
On the beach at Katakai.

BOTTOM
With Ogaeri Yoshio, of Tokyo University, and Ronald Dore, later of London University, on the Tokyo University campus, early 1950s.

With my dear departed friend, Hara Teruo, Kyoto, late 1950s.

TOP

With Kawabata and Harold and Millie Strauss at Echigo Yuzawa, 1957. Yuzawa is the site of Kawabata's novel, *Snow Country*. He took us there to observe the making of a movie version.

BOTTOM

The gathering to soothe our feelings after the "Koestler Incident," 1959. From left: Takahashi Kenji of the Japan P.E.N., myself, Ivan Morris, Koestler, Father Joseph Roggendorf, the dancer Takehara Han, and Yamamoto Yuzo, a novelist and our host.

With Tanizaki and Koyama Itoko, Atami, 1960.

This picture, taken at Tanizaki's last residence in Yugawara, has become famous because Tanizaki is smiling. He was known for his adversarial approach to cameras. This is the last time I saw him; he died a few months later. From left: Howard Hibbett, me, Tanizaki, and Donald Keene.

TOP

A seminar at the University of Michigan. We are immersed in the original of *The Tale of Genji.* My back is to the camera. Father William Currie, on my left, is now president of Sophia University. Carl Taeusch, at the far end of the table, is a Tokyo lawyer. The other two, Cassie Tokushige and Gerry Uyekubo, an investment banker, later married and are living in Honolulu. The fifth member of the seminar, Anthony Chambers, now a professor at Arizona State University, must have taken the picture.

BOTTOM

One of the splendid succession of farewell parties, 1962. Hirabayashi Taiko is addressing the assembly. The others, from left, are Professor Yoshida Seiichi of Tokyo University, Mishima Yukio, Ivan Morris, Kawabata Yasunari, Professor Hisamatsu Sen-ichi of Tokyo University, and Professor Takahashi Masao of Kyushu University.

Atop a mountain in Korea with my friend Kwak So-jin, who occupies the highest elevation, and other Koreans, 1968. We came down the mountain and learned that Kawabata had won the Nobel Prize.

The Nobel lecture at the Swedish Academy, Stockholm, 1968. I read the whole of the lecture and Kawabata read the classical passages in Japanese. Photograph by Kakinuma Kazuo.

TOP
With Muramatsu Hideko and her husband, Nannichi Hideo, at a reception over which she presided, on the occasion of my being decorated by the Japanese government, 1975.

BOTTOM
Utaemon's dog Hanako and my cat Hanako, and Utaemon and I. Utaemon was probably the most distinguished living Kabuki actor. Courtesy *Engekikai*, July 1980.

Hanako in enlightened company. My favorite picture of her, it was taken in the early 1980s by my friend Fukuda Hirokazu, the woodcut artist.

TOP
With one of my two oldest Japanese friends, Shimada (formerly Nakamura) Eiko, 1990s.

BOTTOM
My *kanreki* at Maribel Kilmartin's house in Palo Alto. The ladies are both of the Rubinfien family, old Tokyo and Palo Alto friends. The man is Haruo Shirane, one of my most gifted students, now at Columbia.

possible for Americans to reside in Japan as cultural entrants, as the jargon had it. This meant that they did not have to be associated with the Occupation, which everyone could see was coming to an end, and among the things they could be was a student. I was the first foreign person to take advantage of the possibility.

The university was in Hongō Ku, one of the two proud old names. My new abode was in Koishikawa, the other. It was a *hanare* in the Japanese style in a bit of the city that had survived the fires of 1945. The big dictionary renders *hanare* as, among other things, "an outhouse." This will not quite do, though it points in the right direction. A *hanare* is a secondary residence on the grounds of a primary residence. (My family's claim shanty might possibly have been called a Colorado-style *hanare* had it not been turned over to the chickens.)

Mine had been found for me by a group of youngish men to whom I had given English lessons. Most of them were bureaucrats. I did not accept payment for the lessons, but I was known to accept a favor now and then. The most considerable favor was finding my new abode for me.

Numbers of people in DipSec gave English lessons. Osborn did, and while he was about it sometimes indulged his rich sense of humor a bit dangerously. To a dear little Japanese girl who worked in the consulate he said: "You must remember that the consul was once a missionary, and bring in religion. When something annoys you, you should say: 'Jesus Christ, Mr. B.'" She actually did. I was not present on the occasion, and learned of it from her. The expression on Mr. B's face, she said, told her that something was amiss. He happened to be very pro-Japanese and did nothing by way of censuring her. Presumably the shock passed. She went on working in her corner with her typewriter.

I still have some of the presents which my band of English students brought me. On my Tokyo desk has sat these almost fifty years a lacquer tray in which I keep pencils. It was a farewell gift when I left DipSec and felt that I must stop the lessons. I am still in touch with the only nonbureaucrat among them, Nishikawa Takeo, a nautical engineer who lives in England. I see him and his wife when we are in Tokyo together. He is one of my two oldest Japanese friends. The other is Shimada Eiko, then Nakamura Eiko, who has for many years lived in New York. She was the victim of Osborn's little prank, I do not know why friendships with Japanese who live far away should have proven more durable than with those close at hand, but the fact may possibly tell us something about friendship in general. I have known these two about as long as it would be possible for me to know Japanese.

I did not have the whole of the *hanare.* Some other Americans had the upstairs. Many Japanese preferred foreign tenants to Japanese. A foreign one could be expected to pack and depart without protest if asked to do so. A Japanese might well refuse and indeed hire a lawyer. Tenants had many weapons with which to defend themselves against eviction.

The people upstairs doubtless had better sun in the winter, when it mattered most, but I had the garden and was enchanted with it. In those days I preferred flowerless Japanese gardens to florid European and American ones. It was in general an elegant little abode, two Japanese rooms with only a table and some cushions on the *tatami* mats of the larger one, and only a desk, a chair, and some bookshelves in the smaller.

The situation was neither convenient nor inconvenient. The nearest rapid transportation was a brisk ten-minute walk away, but I did not feel put upon. I sometimes walked to the university, although the walk took the better part of an hour, and more often went by bus and streetcar. I was rather proud to be in one of the old wards. The suburbs that were brought within the city limits only in 1935 begin a few paces west of my first Bunkyō Ku abode. I was barely within the old city limits, and much pleased with myself that I had managed it.

I had a chance, before leaving the Daiichi, to take lodgings in Nihombashi, near DipSec and in the heart of the old mercantile city. I turned them down because I was sure that they could not be very permanent, and I was right. Scarcely anyone lives in that part of the city any more. The schools are going out of business for want of children. The Japanese justly complain about how crowded they are, but there are unpopulated spaces, here and there in the land.

I took a dislike to Tokyo University from the start, and never overcame it. For one thing, it is physically an unlovely place. Of this I had been aware before leaving DipSec, for I had visited the campus numbers of times during my diplomatic career. The ugliness did not matter much then, but it did now that I belonged, so to speak. The campus occupies an estate of the Maeda, lords of Kanazawa, richest of the daimyo during the Tokugawa regime, which ended in the nineteenth century. Traces remain from the Maeda days, conspicuous among them Sanshirō's Pond. It bears the name of the hero of a famous (and very good) early-modern novel, and it is my idea of a dark tarn. The rest of the campus is dark and dank as well, and in those years it was wanting in devices for tempering the elements. We froze in the winter and sweated mightily in the summer. The Japanese academic year, for reasons which I have never understood, has classes running into full summer.

My inanimate surrounds bothered me far less than the animate ones. A generation gap was to be observed, but it was not of the usual sort. The usual sort has young people at war with old people. I got on very well with my professors, who were all of them a generation and more older than I. They were kind and helpful, and I think I may say that a couple of them became my friends. The problem was people of my age. I did not get on well with most of them. I found them cold and even hostile, although there are always exceptions. Among them too were kind and helpful ones. Most were not.

I was better prepared, I think it probable, than most Americans for what was to come after the San Francisco Treaty, which went into effect in 1952. The Japanese media were all sweetness during the Occupation. The campuses were not. They gave a good notion of what the media and the *interi*, the most common rendition of "intelligentsia," were really thinking. The street from the main gate to the main administration building (one of the most hideous buildings in the world) were walled in with handwritten declarations by this and that "group," "circle," and committee, and they were uniformly poisonous. I practiced my Japanese on them, even as young Japanese (very few Tokyo University students among them) practiced their English on me, and may say that it was hard going. I still did not read Japanese with ease, but I took my time, and read, and was appalled.

What I saw up and down that street brought my Tom Paine period to a decisive conclusion. I saw how easily socialism and liberalism can go mad. I will postpone a fuller account, and subsume it in an account of what ruled the media in the years after the treaty, when liberalism and socialism blazed forth and burned away everything in their path. It immediately seemed the sheerest lunacy to someone who had until yesterday been among Tom's disciples.

My trouble was that everyone knew me to be American, and America was the enemy. Had I been French I am sure I would have fared better, and had I been Russian I would have fared far better. Occasionally there was an act of open hostility, as when I would ask directions to the next grubby building I was in search of and be greeted with a snort and an averted countenance. Mostly I got nonrecognition. I was a nonperson. I did not see why I should be so quickly and conclusively tarred with the American and capitalist brush. I may say that it seemed to me a form of prejudice, though in those days, in that student body, it was a given that only Americans could be guilty of prejudice.

With professors it was very different. The one I was closest to in the earliest year or two, when I considered myself a specialist in Heian literature and was still reading and translating the "diary" I had begun in the Daiichi, was Ikeda Kikan, the great *Genji* scholar. Very shortly after I had introduced myself to him, I dropped an idea that I feared would be unfeasible, that a few of us get together and read the *Genji*, in the original, of course. I could scarcely have been more pleased when he agreed. He would recruit a few graduate students, who could not (poor people) disobey the summons, and we would read.

I am astonished now at my presumptuousness. It may have been that in those days we Americans were used to having our way. The students got no academic credit for their efforts, and of course the great scholar can have learned nothing from any of us. They may have been cold personally, but they put up with my academic demands, and I continue to be very grateful to them.

Professor Ikeda was in weak health. Along with the rest of us he sweated in the summer and froze in the winter. We were young and to us he was old, and he was a pitiable sight shivering in his overcoat as winter darkness came on. More than once I considered suggesting that we discontinue our meetings, but I could not bring myself to do it. My Heian Japanese was coming along nicely, and there was a danger of suggesting that the meetings meant nothing to me. Professor Ikeda died, much too young, late in 1956. I learned of his death when I returned from a trip back to Colorado occasioned by my mother's death.

It may be—I find it hard to say—that even before Professor Ikeda's death I was fonder of Professor Hisamatsu Sen-ichi, the head of the Japanese Literature Department, and a scholar of traditional literary criticism and early poetry. There were things about Professor Hisamatsu that one could find fault with. During the nasty years of Japanese nationalism he had been a theorist for that ideology, and he was very difficult to understand, not a good thing for a professor to be. At first I feared that I alone was not following his lectures, but presently I learned that other students were not following them well either. He swallowed his words and had other unfortunate mannerisms, such as a fondness for pre-modern locutions.

But he was unfailingly kind to me. In his gentleness and erudition he reminded me of Tsunoda of Columbia. He may have been somewhat extreme in his nationalism, but I cannot imagine that he was ever noisy about it. Though he lived a longer life than Professor Ikeda, he too is in his grave. When in 1962 I permanently gave up residence in Japan (I have returned every year, but have not since had residential status) and resumed residence in the United States, he gave me by way of farewell a poem of his composition inscribed by brush in his hand on one of the rectangles of cardboard used for such purposes. "A lifetime seeking to unravel the *Manyō*, and the way stretches endlessly ahead." With no attempt at poetry, this is the burden. I find it very touching, especially when I remember the dear man he was. I mean to give the cardboard rectangle to some archive. The *Manyō*, from the eighth century, is the earliest anthology, and many will say the greatest, of Japanese poetry.

There was another faculty member of whom I was fond, the only one not in Japanese literature. This was Ogaeri Yoshio, an instructor in Chinese. He was a small, dark-skinned man who could have been mistaken for a Filipino or some other Malay sort. I went to several China specialists seeking help in my endeavors to learn to read Chinese, and he was more help than the rest of them put together. I much regret that I did not do better. My Chinese continues to be shaky, and when I must use it I always consult an expert.

Here is a part of my diary entry for July 13, 1965. "Down to the Imperial in early afternoon. I fear that place—the Old Imperial, with all its cool pumice—will not be with us much longer, and so take every opportunity to use it as a meeting place. Today it was Mr. Ogaeri I met, and we had lunch in Ginza. He is gloomier than ever—calls himself a *yokei na mono* ["a superfluity," according to the big Japanese-English dictionary], says he likes America second best among the countries of the world and must yet find a country he likes better. . . . A remarkable man, though he will never win the fame he deserves. The wildest reaches of Kyushu to China, and, without a university degree, to Tokyo University and N.H.K. [the Japan Broadcasting Company] and all that. . . .

"I got home at midnight to find the embers of the *mukaebi* still glowing. How nice to be welcoming ancestors into my house. None have been there for rather a long while."

I include the last paragraph because it speaks of one of the pleasant little surprises Tokyo life was always bringing. The *mukaebi* were the little bonfires set out before every house to welcome the spirits of the dead to their summer festival.

Ogaeri died in the summer of 1966, at about the same time as Arthur Waley. Both deaths seem to have occurred during an unfortunate gap in my diary. I never met Waley, but felt bereaved. I felt much more bereaved in the Ogaeri case. He was an interesting, amusing, gifted, and kindhearted man.

I do not remember, for all that they contributed to my education, that any of the students in Professor Ikeda's *Genji* circle was especially friendly. A few other students were. My best friend, Takahashi Osamu, has since become a famous novelist. He is from Chiba Prefecture, which closes off the east side of Tokyo Bay from the ocean. Because of him and his brother-in-law, Hara Teruo, a potter, I spent several marvelous summers on the outer or eastern coast of the Chiba Peninsula.

Of the prefectures bordering on Tokyo, I have always liked Chiba the best. In this I am part of a small minority, perhaps, outside of Chiba itself, a minority of one. Most Tokyo people are a little ashamed to have Chiba so close at hand. It is a place of gangsters and corrupt politicians. To this I reply: all of Japan is even so, and Chiba has a rough-and-ready honesty in which the other neighboring prefectures, so much better integrated into Greater Tokyo, are wanting. Chiba is more open in its disorder and distaste for propriety than most other places that have these qualities in equal measure, and this I like.

In Tanizaki Jun-ichirō's *The Makioka Sisters,* which I was later to translate, one of the family doctors, doubtless based on a living model, has the warmth of what I translate as "his East Country origins." I did not want to clutter the translation with proper names that would convey nothing to the reader in English. In the original he is from Chiba. One of the eminent writers whom I was to know best and become fondest of, Tateno Nobuyuki, was from Chiba. Takahashi is, and Hara was (he is no longer living, having died some years ago in the United States), from Chiba. There is something about the place, an earthiness, an unpretentiousness, something.

The marvelous summers, six in number, were all in the fifties, the earliest of them 1951. I rented the second floor of a pharmacy in the village of Katakai, on Kujūkurihama, which might be rendered "Ninety-nine Mile

Beach," though it is by no means that long. I had a stream of guests from Tokyo and Chiba. During a couple of the summers, Hara stayed with me and cooked for me. During the others, the family downstairs kept me fed.

I have never learned to do anything more complex in the realm of the cuisine than boil an egg. This is because in the years when I should have been learning to cook I always had a housekeeper. I did not live extravagantly, but domestic help was cheap. Though my housekeeper never came to the beach with me, she was always there in Tokyo awaiting my return. It was late in the sixties that I found myself unable to afford help, for the Japanese were getting rich and prices were shooting up. By then all culinary ambitions had left me.

Katakai, which is no longer to be found on maps, for it has become part of a larger entity, was a fishing and farming village. The farming part did not much hold my attention except when it was having one of its festivals, usually centered upon fires in the night, which could be most splendid, or when the fireflies were out, turning the paddies into carpets of sparkling emeralds. Occasionally a firefly strayed into my rooms and sparkled the night away in my mosquito net.

The fishing part, the fisherfolk and their boats, the surf, even the four-footed habitués, quite delighted me. There was a lovable monster of an Akita dog that thought itself a lap dog. I would be sitting on the beach trying to read, and it would amble up and sit on my lap, walling off the rest of the world. It must have died long, long ago. I think the fisherfolk were the hardest-working people I have ever seen. There was no harbor, and so, at the end of a day's fishing, they had to pull their boats, by no means tiny, up on the beach. The nearest thing possible to stark nakedness prevailed. Occasionally I went out on a boat to watch the fishing. Pulling in the nets was labor of a sort I could not have survived for a half hour.

And it was all so full of laughter and bawdy singing. The women were the bawdiest. They were not allowed aboard the boats, but they helped mightily with unloading fish and pulling the ships up on the beach. I loved them, and their menfolk too, and their village.

And then it all went to pieces, most tragically. The pharmacist's wife, the really strong member of the family, had a stroke, was bedridden for some months, and died. The only son killed himself, I have little notion why, though it may have been at least in part because he no longer had his mother's support. The pharmacist was a genial but weak man. The pharmacy was closed, the surviving family, father and two grown daughters, dispersed. For some years I went back to put flowers on the graves. Then I stopped, I do not know why. When last I visited Katakai, the building on whose second floor I passed such happy summer days had disappeared to make way for a parking lot. I could probably have found another place in Katakai after the death of the pharmacist's wife, but I did not want to.

Here is part of a diary entry from June 1967:

"I have chosen to observe the longest day of the year . . . by a visit to Katakai. I stay at the Chiyomoto [the best inn in the village]. It seems to be inhabited largely by female impersonators whose business is to advertise Oriental Curry. Otherwise it is a rather sad place with a run-down look, and, so far as I can tell, a single sullen maid to do the serving. I have not had the heart to ask what has happened to maids known long ago, such as the one with the Japanese coiffure. The *wakadanna* ["young master"] was killed in an automobile accident some months ago, driving back from Tōgane.

"My room faces north, towards a thatched roof unfortunately rimmed with aquamarine plastic, and the pine groves of such rich memories. Outside in the twilight the spiders spin and spin. I had forgotten what a town of spiders this is. . . .

"The grandeur of the entry into Katakai on that clanking train is no longer permitted us. Somehow the green of the fields seems a touch faded when you come through them by bus. Very green all the same, and heavy with summer. Just for one moment, as we passed the clinic where I offered an ear infection for treatment one summer, I had the illusion that I was coming this summer, too, to stay. And why not, if I want to so badly?

"I guess I really don't. It would not be the fun it once was, old Katakai. I have changed, the town, and especially the beach, has changed. I spent most of the afternoon down there, despite the gray, blustery weather. There are not many bathers yet, but the beach is a clutter of beach stalls, or whatever they are called. I watched the boats come in, and should have been taken back a decade. Alas, it seemed a forlorn shadow of its old self. The horns to summon the women are gone, the fine ritual of drying the nets is gone. Far worse, the naked vitality is gone. . . .

"I had a talk with the head of the Hanza enterprises [Hanza was the business name of one of the net owners, the aristocrats of the village], son of him who was the head of the Hanza enterprises when, a decade and a half ago, I bummed rides on Hanza boats and then wrote nasty articles about feudal survivals. The old man has been in his grave seven years now. . . . Genshichi [the net owner with whom I was on the most familiar terms] has gone broke—there too the old man is in his grave—but the number of net owners is still the same, certain of the shell gatherers having combined and expanded. Mr. Yamaguchi—that, if memory serves, is the Hanza family name—was bitter on one subject, the bureaucracy.

"As I stood surveying the melancholy scene, I was addressed by a young man who, awful thought, had scarcely been born when I first visited Katakai. He told me how young people feel about fishing. They want to get away from it, and as soon as possible. And so maybe the Katakai fisheries are among the things our most destructive of ages has succeeded in destroying. In a way it serves the net owners right. They did exploit their men dreadfully, there were feudal remains. And yet one is sorry. And yet again—perhaps—things are not really so bad. There still seem to be, among the youth of the land, lads like Kazuo of yore, who so love the sea and fishing that they do not mind being exploited. I wonder where Kazuo is. I did not see a single familiar face, save only Yamaguchi's, among the people bringing in the boats.

"Another change: the clam rakers have been outlawed."

And from the next day:

"Down to the beach again in the evening. The tide was very high, the waves biting at the underpinnings of the boats. The Hanza man was there, ordering them back, and when they had obeyed we had another conversation, or rather I listened to his views on a variety of subjects, from Hegel to the future of the fisheries. On most subjects I found myself in agreement with him . . . when fifteen years ago I would have been in violent disagreement. It is I who have changed, not he. He deplores the flight to the cities, muses, not without bitter humor, that when the bomb comes a fisherman will have more chance of escaping than most people—and will again be recognized for the important person he is. . . . Naturally he is in favor of rearmament. Who is going to take care of you if you aren't ready to take care of yourself, he says. All in all Mr. Yamaguchi, whom I thought to be something of a prig in the old days, has been the liveliest part of this encounter with Katakai."

And from a third day:

"Back through the green fields very early. The connections were very good, and I was back in Ueno well before noon. The fields seem greener than on the way out, and I suppose I was, after all, despite the disappearance of so many of the joys of other years, sorry to be leaving. If rough vitality seems to have gone from the beach, it is still to be felt in the paddies—or so it seemed, at least, as one watched the brown folk, sturdy and grinning, get on and off the bus. In Tōgane, a sad sight: rows of cars from the old Kujūkuri Railroad, just rusting away, never again to clank us into Katakai."

In the summer of 1950 I went down to Taiwan to spend a couple of weeks with Osborn. He had married in Tokyo the year before and I was much honored to be the best man. His wife had been evacuated, since an invasion from the mainland was feared. I went both ways by ship. On the southward passage I saw Okinawa for the first time. It had scarcely begun to recover from the war, which was crueler to it than to any other part of Japan. It seemed to me infinitely sadder than Nagasaki, the recipient of so much more attention. I quickly saw that it had its own culture, different from that of Japan proper, and wondered why it could not become an independent country when it left American control. When I ask why it could not have gone the way of Singapore, the usual answer is that Okinawans do not have it in them. This may be true. We will never know for sure.

Okinawa was not returned to Japan until 1972, two decades after Japan itself ceased to be occupied. Memories of the Korean War were still fresh when occupation of the main islands ended. If the United States was to be responsible for the security of Japan, as it clearly was, then it needed bases. The largest concentration of them was on Okinawa, and it continued to be. Why Okinawa could not have been returned to Japanese jurisdiction in 1952 as in 1972 is not clear, but the military is reluctant to see anything go, and has influence.

My ability to read Japanese was still shaky. A trouble with reading Heian literature was that it brought little contact with Chinese characters. It is written mostly in the Japanese *hiragana* syllabary, phonetic and not ideographic. Modern written Japanese, by contrast, is infested with Chinese characters. So I still had some learning to do. I was determined to get it done in the course of the two sea passages.

I took along a dictionary containing four thousand Chinese characters and was determined to have it memorized by the time I returned to Tokyo. I actually did. Back in Tokyo, I found that I no longer had to carry a dictionary or keep popping into a bookstore to consult its dictionaries. The exhilaration of this discovery was similar to that of being able to walk unassisted after breaking a leg. When asked the best way to learn Japanese I reply: "Memorize a dictionary." People think I am joking.

The time in Taiwan was great fun. I did the circuit of the island by myself, and in Taipei I relied on Osborn for fun, which was plentiful. In charge of the information section of the embassy, he did broadcasts to help people with their English. Listeners sent in answers to questionnaires, and the winners received prizes, two-bit pens or something of the sort. The broadcasts took the form of dramatic skits, and Osborn played all the parts, male and female.

I was required to splash water for sound effects for one of them, from time to time splashing with increased vigor to cover my half-stifled laughter. Osborn was a superb mimic, and his talent must have had something to do with the fact that he was also a superb linguist; but, mystery of mysteries, he was unable to carry a tune. He would say that his big challenge as information officer was not to make people like the United States but to keep them from liking it too much.

I was not frightened in Taiwan as I had been earlier in the summer, when the Korean War broke out. I had quite expected North Korea to overrun the peninsula and immediately move on to Japan. The indifference of the Japanese to what was happening in the country next door passed belief. They seemed to assume that someone would do something. They were right, of course; and mixed in with the indifference was a certain feeling that the damned Koreans were getting no more than they deserved.

The sense of emergency was diminishing all over Taiwan. That it was there at all tells us that not many people among native Taiwanese, who had been badly mistreated by Chiang Kai-shek's mainland bureaucracy, wanted to become a part of the People's Republic. By the time I left people were beginning to talk about "the fluke that saved Taiwan." I do not know how much truth there was in the assertion, but it was held that a type of liver fluke (*Fasciola hepatica*) attacked and felled thousands of troops training for the invasion in the mainland canals across the straits from Taiwan.

There came another change in my life during my Tokyo University years. Early in 1951 I had a falling out with the American bureaucracy, which said that I was not being sufficiently diligent in my attendance at the university. I argued that I was being as diligent as it was in my power to be, but in vain. I had been receiving support from the American government under the GI Bill, and the support was withdrawn. I applied to the Ford Foundation, which had just begun its overseas fellowship program.

Shortly before I set off by ship to spend most of the summer in Colorado, I had word that my application had been turned down.

I set off cheerfully all the same, sure that something would happen. Something did. I have been very lucky in this regard. Something good has always come along to rescue me when I have been in trouble.

The trip was the best among my many Pacific crossings. My erstwhile band of students of English did me yet another favor. They arranged for me to be the only passenger on a Japanese whaler bound for San Francisco. During the off season, when winter prevailed down in the Antarctic whaling grounds, the whaler was used as a freighter. It was empty on the passage eastwards, and carried oil on the westward return. If ships of the sort still do that sort of thing, it must be with them the opposite. They must carry all manner of Japanese gadgetry eastwards, and make the westward passage empty. Because it was empty, the ship bounced about like a cork. I have never been troubled by seasickness and enjoyed the bouncing. It was like being on a roller coaster. I had no other passengers to distract me, and spent my days revising the *Kagerō Nikki* translation. It was my first experience of a condition that prevailed all through my career as a translator: reworking a rough translation into English of a certain fluency was always the most difficult stage in the process of translating. I took my meals with the officers. They kept telling me that the sailor's lot was not a happy one. Sure that this was true, I listened sympathetically. I may have implied above that my translations go through many stages, but there are essentially two, ever since the first one, begun with my sage in the Daiichi Hotel. I first make as literal a translation as possible. This is inevitably lame. The second stage is putting it into something that will pass as fluent, literate English.

On the night before we arrived in San Francisco, I got cold feet. I had with me a little Japanese book which, though undeniably pornographic, I thought rather charming. I had not left it in Tokyo, because I had not wanted it to be among my effects should someone else have to go through them. Doubts overcame me about the advisability of trying to smuggle it through American customs. So I dismembered it and threw it overboard. A gust of wind brought it back again. It lay scattered over the deck. I fled. When I looked out the next morning the sailors were having a delightful time trying to reassemble it. Why I did not heave it overboard whole I will never know.

The good thing awaited me when I arrived by train in Denver. In the mail my mother brought to the Union Station was a message from the Ford Foundation. It had had second thoughts. Would it be convenient for me to come to San Francisco for an interview? I was very soon on another train, bound for San Francisco, with far more luxurious accommodations provided by the foundation. I liked the thought of being in San Francisco again. My Yokohama aunt and uncle, of whom I was very fond, were living in Marin County, across the Golden Gate Bridge. I was happier than ever this time, because I thought it most unlikely that my application would be rejected a second time. The summons to San Francisco seemed almost a promise.

I was right. It is good to be from Colorado, I was thinking all the while. I had thought it many times in many circumstances (as when I learned that the kindly gentleman in Washington was also from Colorado), and here was a new set of them. I immediately suspected that the reason for the summons was that the foundation wanted wide geographic distribution and had no other applications from Colorado. Such evidence as I have been able to gather since supports the theory.

Soon after I returned to Colorado I had another message from the Ford Foundation. I was pleased and grateful, though not surprised. I had received my fellowship. I would go back to Tokyo as a member of an elite band, the first band of Ford overseas fellows, and I would study modern Japanese literature, because that is what I had said in my application I would study. The shift from Heian literature to modern literature was a big change in my life. I do not think it in any degree cynical of me. I would want to read modern literature some day in any case, and the *Kagerō* translation was finished in the course of the summer. My sister and one of my cousins did the final typing. The time was propitious.

It was a good summer. I did not know that it would be my last Colorado summer. I have been back many times since, but not for so long a time. Besides working on the translation, I walked and swam and gardened and saw family. I was the only one who really cared about the garden. It had grown weedy. My mother died before I was again in Colorado, and so it came to seem not quite so much home.

I returned to Japan by ship, from Los Angeles to Kobe, and from the latter place to Tokyo by train. I quickly went around to the university and announced my change of course. No one objected, not even the professor for whom I would now be a burden. Actually he was not a professor but a lecturer. The university had through most of its career paid no attention to modern literature. It edged its way into the subject, hiring first as lecturer a professor in another major Tokyo university (many a person at Tokyo University would deny that there is such an entity, but that is another matter), and then making him its first professor of modern Japanese literature.

This was Yoshida Seiichi, at the time a professor at Tokyo University of Education, another state-supported university. I did not get on as well with him as with Professor Ikeda and Professor Hisamatsu. He showed me no enmity, but neither did he offer the warmth the other two had offered. I had nothing to complain about, and on the other hand I had nothing to cherish.

I rather think he did not like me, and it is often the case, certainly very often the case with me, that a person does not like a person who does not like the person. Professor Yoshida once said in a newspaper interview that my Japanese, and he must have meant my command of written Japanese, was at about Japanese high-school level. I might have been amused at having this from Professor Hisamatsu, but I was not, somehow, at having it from Professor Yoshida. He was always available when I needed advice, and for this I had to be grateful. The trouble was that I did not like going to him. I had felt no such inhibitions with Professor Ikeda.

So I started reading modern fiction. My knowledge of modern poetry and drama has always been spotty. In a sense I obeyed the Japanese command. The novel has reigned supreme in modern Japan, clearly under the influence of the West. Other genres have been in its shadow. This has in a way been good, and in a way not so good. The best modern Japanese fiction is better than any since Heian, a millennium ago; but on the other hand, some very talented writers whose talents have been of a different sort have worked in the novel, because therein lie fame and money.

In my remaining Tokyo University years I read virtually the whole of the canon of modern Japanese fiction. The canon is astonishingly stable. There is no country in the world, I should think, in which "all the works" of some person or period so flourish. They certainly do not in the United States. In Japan a writer is not really established until someone publishes "all his works" in uniform edition. This can be long before his career has ended.

So it is too with "all the Japanese classics" and "all of modern Japanese literature." These last expressions should be taken as signifying the canon, again in uniform edition. Such collections scarcely vary one from another.

I have never bought one, though I have received complimentary sets. If I were to buy one I would shop around for the cheapest, being confident that my cheap set would differ little from someone else's grand, expensive set. Soon I started translating. My first published translation, as I have indicated, was a classical one, the *Kagerō Nikki.* During my Tokyo University years I published short modern translations.

The San Francisco Treaty was signed in the autumn of 1951 and went into effect in the spring of 1952. The floodgates opened and we were all swept under. The great day began for the left-wing intelligentsia, which dominated the media and the universities, saw things in black and white, and admitted no grays. The world was divided between good guys and bad guys. The former were called peaceful and socialist, and their headquarters were in Moscow. This was before the break between China and the Soviet Union. The latter were capitalist warmongers, and their headquarters were in Washington, D.C. There was a simple explanation for all the unpleasantness in the world: warmongering capitalism. Some of us who did not much like the peaceful socialists had other designations, peace mongers and culture mongers among them.

If the explanation that the intellies (as the *interi* called themselves and we called them, too, with a certain glee) had for the world was so simple as to be simple-minded, explanation of the intellies themselves was difficult. All manner of theories were advanced as to why they came to be what they were. It was said, for instance, that they were doing penance for their failure to oppose the "Fascists" before 1945. It is an explanation I found and find hard to accept. Surely a better act of contrition would have taken the form of a clear look at the world and all its problems. My own favorite theory is that they had their clocks stopped. They were back in the days of the Spanish Civil War, when totalitarianism came to Japan, but they had no George Orwell or Arthur Koestler.

I have already suggested that I had intimations, from all those declarations on the university campus, of what would happen. Clearer intimations were to be had on the beach at Katakai. They took the form of peace festivals, and they were made up mostly of students, although the socialist peace lovers who raised such a stir in the media were much older. The peace that came to our beach was very noisy and belligerent. It did not frighten the fish away. The fisherfolk went on plying their humble trade. Fish must not have very good ears.

I fought back. There was never physical violence, but there was many a shouting match. I did not like their peace and their socialism, and I said so. I may give them credit for deigning to shout at me. These days, young believers in peace and socialism (they are much fewer in number) merely sniff.

They had songs, which I found execrable.

Oh do not drop the atom bomb,
No, not through my skies.

Actually the floodgates had already begun to open in the great world of the Tokyo intellectual and opinion makers. Television was not a powerful force in those days. So the peaceful, progressive forces were focused upon the printed media, and especially on a magazine, *Sekai (The World)*, a monthly that came out from probably the most highly esteemed publisher in the land, the Iwanami Shoten, and the *Asahi Shimbun*, a newspaper that was read by everyone who was anyone in the intellectual world. *Sekai* has in the years since fallen into obscurity. The *Asahi* no longer has the largest circulation in the land, but it goes on being the newspaper of the *interi*.

Even before the 1951 signing in San Francisco of two treaties—a multilateral one that brought peace and Japanese independence, and a bilateral military alliance, the Security Treaty, between Japan and the United States—peaceful, progressive people were opposed to them. They wanted what they called "universal peace." *Sekai* and the *Asahi* were all in favor of this thing. What it referred to was a treaty signed by all the nations with which Japan had been at war. The People's Republic of China was not invited to San Francisco. Neither was Taiwan. The Soviet Union sent a delegation but did not sign the treaty. What "universal peace" meant in practical terms was a treaty the Soviet Union would sign. It meant the Soviet Union could go on refusing forever, and there would be no treaty forever. It meant giving the Soviet Union a veto.

The prime minister of the day, Yoshida Shigeru, was a strong man and a practical man, and he would have none of this. He wished to get rid of the Americans so that economic miracles and such things might blast their way ahead. He had his way, of course, but that did not keep the *interi* from making noise. A noisy time it was too.

I have said that the fifties were the most interesting years of my life. They were, but I was angry much of the time. Thinking myself *interi* in my small way, I read the *Asahi*. It spoiled many a breakfast with its peace, progress, and socialism. Presently, having decided that it was not worth ulcers, I stopped reading it. Socialism is not what it used to be, and the *Asahi* has changed in subtle ways, but I do not think that I will ever go back to it. The sight of it would probably spoil a few breakfasts.

I used to say that Japan was remarkable for the fact that the best newspaper (the *Asahi*) was the most widely read. In point of fact there is little to choose among the big national dailies. The *Asahi* may be the most widely read by the *interi* (as well as the most obnoxious), but it is little if any better than the other four. The Japanese have a marvelous expression to indicate a choice that is no choice: *donguri no sekurabe.* This is literally "acorns comparing height." The five national dailies are a fistful of acorns.

From the declarations on the Tokyo University campus I had a good notion of the progressive platform—not only were capitalists all bad guys and socialists all good guys, but all evil lay on the side of the former and all good on the side of the latter, which must prevail, making everything good. If one definition of lunacy is a loss of touch with reality, then this was lunacy.

I never argued that the United States is always right. American policy in Central America, for instance, has been deplorable. But if the United States was responsible for everything, from the halls of Montezuma to the shores of Tripoli, then it must be a pretty smart country, and anyone in his right senses would be joining it rather than trying to beat it. The Japanese Left gave us credit for far more than we were capable of, meanwhile holding that our internal contradictions must inevitably bring us down. It was ludicrous and maddening.

Signs that China and the Soviet Union did not like each other hugely, and that Yugoslavs and Magyars did not uniformly like the Soviet Union, were so much dust to be swept under the carpet. I think it particularly bothered me that the U.S. was held responsible for the Berlin blockade and wall, and for the Korean War. The peaceful socialists, the line had it, were only doing what they had to do in the face of evil.

This, in rough outline, was the Japanese (or progressive socialist) orthodoxy of the day. Not everyone subscribed to it, but *Sekai* and the *Asahi* did, and many an intellectual who should have known better did. Some of them may have been cynical, doing what would bring them fame and money, but I do not think that cynicism is strong or common among Japanese intellectuals. (It may be that they do not have a robust enough sense of humor to accommodate the requisite irony.)

In one respect they may indeed have been cynical. They called themselves "The Resistance." They must have known what claptrap this was. They had done nothing at all during the decade before 1945, when opposition to the political establishment would have been dangerous, and now that it was perfectly safe, they claimed to the world that they were brave resisters. Nothing, absolutely nothing, was less risky in those days than criticizing the United States. A person who did it need fear no punishment at all, not obloquy or poverty or incarceration or ostracism.

It is very easy to exaggerate in such matters, and I have exaggerated in suggesting that the new Resistance swept everything before it. There was resistance to The Resistance, and I was fortunate to be a part of it. Largely because of my friend Takahashi Osamu, I made my debut in the brilliant world of the *hyōronka.*

The big dictionary renders this as: "a critic; a reviewer; a commentator." None of these catches the full import of the expression. A *hyōronka* is more like a guru, happy to express an opinion on anything. And people listen respectfully. I suppose I may have been called a scrawny little *hyōronka* through most of the decade down to 1962, when I gave up residence in Japan. But the resistance to The Resistance, although it existed, was far less powerful than The Resistance.

I did not then keep a diary and cannot be entirely sure, but it must have been in the winter of 1951 and 1952 that Takahashi and I took a trip down the "back side" of the main Japanese island. The back side is the Japan Sea side, the front side lying along the Pacific and the Inland Sea. We were three when we departed Tokyo. We had with us Suzanne Le Blond, a young French woman whom I had known at Harvard. She turned back to Tokyo from our first stop, Kanazawa, because she worked in the French embassy and France was again without a government.

Takahashi and I proceeded down the back side. When we returned to Tokyo, more swiftly along the front side, I wrote a chronicle of the journey in English and he did one in Japanese. His was the influential one. I sold mine to an English-language daily and his went to an important weekly magazine, the *Sunday Mainichi.* Takahashi's deserved and got much more attention. As a result of it Matsuda Fumiko, an editor of the magazine and among the earlier Japanese career women of significance, picked me up, but not him, for he was just another Japanese schoolboy.

My first considerable public brush with the progressives was on the pages of *Sunday Mainichi.* Miss Matsuda arranged a *taidan,* which may be rendered "dialogue," between me and Nakano Yoshio, an eminent intellectual and *hyōronka.* Japanese journalism is much given to dialogues, trialogues, and panels which purport to be faithful transcripts of words exchanged among a number of people assembled over tea or beer or something of the sort. Nakano's remarks had been thoroughly rewritten when they appeared in print. Mine had scarcely been rewritten at all. He of course made me look rather silly. I have since avoided such traps. I do not accuse Miss Matsuda of deceit. She probably thought I knew.

I had been acquainted with Nakano at Tokyo University, where, before he resigned to give all his time to being a *hyōronka,* he had been a professor of English. He made a great deal of money from translations of Somerset Maugham. He had been kind in his help with such problems as wresting a copy of de Tocqueville from the grasp of the law school. He became editor of a magazine called *Heiwa,* which means (yes) *Peace.* One knew what to expect in a magazine named *Peace.* One might expect the new orthodoxy at its most virulent.

I had no right to feel betrayed. He had not lied to me. He had merely said nothing at all. I have often asked people what made him behave as he did. The commonest answer is that he was doing penance for not having resisted the ultranationalists. The answer to the answer is all too obvious. Replacing one set of lies by another seems a strange way of doing penance.

There were plenty of others to dislike. I greatly disliked the people who were educated in the United States and then joined so vigorously in the anti-American orthodoxy. They were aggressive in what seemed to me to be mass lunacy. The professional cultural exchangers who thought that if we got to know one another we would love one another were wrong. The Japanese who knew Americans best could not say anything good about us.

There were quite a number of them. There was Matsuoka Yōko, the venomous office manager of the Japan PEN Center. I kept wondering why Kawabata Yasunari, the great novelist and the president of the center, put up with her. Weakness, I thought; until one day he proved to be not at all weak. "Thank you, Miss Matsuoka, for all you have done for us," he said, and turned her out. There were the Tsurumi siblings, Kazuko and Shunsuke, of whom the latter is much the sourer. There was Ishigaki Ayako, who at least had exhibited similar tendencies during her New York years. There was Minami Hiroshi, a well-known psychologist.

The economist Tsuru Shigeto stands out among them. Tsuru was for a number of years on the editorial board of the *Asahi,* and in its heyday *Sekai* published more articles by him than by any other guru. A Harvard man, he made one point endlessly, that a capitalist economy can maintain its prosperity only by spending a lot of money on arms. Yoshida Shigeru wanted no armed forces at all; his diplomatic career had been cut short by them, and he had been arrested as too friendly toward the English and the American enemies. Yet Japan was undergoing an economic miracle.

Not all the people with prewar experience in America turned against America. There was Sakanishi Shio. Before the war she was with the Library of Congress; after the war she was with every good cause she could find, and she was one of the sturdiest friends the United States had anywhere. I loved going to her very beautiful old house in Oiso, on the coast southwest of Tokyo. It had belonged to an eminent statesman in days of yore.

Here is a part of my diary entry after my first visit to the house, late in the summer of 1964: "She has a truly lovely place, of a sort I did not know existed in this part of the country: moss in the garden and along the walk, great old plum trees, and, outside the *hanare* [annex or outbuilding], where we sat sipping booze in the evening light, great, pale-green stems of bamboo, the quiet, luminous sort that one associates with the western sections of Kyoto—the sort that demands a Kōrin to paint it. . . . Cats everywhere.

"She has been getting threats from rightists because of her opposition to immediate revision of the constitution, and has been offered a bodyguard—but says she would prefer to be assassinated."

Here is part of a 1966 entry with adumbrations of things to come. On a summer day, at her Oiso house, I was honored with the presence of Dr. Yashiro Yukio, a historian and critic of art. He was a good friend of Sir George Sansom, and that is always a recommendation.

"Dr. Yashiro told us in much detail how good the Japanese were to the Koreans in matters of art, largely because General Terauchi was under the influence of Bernard Leach."

The notion that the Japanese overran much of Asia for benevolent reasons, killing quite a few million Asians in the process, has gained a large following in recent years. The Japanese occupation of Korea was harsh. General Terauchi Masatake presided over the annexation of Korea in 1910 and was the first governor-general or viceroy.

At the end of the same entry there is another instance of a good mind gone astray, which gives a good indication of how things were in those far-away years. I went to a dinner party at the house of a friend in Tokyo, the late Theodore Cohen, who had been director of General MacArthur's Labor Division. The guest of honor was an illustrious gentleman from the Ford Foundation. He "thinks that the big problem in *his* racket is going to be the fact that the United States is getting too far ahead of the world. Computers and all that. But when it comes to turning the world into one enormous computer, I'll just bet that the Nippies manage to hold their own." It was not long afterwards that the United States started having a trade deficit with Japan.

On a summer day in 1967 Miss Sakanishi was a source of unexpected comfort. I will quote a few preceding sentences, because they tell us how things were at Tokyo University, a very important place: "A drink at the Imperial with our student Harper. He is still collecting sheafs of paper for submission to Tokyo University. The forms require that he call upon both the head of the department and the acting dean of the college. Both turned out to be Professor Gomi, and so he was interviewed by the professor first at the departmental desk and then at the doyenal. All this, he said, passed without a smile. Miss Sakanishi was also in the Imperial lobby, awaiting an *Asahi* personage. Of that little article in the *Tokyo Shimbun* she said: 'You don't amount to anything unless these people have nasty things to say about you.'"

The little article, which was anonymous and nasty, for the nastiest ones tend to be anonymous, accused me of ignorance and illiteracy. I may indeed suffer from these defects, but the famous good manners of the Japanese sometimes desert them, especially when anonymity prevails.

The last meeting with her recorded in my diary was in the spring of 1975. We had lunch together. I found that she had "aged disquietingly since last we met. She does not talk very distinctly, and her mouth is drawn and puckered, and some of her old optimism has left her. . . . But she continues to serve on every committee in sight . . . and she manages to take care of cats and house and garden all by herself, and says she will never move into an apartment."

The next entry in which she figures is that for January 30, 1976, the day of her funeral, which I attended, in the Aoyama Cemetery.

I have a score of cards and letters from her. With one exception, they are in English. Her written English contains a minor flaw from time to time, but is better than that of most American university students. Her spoken English I would have described as impeccably American. The single exception, from 1972, is a letter thanking me for a book I had sent her, indited by me in English and published in Japanese. She comments upon the argument, or several arguments, for it is a miscellany, in such detail as to make it amply clear that she has read the book. (Not many of the people to whom one sends one's books do read them, nor indeed do all of those who review one's books.) Among other things, she advises me to be patient with Mishima Yukio. Since he was no longer among the living, she meant that I must let his writings age a while before passing final judgment upon them. I do not doubt that it is wise advice, and I have not followed it. Almost thirty years after his death, I go on being fascinated with Mishima, the man, and dissatisfied with his fiction, which to me seems mannered, overly decorated, often dishonest, and generally unworthy of a man of such extraordinary talents.

The earliest cluster of letters is from 1954, when she was writing an article for a supplement to the *Atlantic* being edited by James Laughlin of New Directions. She had trouble writing it, and expressed dissatisfaction with the result. Her subject was the Japanese character. Of the subject she complains that in 1954 there was not "what you can call the Japanese character." This is from August. And in October, when the article was finished: "I am still rather unhappy about the article, but could not find any way to get around the terrific confusion. . . . If something comes out from this hopeless muddle, we do well, but what we need most at present is strong leadership."

If this was so then, it is far more so now. As Japanese prime ministers go, Yoshida Shigeru was a strong one. Through most of the years since, the country has been run not by far-sighted statesmen but by bureaucrats whose vision goes no further than rich sinecures with big companies after their retirement.

About the progressive types I have mentioned thus far my feelings are not ambivalent. I felt unadulterated hostility towards them. Of others I could not make up my mind. There was, for instance, the famous political thinker Maruyama Masao. It was with him somewhat as with Fairbank at Harvard. He had many interesting and indeed brilliant things to say, but through them ran a prejudice. In Maruyama's case it was the orthodox one in favor of "socialism." When in the summer of 1960 anti-Americanism briefly turned violent, Maruyama was conspicuous among those out on the streets showing where their sympathies lay. He seems to have mellowed thereafter.

So did numbers of others, such as Shimizu Ikutarō, among the more powerful of the progressive gurus. I heard him lecture more than once in the golden days of the progressives, and I think that there must be a masochistic strain in me that I should have gone back for more. The sneering hostility was scarcely to be borne. After 1960 it was turned upon his erstwhile fellows. At any rate I may assume that it was. I never went back to find out.

The Japan PEN branch was forty years ago a far more interesting organization than it is now. I am not sure how I became a member of the Japan Center. I never applied for membership, and yet there I was, a member, from the mid-fifties. I would imagine that this was Kawabata's doing. He was the first eminent writer I met, and we were by then on friendly terms. The Japan PEN was an important battleground in the unequal conflict between the progressives and the sensible people. The progressives were the noisy ones, and Miss Matsuoka, the office manager, whom one might have expected to be neutral, was by no means that. A gifted and intelligent woman whose talents were, I think, misdirected, she did everything she could, and she was very successful, to see that the position of the Japan PEN and that of the Soviet Union coincided. She had the support of the most influential and outspoken members. Kawabata may have been influential but he was not outspoken. He really did seem to be neutral, at a time when neutrality seemed to me to do the work of the enemy. I have already told of the day when he announced himself, most decisively, and fired Miss Matsuoka. It was a turning point.

The most influential enemy, Aono Suekichi, among the intellectual satraps, as I liked to call them, was president or a director of almost everything. An important dictionary of modern Japanese literature says that he "stood between literature and politics." This is true after its rough fashion. The sort of politics he stood with, or beside, is apparent from the fact that he was editor of *Shakai Times.* The second word of the name is a phonetic transcription of the English, and the first means "social." It followed the line of the huge Sōhyō labor federation and the Socialist Party. I disliked the Socialist Party, which has almost disappeared, more than the Communist Party. The latter was honest about where it stood. The former waffled, as did its intellectual supporters. It said it was in favor of peace.

There was, however, opposition. I might have become friends with its leaders in any event, but their bravery as members of a small opposition made it inevitable that I would. It is a painful thing for a Japanese to be in a minority. To be an outspoken member of a small minority can be especially painful, even if there is no risk of going to jail.

There was Komatsu Kiyoshi, who died in 1962, still in his early sixties. A specialist in French literature, he was a friend of Gide and Malraux. He spent several wartime years in Vietnam, where he was sympathetic with the independence movement. When I knew him he had thrown his leftist inclinations aside and was if anything Gaullist in his view of France. He did not like America. One evening, at his house, he told me, for no very good reason, that no American understood Picasso. I let the remark pass, though I thought that he must have interviewed a great many people to come to this conclusion. For me, the fact that he was unfriendly to the United States was less important than that he was unfriendly to Aono. This he was, stalwartly so.

Then there was Hirabayashi Taiko, one of the Japanese of whom I have been fondest. She was a novelist, and a dear, brave lady. She died in the spring of 1972, which was an eventful spring. Kawabata also died in the course of it, and control of Okinawa was returned to Japan. She was from the mountains of central Japan and was, in her youth, a participant in the proletarian literary movement, a leftist movement, I need not say. This was long behind her when first I knew her.

I met her through the Tokyo office of the Congress for Cultural Freedom, an anti-Communist organization based in Paris. She was one of its strongest supporters in Tokyo. I thought her most marvelous when she would arise at a PEN meeting and talk what seemed to me the commonest sense to Aono, who gave forth with the usual leftist line about peaceful socialism and warmongering capitalism and the need to further the interests of the former. Marching through an unfriendly gathering as she made her departure, she seemed to me like Joan of Arc. She was not to appearances a battling sort. She was gentle and soft-spoken and utterly womanly, and was still a very handsome woman, though somewhat portly, at the end of her life.

I saw Mrs. Hirabayashi in the course of each of the nine summers between my departure for California in 1962 and her death. Sometimes she was by herself and sometimes she was with company, usually of her choosing. She was always interesting by herself, and the company was always interesting too. When dinner was at her house in the western part of Tokyo, we always had the company of her mynah bird, a cheerful creature. It talked, but made only one remark, "Kōfuku yo," something like "I'm so happy."

"The evening at the Happōoen [an elegant restaurant in the Japanese style], guest of Hirabayashi Taiko. She also had Enchi Fumiko, Ishihara, and Herb Passin. . . . Mrs. H. and Mrs. E. are a fine pair, managing to communicate their scorn for certain of their fellows without seeming in the least malicious. Among those scorned: Mishima (he has everything, said Mrs. E., but he does not add up to anything), Oe Kenzaburō, Ariyoshi Sawako.

"Mrs. E. is really a most likeable person (nothing more need be said of Mrs. H., admirable woman), with her bubbly laugh, her quiet air of good breeding, her intelligence. 'Well, bridges are made to be stepped on,' she said, when Ishihara remarked upon what a pity it is that such purveyors of Japanese culture as myself are not better treated. . . .

"Forty years ago tonight the city lay a-burning. One year ago tonight I lay a-snoring in Palo Alto, California. Two weeks from tomorrow, I will have had my last snore in Tokyo."

The reference to the great earthquake of September 1, 1923, dates the entry. Ishihara Hōki in the early 1960s was director of the Japan Culture Forum, the Tokyo branch of the Congress for Cultural Freedom. All of the Japanese writers scorned by the two ladies have been translated into English, and Oe Kenzaburō is the second (after Kawabata) Japanese Nobel laureate in literature.

In 1967 Mrs. Hirabayashi and I went to Korea together. Despite my liking and admiration, she made me very nervous, chiefly because of her propensity for suddenly changing her plans. Because of one such change I found myself alone in Kwangju, the southwestern city built by the Japanese as a railway junction and later to become famous for a student massacre. I did not like Kwangju, and thought that the only thing to be done was bulldoze it and start over somewhere else. As a result I was not as devastated by the massacre as I should have been. In balance, however, it was a memorable journey, including my only visit to Chejudo, the large island province off the beautiful south coast.

"The first thing we did was, we had an accident. We came tearing out the hotel entrance, rounded a corner, and gave another jeep a glancing blow. The drivers got out and shouted at each other for a while, and then we went on. . . .

"We had lunch at Mosulpo, at the southwestern tip of the island. A shabby, smelly little Korean place, with splendid old Korean chests, myriads of children, and myriads of myriads of flies—and splendid food. . . .

really one of the best lunches I can remember having had anywhere, the better for its coming as such a surprise.

"After dinner [in the provincial capital] we all went down to the breakwater to watch the fishing. It was very beautiful. I do get tired of that word. Shall we say that it was very *aware* ["moving"]? Utter silence save for the calls of the fishermen, some of them spearing octopus, some of them diving for shellfish and sea slugs, and utterly dark but for their torches. . . . Tired of the modern world, what could you find less modern than a Korean lad diving for sea slugs in the waters of the farthest reaches of Korea in the middle of the night?"

I have had a modest career as a smuggler, getting things past what have seemed to me utterly unreasonable customs inspectors. The most memorable incident was at the end of the trip with Mrs. Hirabayashi, who had changed her plans yet again and already gone back to Japan. Korean customs were even more unreasonable than usual, not letting anything pre-modern out of the country, regardless of rarity and quality. The pre-modern era ended, by their lights, with the Japanese annexation in 1910. I had some not at all distinguished nineteenth-century ceramics. I knew that I would not be permitted to take them out. Having them leave the country would have taken nothing at all from the Korean national heritage. So I sought devices. I left them with a friend in the American embassy, asking him to send them out with someone who had diplomatic immunity. He sent them with Hubert Humphrey. I went to Washington in the fall to pick them up.

A sad diary entry in the spring of 1969 describes how Ishihara Hōki told her of his intention to resign his position. She pleaded with him to stay yet a while, because, she said, her doctors gave her only another year to live. In fact, as we have seen, she lived until the spring of 1972.

I went to Mrs. Hirabayashi's funeral, but there is no entry for the day in my diary. I think I may have been drinking. That is the usual explanation for lacunae in my diary. I do not often drink to drown my sorrows. Happiness is (or was, before I became temperate) for me a far stronger incentive to drink than sorrow. But very probably I was drowning sorrows that day. I quite adored the woman, for all her little foibles.

Despite the Ishihara remark that led to Mrs. Enchi's remark about bridges, the Japanese were on the whole rather good to those of us who translated and otherwise purveyed their culture. There are not many places, and certainly the United States is not among them, where such attention is paid to translators. Early in September of 1964, Shimanaka Hōji, the president of Chūō Kōron, prevailed upon the foreign minister, Shiina Etsusaburō, from Iwate, my favorite Japanese prefecture after Tokyo, to throw a party for several of us bridges, American ones all. Mishima and Kawabata were also present. It was a very elegant dinner in a restaurant in the Japanese style, and doubtless, although of course I did not see the bill, among the most expensive meals I have ever sat down to.

"The minister a dry and not very exciting man, though on one subject he was extremely interesting, the riots of 1960. He was chief cabinet secretary at the time and said that no one was really frightened because the contrast with the anti-Rhee riots in Korea was too apparent. In Korea the size of the demonstrations would grow as bystanders joined the initial demonstrators. In Japan nothing of the sort happened. Proprietors of drinking places, . . . he said, went around afterwards to thank Kishi [the prime minister] for the business he brought them.

"Mishima in great form. When Shimanaka . . . said that we were products of the war and were not likely to have . . . successors, he said that the obvious solution was to have another war."

Shiina's account of the 1960 events does not agree completely with what I have heard from other presumably unimpeachable sources. The latter have it that the prime minister panicked, wanted to call out the army, and was dissuaded by the sensible advice of his confidantes. Shiina's generalization is as good as most of them if he means "no one except the prime minister."

I have been invited to this and that event by Japanese of great eminence. I have done by no means as well in the United States. Here is an instance rendered memorable by a harmless little mixup. It occurred on the Shōwa emperor's birthday, here called Charlie's birthday, April 29. We all called him Charlie in the days of the Occupation, but the designation had fallen into disuse before he went to join his ancestors.

"Thence to Charlie's birthday party, the foreign minister's reception, at the prime minister's residence. There was a bit of confusion. The young man . . . asked me which ambassador I was. When I said I was not an ambassador, he said, 'Oh, the Norwegian ambassador,' and refused to understand my Japanese. The foreign minister seemed unaware of the mistake, though he may have thought it odd that there were two Norwegian ambassadors present."

It was a different foreign minister, an unfortunate man who died a couple of years later of some sort of seizure because the emergency ambulance could not find his address. Tokyo addresses presented difficulties in those days even to professionals. They are somewhat simpler now, though not ideally so.

There was another lady novelist of whom I was fond, Koyama Itoko. She was not popular in the literary world. An important editor once remarked, in my hearing, that she had an uncommon faculty for enmity. I got on beautifully with her, however. She was among my favorite roistering companions back in the days when I was a vigorous roisterer. We spent many a jolly evening together at the Shinjuku Westmouth. I may not have been as fond as she of shark-fin sake, but I did not let her drink it alone. Two decades older than I, she too is in her grave.

She was not as effective at answering Aono and the other PEN leftists as were Komatsu and Hirabayashi, I think because she had a less orderly mind, but she did her bit. She did more than her bit in her reportorial writing. She went to Europe in 1956, the year of the Hungarian uprising, and on her return wrote several articles that were very stern in their treatment of the Russians. She may have helped turn the tide.

I think that, given the sexist nature of Japanese society in those days (and nowadays to a lesser extent), it took a man to turn the tide conclusively. As to who the man proved to be, I will have something to say shortly. Actually it was a pair of men working together. I counted them too among my friends, and think I have been very fortunate in the matter of friends. Not being a prophet or the most sensitive of political observers, I was not aware then that the tide was turning, and indeed the biggest time for the progressives, the riots of 1960, lay ahead. With the advantage of almost a half century to look back over, I now think that it was.

My flashiest battle with the *interi* establishment had its origins in Matsuoka's and Aono's PEN. When Boris Pasternak won the Nobel Prize in 1958 and then was required to decline it, the attitude of the PEN was, to put it as charitably as possible, mealymouthed. There was a great deal of "on the one hand" and "on the other," and the conclusion was that the PEN did not think it had the privilege to say much of anything at all. Coming from a branch of an organization dedicated to supporting free speech, this was not what a person wanted.

I protested to Kawabata that it was a political act on the part of an organization that should be non-political except as regards infringements upon free expression. There came a polite answer, not as beautiful to look at as some Kawabata letters. He was a famous calligrapher, and the most beautiful ones are in brush on Japanese paper. This is in pen on glossy, ruled manuscript paper. The less beautiful ones have the advantage of being easier to read. The beautiful ones are sometimes next to illegible, for me, at any rate, though there are people who read such things easily. In Japanese calligraphy, however matters may be with Chinese and Korean, elegance and illegibility commonly go together. The letter was written from a hospital. I do not remember why he was hospitalized; nothing serious, says he. The date is the twenty-seventh, of what month I cannot say. I seem most foolishly to have discarded the envelope.

At almost exactly the time when Pasternak would have been receiving the prize in Stockholm, had he been permitted to receive it, the Japan PEN was entertaining some Russian hacks. The assembly rocked with song and laughter, a famous professional entertainer having been brought in to liven things up. I choked with anger.

Ivan Morris, an eminent scholar and translator of Japanese literature, was also at the meeting. Whether or not he was choking I cannot be sure, but he was amply indignant. Something, I do not remember what, was on at the British Embassy that evening. We walked to the embassy together, and decided that something must be done. Morris had an American father, but everyone considered him British, which served our purposes well. We would not have wished it to be an all-American thing.

We thought it a good idea to bring in yet another blue-eyed country (in Japan, all persons of European stock are held to have blue eyes). The obvious choice was Father Joseph Roggendorf, a German Jesuit on the faculty of Sophia University (Jōchi Daigaku) in Tokyo. Both of us considered him a good friend, and the Japanese held him in high esteem.

So we drafted a statement that made its way to the front page of the *Mainichi*, another of the five national dailies. We deplored the insensitivity of an organization of writers to the plight of a fellow writer. It was I who gave it to the *Mainichi* reporter, and thus I made for him a modest scoop. In Japan this is not a good idea. Favoring one reporter, a person makes enemies of all the rest. The correct thing is to call a conference and give news simultaneously to all the boys in the club. I might or might not have given the story to a single reporter if I had had the slightest expectation that it would be front-page news.

The timing was beautiful if fortuitous. An international celebrity came upon the scene, just in time to read of the affair in the English edition of the *Mainichi.* This was Arthur Koestler, who was brought by the Congress for Cultural Freedom. Most people are suckers for international celebrities, but the Japanese must be among the foremost in that regard. What had been "the incident of the three foreigners" now became "the Koestler incident." Thus it was assured of more attention in the media than it would otherwise have had.

Here is a part of my recounting of the affair, which appeared in the English edition of the *Yomiuri* for March 7, 1959. The "it" in the first sentence is the article in the English *Mainichi* which had attracted Koestler's attention. "He was incensed by it, and wrote a public letter declining to appear before the PEN and stating his reasons in detail. One passage in particular incensed him, a statement attributed by the *Mainichi* to Takami Jun, the PEN secretary. It appeared thus in the English edition: 'The Pasternak incident may be a grave problem as Mr. Seidensticker and Mr. Morris [no mention of Father Roggendorf, perhaps because it would be impolite to accuse a gentleman of the cloth of insensitivity] say from the point of view of principle. But one must also think of the repercussions that might have been created if a statement were issued by us. I do not know if it is wise to stick to principles always.'

"This, said Koestler, was the language of politicians, and, since he had announced in advance his intention of avoiding political gatherings, he thought it best to avoid the PEN. He then summarized the facts of the Pasternak case as he saw them, and added that he would probably not be here if European intellectuals at the time of the Spanish Civil War had been as timid in their protests as Japanese intellectuals seem to be now. He was saved from a Franco death cell by protests that were by no means timid."

At the PEN meeting, which he refused to attend, the red herrings flew, I say, making it impossible to have a rational argument, and "almost no one got down to the simple issues he raised: the fundamental immorality of Takami's *Mainichi* statement, if he was quoted correctly, and the fact that, for what seemed to be political reasons, the Japan PEN was not disposed to speak out in support of Boris Pasternak."

The 1959 article ends thus: "There is a bright spot in the dreary picture, however. On Tuesday the *Yomiuri* quoted the novelist Tamura Taijirō as saying ruefully that foreigners seemed to worry more about matters of principle than did the Japanese.

"Than which an apter remark could not have been made.

"Since the above was written, the PEN has sent a long letter to Koestler. It does not answer his charges, however, and only makes one feel more strongly how hard it is to have an argument with the Japanese."

Tamura was a good friend and an important minor writer. He would probably be on no one's list of the dozen most important postwar Japanese writers, but he calls back the mood of those desperate years better than almost anyone. His best work, *Flesh Gate,* a novella published in 1947, is about a band of Tokyo streetwalkers and the code by which they survive.

The incriminations flew, and a foreigner is at a great disadvantage in flinging them about, since the matter was widely held to be no business of foreigners. There is some element of truth in this view, but a person choking with anger is not easily restrained. I think the common view was probably that we three lost. The PEN never admitted to improper behavior, and Matsuoka and Aono continued to be the most influential members. It was hard not to conclude that free speech, though of universal validity, was more valid in some places than others.

We three foreign ones had eloquent support, however. Takeyama Michio, a writer probably best known for *Harp of Burma,* was the most eloquent and influential. *Harp of Burma* was written for children but is widely read by adults. It is about a Japanese soldier who remains in Burma at the end of the war and becomes a Buddhist monk. I knew Takeyama through the Tokyo office of the Congress for Cultural Freedom. He was also a friend of Father Roggendorf, though they later had a falling out over whether Christianity was good for Japan. The good father's missionary zeal insisted that it was, and Takeyama's patriotism caused him to have doubts.

The only written message I had from him, or at any rate the only one I can find, was a card in reply to a letter thanking him for his article. After thanking me for my thanks and indicating appreciation for my efforts and Father Roggendorf's (he does not mention the third alien person, Ivan Morris), he says: "The mood of the day is deplorable, but all we can do is be patient. Things are much better than they were five years ago." I did not think so, but he was right. The date on the postmark is May 15, 1959.

There were other bits of silver in the dark cloud, other bits of good blown by the ill wind. Yamamoto Yūzō, one of the revered elders of the literary world, threw a party for the four of us, Koestler and we three of the original protest, and quite a party it was, too, and quite a heap it must have cost him. He said he did not want a man like Koestler to go home angry at Japan. We had dinner at Han's, as we might render Hankyo, a restaurant a little south of the palace owned by Takehara Han, an exceedingly famous dancer in an Osaka style. Han herself danced for us. It was a beautiful evening, in every sense of the word. I was most grateful to Yamamoto. It did not, however, change my view of the PEN.

I may say here, because it needs to be said somewhere, that scarcely anyone figures in this book whom I did not know personally. I even knew Yoshida from my DipSec days, and Prime Minister Kishi Nobusuke and I appeared together a couple of times on panels. Kishi had an engaging chipmunk smile that did not show in photographs. Perhaps it was censored by the press, which did not like him. Though he is much castigated for his not at all unsuccessful endeavors to preserve the spirit and body of the notorious imperialist bureaucracy, he was a very intelligent man, arguably the most intelligent prime minister Japan has had since the war. At a time, shortly before his fall in 1960, when all the media were down on him, he referred to his supporters as "the voiceless voice." By this he meant that they were denied space in the media but were numerous and strong. The *interi* has had great fun over the expression, but it was far from beside the point and has not been forgotten.

Sometimes I am required to admit that I have never met Oe Kenzaburō, the second Japanese Nobel laureate in literature. The reaction is disbelief. Finding both his fiction and his politics distasteful, I never sought to be introduced to him. The fiction seems pompous and monotonous, and the politics are of a sort that I might have found congenial back in my Tom Paine days but do no more. Clearly he never felt a need to be introduced to me. I have occasionally seen him at large gatherings, but we have never exchanged words. For me he has been a distant presence. I doubt that I have been anything at all for him.

To return to the three-foreigner mafia, I saw rather a lot of Koestler because I was working for the Congress for Cultural Freedom. He was a difficult man. He always had his way, against the advice of those attempting to see him around. Though warned that it was very dangerous in the flashier parts of Tokyo to go into an unfamiliar place that was full of beautiful women, he would advance on a bar that caught his fancy, and then, confronted with the bill, enormous, of course, refuse to pay. Such places very often have gangster protection and are immune from the scrutiny of the police. So someone else would pay.

One evening he angrily and noisily marched out on a dinner party because he thought that someone was denigrating his native land, Hungary. I doubt that anyone was. Most of the guests were foreigners, and in those years after the anti-Soviet uprising, Hungary was held in very high esteem by the foreign set, however matters may have been with the Japanese. He may have misunderstood someone, and he may just have wanted to create a scene. Someone in the British embassy who had known him earlier said that he was unaccustomed to not knowing the language of the country he was in, and the impenetrability of Japanese unhinged him. It may be so, but I am inclined to think, merely, that he was a difficult man. He was certainly right, however, in his argument with the PEN.

All the reporters doubtless knew, through their clubs, that I was the one behind the knavish doings of the foreign mafia. I was the victim of such abuse, most of it in anonymous columns, that I consulted a lawyer about the possibility of suing. Forget about it, said he—it will get you nowhere. I was accused of being a C.I.A. agent. I was never any such thing, though I occasionally translated documents for a friend in the agency. Then there is the fact that from the late fifties into the early sixties, I worked at liaison between the Japan Cultural Forum, as the Tokyo office was called, and the main Paris office of the CCF. Liaison persons were needed, since competence in English and French was not high in the Tokyo office and Parisian competence in Japanese was perhaps even lower, except when Herbert Passin was in residence.

It was presently to become public knowledge that the congress had taken money from the agency. So I suppose it may be said that, remotely, I had worked for the latter. I did not, however, feel overwhelmed by guilt. I wrote in my diary on May 9, 1966: "In the *New York Times* this morning, or it could have been yesterday morning, since they were delivered together, four Famous People, two clever boys from Harvard, Kenneth Galbraith and Arthur Schlesinger, Jr., and two American saints, George Kennan and Robert Oppenheimer, have a letter to the editor affirming their confidence that the Congress for Cultural Freedom never had money from the C.I.A. I of course know differently because of things that happened in Tokyo, and so the document is an indication of a certain gullibility on the part of Famous People. Not that I myself see that the presence or absence of C.I.A. money makes all that much difference."

The agency was one of the Great Satans, and to accuse me of being among its catspaws was a very dark accusation indeed. There was no corresponding Satan on the other side. Everyone knew that the Soviet embassy was infested with intelligence agents and that accredited newspaper correspondents were agents too; and no one said anything. I more than once had it in a signed column as the position of an important "opinion maker" that he would accept money from the Soviet government but not from the American, because there would be strings attached in the latter case. Governments the world over give money to people of whose work they approve. Such are the strings that are attached, everywhere.

The PEN still had not changed its ways by the summer of 1960, when the streets of Tokyo were taken over by huge demonstrations opposing a revised version of the Security Treaty with the United States. I was greatly alarmed. I thought that if they had the energy and imagination to march upon the television stations, the equivalent in our day of the Winter Palace, they might accomplish a revolution. I was not alone in my alarm. Prime Minister Kishi wanted to call out the armed forces. He was wisely dissuaded by advisers, and the police managed the crisis. I doubt very much that Kishi was wanting in political acumen, but I did not have enough to see that the tide had already turned.

I could not, in 1960, see what they were all in such a tizzy about. The treaty was revised at Japanese request and answered many objections to the original treaty. In this view, too, I had eminent support. Hayashi Kentarō, a famous professor of European history at Tokyo University, was in Europe at the time of the disturbances. He told me after he came back that he could not, from Germany, understand what it was about. I knew him through the Culture Forum. All the eminent and to my mind sensible people associated with that organization persuade me that things can never have been as bad as I thought they were. The progressive *interi* were raising a huge din, and I let myself be distracted by it.

Hayashi had quite a time of it during the student troubles of the late sixties. He was dean of the Faculty of Letters, and was held captive by student rebels for several weeks. He had refused to let them have their way or even to compromise with them. Father Roggendorf and I went to see him in a hospital shortly after his release.

Here is part of a diary entry for late in 1968: "It was one of those afternoons. I kept getting farther and farther behind schedule . . . because traffic in the plebeian parts of town through which we passed has reached a stage of near paralysis. Most of the money thus far has gone into improving things for the rich people who live in the southern and western parts of the city.

"Anyway. It was nearly two when I reached Kanda, and well after when, bouquets in hand, we reached Kuramae on the Sumida. Mr. Hayashi looked well enough, though he was more talkative than is his wont, and that may have been a sign of nervousness. He said that he did not feel in danger at any time through the ordeal, though the language of the students was frightful. . . . He had little to say of Ogōchi [president of the university when the students took it over], but what he did have to say indicated contempt. Father R. quoted Professor Aoki, he who is in English literature and teaches at both Tokyo University and Sophia, to the effect that the students too have great contempt for Ogōchi—and great respect for Hayashi himself."

Later Hayashi was called back from retirement to become president of the university. It was very rare for a retired professor to be honored with the position, and rare as well for someone from the Faculty of Letters to be. Presidents tended to come from the social science, pure science, and professional faculties. There can be no doubt that his brave and dignified response to the crisis was the reason. Here, possibly, we may see Kishi's voiceless voice having its way.

The PEN issued a statement opposing the revised treaty, which had already been "forced" through the Diet, the national parliament, by the ruling Liberal Democratic Party, which had enough votes to do it unassisted. I protested to Kawabata, still president of the Japan PEN, that this was a political act on the part of an organization that should be nonpolitical except with regard to freedom of expression.

Here is a part of Kawabata's reply. "While the declaration is 'political,' there are points which show an endeavor not to be political. It does not say whether it is for or against revision of the treaty. This it cannot do. It protests the less than complete respect for free speech in the deliberation and passage of the measure by a single party. (The obstructionist tactics of the Socialist Party and others were of course wrong, but it was wrong of the Liberal Democratic Party to force revision through by its vote alone.)"

Well, maybe. I liked and admired Kawabata, but his comportment as president of the Japan PEN did not give cause for great admiration until he dismissed Matsuoka. The third sentence of the quotation above is an interlinear amplification. I do not know what it means. It might be rendered: "This would not be possible."

In the card from him which I have quoted above, Takeyama Michio says that things are much better than they were five years ago. This would take us back to 1954, the year in which the progressive tide started withdrawing. A controversial article by the playwright, critic, and translator Fukuda Tsuneari appeared in the December 1954 issue of *Chūō Kōron.* (Fukuda was a classmate of Hayashi Kentarō at Tokyo University.) The article was titled "Doubts about Pacifism" *(Heiwaron ni taisuru gimon),* and the president of the Chūō Kōron Publishing Company, Shimanaka Hōji, went over the heads of his editors to insist that it be published. This was very brave of him; in that day "pacifism" was close to being dogma. There was no telling of course what the effect on the readership would be. In fact that issue of the magazine sold out almost immediately. Shimanaka printed an apology to the readership for his presumptuousness. It greatly annoyed Fukuda, but it was a necessary sop. The Japanese are much given to apologizing for nothing. When there is nothing to apologize for, I often think, they apologize profusely, and when there is something that genuinely asks for an apology, none is forthcoming.

I had known Shimanaka for some years. His company, Chūō Kōron, was the publisher of Tanizaki Jun-ichirō, the author of the first novel I translated. He was very kind in helping me acquire rights to publish the translation, but I did not find it easy to be friends with him. "Out to Chūō Kōron in the afternoon," I say in my diary entry for the summer solstice of 1965. "Shimanaka continues to make me nervous—the sudden coldness that comes like a gaping hole in the roof." He did blow hot and cold. But this did not really matter. I had huge respect for him.

I knew Fukuda by reputation, but had not met him at the time the article appeared. He was well known as a translator of Shakespeare, a playwright, and a critic. I was once asked to name the Japanese opinion maker from whom I expected the best things, and why. I gave his name, and what seemed to me the brilliant but altogether sensible quality of his social and political essays as my reason. I did not expect him to take notice, but he did. He asked the Culture Forum to introduce us.

Many thought him a forbidding man. He rarely smiled, and was of stern mien. I got on well with him, however, and I saw him as frequently as I saw any of my Japanese intellectual acquaintances, and went on seeing him until his last illness made it impossible for him to come to Tokyo and almost impossible to receive callers. I occasionally visited his house in Oiso, on the seacoast southwest of Tokyo, very near Sakanishi Shio's, and, like hers, beautiful. Most commonly I saw him in the hotel room he kept near the Kabuki Theater in Tokyo and used when theatrical business required him to be in Tokyo for extended periods. In addition to being a playwright and translator, he was a director and producer.

"Doubts about Pacifism" is closely reasoned and tightly written. After castigating the progressive know-it-alls and the Japanese pacifist view that no problem, such as the unfortunate effects of American bases on schoolchildren, can be solved until the biggest problem, essentially the Cold War, is solved, he lists five specific objections to the Japanese pacifist movement.

"First, the pacifists believe in the peaceful coexistence of the two worlds, but where do they find evidence to support the belief? . . .

"Second, the choice between war and peace . . . becomes a choice between capitalism and communism. . . . For the young people who take the pacifist movement seriously, the capitalists become the bad ones in all regards. It is the communist countries who argue for peaceful coexistence, and the capitalists, who proceed on the assumption that this is impossible, become the belligerent ones."

After discussing the tendency of journalists, intellectuals, and such types to think that Great Britain holds a warmongering America in check, Fukuda proceeds: "Third, do the pacifists really put their faith in England? . . . I do not for a moment think that England believes in peaceful coexistence.

"Fourth, do the pacifists think that the Soviet Union believes in peaceful coexistence and is striving to bring it about? . . .

"Fifth, I do not understand why Nehru has become such an object of adulation. Would the pacifists really want such a man to lead Japan?"

Fukuda concludes that there is no such thing as complete independence in this world. Nations are bound to one another, and it is inevitable that the stronger of two nations has the stronger voice. "If this is recognized, then why is cooperation with the United States wrong? . . . There is nothing absolute about it. When it seems wrong it can always be corrected."

Many years later Fukuda was to say that everything in the article had since become common sense. This is probably true. Yet the recriminations were thunderous. They tell us how thoroughly the progressive intelligentsia had become lost in mazes of its own making.

Two months later, in the *Chūō Kōron* issue for February 1955, Fukuda replied to the attacks. He never contributed another article to the magazine. He led me to believe that this was because of the apologetic manner in which the first article had been presented to the world. I did not have Shimanaka's side of the story, and never will, for neither of these most estimable men is still among the living.

Early in the second article comes one of my favorite passages in Fukuda's writing. The "Mr. Kuno" is Kuno Osamu, a philosopher and polemicist. The *Yomiuri Shimbun* now has the largest circulation among the five national dailies. "Mr. Kuno, in his criticism of me in the *Yomiuri*, says: 'My own opposition to America is thorough and emphatic opposition to the particular policies of the government. My attitude toward American culture and the American people must be distinctly separated from this.' With me it is the opposite."

In the sentences that follow, Fukuda does not quite come out and say what is clearly implied by this, but the implication is certainly there, that he dislikes American culture but approves of American policy. This delighted me. Dozens, scores, hundreds of times I had from progressives what Fukuda here has had from Kuno. I was not to take umbrage, I would be told, at the dreadful things that were about to be said of America, because they were directed at the American government and not at the American people.

This seemed to me ignorant or hypocritical or both. Any fool could see that most Americans approved of American foreign policy, essentially the policy of containment, not at all compatible with the "peaceful coexistence" so beloved of the Japanese progressives. For my part, I would much prefer to have American culture rejected, and myself personally, than American policy, surely the more important of the two for the world, including (we may say with confidence) Japan.

One of the persons prominently addressed in the article is Minami Hiroshi, the American-educated and strongly anti-American psychologist who has been mentioned earlier. Fukuda thus quotes a Minami magazine article: "Among the women known as *pampan* are many who cast themselves away that they may feed themselves, and many who, raped by American soldiers, go into the trade from utter desperation." Fukuda wondered where Minami got his information.

I do not remember having seen the Minami article in question, but it is the sort of thing he would have said, without giving his sources. *Pampan,* etymology unclear, is a word much used at the time to designate a streetwalker, and, in particular, one specializing in American soldiers.

I am reminded of an enchanting little skit I saw in an Asakusa strip theater in the late fifties. The heroine is a *pampan* in Tachikawa, in the western part of Tokyo prefecture, where there was a large American air base. She has acquired a loathsome disease from an American who raped her, and is having her revenge by passing it on to other Americans. The impression is strong that in Tachikawa a person cannot see the ground for the carpet of rape spread all over it. A newspaper wryly remarked, whether it was true or not, that Tachikawa had suddenly become a sightseeing center.

Fukuda thought of himself as a man of the theater. He had his own company and was presently to build his own theater. In the summer of 1962, shortly before I left for California to start professing Japanese literature, I had a letter from him which touched upon the matter. "Modern Japan, in which a person like myself writes about politics and society and is read, is a most peculiar sort of country. I am sure that you are going home because you are so keenly aware of this."

Politics provided the occasion for our becoming acquainted, and were seldom distant from our conversations, which occurred in at least three places, Oiso, Tokyo, and New York. Excerpts from my diary will provide a sense of the variety, and may also give some sense of a powerful mind at work. I listened much more than I talked. The entries take us somewhat ahead of our story, beyond my departure for California, but that, I think, need not worry us.

"I left . . . to meet Fukuda Tsuneari at the New Japan. . . . Being, as I have said, tired, I looked forward to the meeting with considerable apprehension, and at first I did find it rather hard work. But then, presently, I think because his quite open . . . manner makes you forget that an ocean lies between, . . . I got all wrapped up, and when I looked at my watch it was eleven and time for him to catch the last train home. . . .

"I could not begin to set down all the things I would have set down had I had this notebook with me and been in a position to use it. On translating Shakespeare: the amount of time it takes to say something in translation quite ruins the effect, and makes it next to impossible to produce a full play in Japanese. Akutagawa, who must do something with Hamlet's "vengeance," says that he sounds like a leaky tire when he must say *fukushū*. . . .

"One may speak of modernization, he says, as if the same thing happened to every country concerned; and yet matters are obviously different between countries to which movies and a realistic theater came simultaneously and countries in which this was not the case. . . .

"Of Etō Jun . . . he says, the quick change to anti-*Ampo Hantai* came too quickly, inviting suspicion of opportunism.

"I no longer think myself very sound in my judgments of people, but Fukuda seems wholly admirable—and there are not, alas, many Japanese I would put in that category."

The Akutagawa in question is Hiroshi, a well-known actor and the son of the writer Ryūnosuke. Etō a well-known critic, killed himself in 1999. He turned coat and was suddenly conservative at the time of the 1960 riots against revision of the security treaty with the United States. *Ampo Hantai* means roughly "down with the treaty." Japanese demonstrators are much given to chanting four-syllable slogans.

"In the evening, at the Akabane, a dialogue with Fukuda Tsuneari, for *Jiyū* . . . Perhaps he was most interesting on the modern theater. You have to write an artificial language, he said, and the actor has to give it artificial enunciation if it is to be understood from the stage. Ordinary language delivered in an ordinary manner becomes a mishmash of vowels. Maybe the Japanese, too, have trouble eavesdropping. However hard I try, I cannot really overhear a conversation on a bus or a train. Maybe they can't either. Maybe all they need to do is talk fast and natural and they defeat electronic devices." *Jiyū* is a monthly magazine originally published by the Japan Culture Forum.

"Finally we talked of C.I.A. funds. 'I wish I knew where to make application,' said Fukuda."

I found Fukuda's willingness to accept tainted money most refreshing.

"Fukuda was close to an hour late. . . . Presently he did arrive, and we went off to dinner at a very elegant place in the direction of the Diet. . . . We talked, of course, of politics and of the intellies and the 'little children,' as he calls them, which is to say, the students. It seems that in the Oji agitation they have been turning out the proper Red Guards, high-school students. Fukuda, being a much less flamboyant person than Mishima, leaves one with far fewer flashy remarks to set down. He thinks democracy a pretty poor thing, but it's all we've got. And he agrees that what is happening in America will have more to do with the future of Japan than anything the intellies and the little children are doing. 'As long as you hold together we can make do.'"

This is from a summer late in the sixties, when anti-war agitation was sweeping the United States. There was agitation against putting a military hospital at Oji, in the northern part of Tokyo, to the uses of war. "Down to Oiso in the afternoon to be the dinner guest, at his house, of Fukuda Tsuneari. I went peacefully to sleep as the train pulled out of Fujisawa, and when I awoke it was about to pull into Ninomiya. The man at the gate said it would be more expedient to wait for the next Tokyo-bound train than to take a taxi back to Oiso, and so that is just what I did. Naturally I was rather late, but . . . Mr. and Mrs. Fukuda were much amused at the story of my folly, and so I suppose it served a purpose. We had dinner, Mr. Fukuda and I, and a most wonderfully prepared one it was, while darkness came over a mossy . . . garden. There were interruptions, the longest of them when Mr. F. was called upon to communicate to the *Yomiuri* his thoughts about Hayashi Takeshi, who died today. My own chief recollection of Mr. Hayashi has to do with how he kept stepping on my toes at a concert somewhere long ago, one evening.

"We talked of politics. Mr. F. continues to worry about the unwillingness of his countrymen to face up to the task of defending themselves. . . .

"We talked of art. He has beautiful things, the most remarkable a couple of bronzes said to be Heian, acquired through the father of a well-known playwright. The father was a restorer of art, and would secure pieces by putting a low appraisal on them. 'That is fraud,' said I. 'It is fraud,' said he serenely. . . .

"Mr. F. says that just after the war Kobayashi Hideo recommended most earnestly that he give up the stupid business of writing and become a curio dealer."

The name of the playwright is suppressed, for obvious reasons. Kobeyashi Hideo was perhaps the most highly esteemed of modern Japanese critics. He was conservative and mildly nationalist. I considered him an eminent acquaintance even as I considered Fukuda an eminent friend. It is of course difficult to distinguish between the two, but one has a feeling. Hayashi Takeshi was a famous painter in the Western style.

Those who are familiar with Japanese customs and manners will not be surprised that Mrs. Fukuda did not join the two of us for dinner. In conservative Japanese households there is little entertaining at home, and when there is the guests are usually the husband's. The wife may wait upon table as if she were the maid, but she does not sit at it.

"Out in the afternoon to meet Fukuda Tsuneari at the Okura. . . . He did most of the talking. What a concentration of energy and ideas he is—I felt like a great, fat sloth beside him. He thinks the solution in Vietnam is for the Japanese to take over. None of this 'understanding the Asians' mystification—he simply thinks that Japan is the country most interested and the country that ought to be doing the work. . . . Buried beneath his remarks was a sense that the Japanese would not be as soft as we have been. But of course he has no illusions about the possibility that anyone will do what he wants done."

Fukuda was one of the most interesting men I have known. He may not have been a great writer, but he wrote very well, and he had a brilliant mind. Though it was a mind that frequently left my own mind helpless in its wake, I never felt that it was trying to deceive me. He was important for Japan and he was important for me. He summarized most skillfully and succinctly what it was that we were both so opposed to.

In looking over correspondence from literary eminences, I find that, after Kawabata's death in 1972, Fukuda was the one from whom I had the most numerous written communications. (I have left my relations with Kawabata for the next chapter.) Most of them are pleasant answers to hopes expressed by me that I might see him. Even after the end of the Cold War, when the Soviet Union was no longer around to be sycophantic towards, the Japanese intellectual world seemed a bit flaky. Among them he was, as Huck Finn said of someone he admired, chock full of sand. He was so sensible, as I understand that term, and withal so erudite and intelligent. I think he was essentially a pragmatist. The important thing was whether something worked. Relations with the United States were working well, and nothing better was in sight. Therefore he was friendly towards them.

The last precisely datable communication I have from him is postmarked May 18, 1992. He has not been out of the house even for a walk since the first of the year, he says. To characterize his physical condition he uses an unusual word, perhaps of his own fabricating. It may mean something like "jellyfish" or "squid," something boneless and flabby in any event. I did not see him again. He is greatly missed. There was no one else quite like him.

In 1954 I bought a little house, and moved from the rented rooms my students of English had found for me. The two were only a few minutes' walk apart, both in the Koishikawa part of Bunkyō Ku. It was a sweet (the word seems right) little house, completely in the Japanese style, two rooms downstairs and two rooms up. I provided the larger of the upstairs rooms with Occidental furniture. The other three remained completely

Japanese. There was a small garden, dominated by a maple tree. I was never able to learn much about the history of the house. Old residents of the neighborhood told me that it had been put up shortly after the great earthquake of 1923, when the old city was expanding into the suburbs and the paddies were disappearing. All I could say for certain was that it had survived the fires of 1945.

It did not look so sweet when, with my housekeeper and her daughter, I walked the short distance from the rented rooms and sat waiting for the carter, an old person who had shipped bedding to me for those summers on the beach. My housekeeper had been Takahashi Osamu's landlady in Kanazawa, where he had attended one of the esteemed national high schools.

It was about as starkly empty as a house could be—floor, roof, a telephone, and nothing more. The previous owner had taken everything, even the light bulbs. The telephone was there because of the agent through whom I had bought the house. Telephones were in those days not easy to come by, but he said that he had ways. He needed a little money, however. Clearly he did have ways, and clearly bribery was among them.

There, in any event, was the telephone. I was using it to inform friends of my new circumstances.

"They're taking out everything but the kitchen sink," I said to one of them; and just then the sink went past.

Not a great amount of work was required to turn it into something that could indeed be called sweet. I became very fond of it, and would not have left it except that changing circumstances, as changing circumstances will, forced me to do so. Of these I will speak later.

Arrangements with regard to title were of a sort very common in Japan. I owned the building but not the land. This is not a wise arrangement, since land is far more valuable in Tokyo than buildings, which can on occasion be held to have a negative value. I should have tried to buy the land, but I was negligent and parsimonious. When finally I had to sell the house I found that it sat on rights of a complexity I would not have thought possible. These too I will describe later. The only person I could sell to without very great complications was the landlord, and he took me to court. It was the only time I had the experience of being taken to court.

I went on being angry much of the time with the interi, but I can see now that the years until my return to the United States in 1962 were my happiest Tokyo years. Having squeezed all I could out of the fellowship circuit, I went to work as a lecturer in both Japanese and American literature at Sophia University.

I liked Sophia, though the work was hard, especially that with the Japanese part of the university. I wished that the students might be more responsive. Unresponsiveness tends to be characteristic of Japanese in general. Father Roggendorf, my best friend among the Jesuits, once said: "When we have our international conferences, there are always two problems. One is to keep the Indians from talking, and the other is to make the Japanese talk."

I liked going to Kyoto in those years. I do not much any more. I have seen all the beautiful sights and have trouble summoning up resolve to go see them again. As a city, rather than as a tourist attraction, it is rather dull. My favorite place in that part of the country is Osaka, which I find endlessly interesting. It may not be quite as lively and diversified as Tokyo, but it is not far behind. It is just right for a short visit. A walk through the bustling centers for entertainment, dissipation, and so forth, is long but not impossible. A walk through corresponding districts of Tokyo without the help of wheels would be wholly impossible.

The great novelist Tanizaki was in the Hakone Mountains, southwest of Tokyo, when the earthquake of 1923 struck. He took refuge in the Osaka region without going back to Tokyo to inquire after his family. Most refugees from the earthquake went back to Tokyo as swiftly as was possible. Tanizaki stayed on in the west, which is to say, the Osaka region.

The common view is that he found there an old tradition to which he was drawn ever more strongly. I suspect that this is only part of the story, and a minor part. In his personal life, he was not such a traditional sort of man. I suspect that his strongest reasons for liking Osaka were not greatly different from my own. In the fewest possible words, I like Osaka because of its freedom from inhibitions. It is a lusty city. It does not have the hangups of Tokyo. In the matter of hangups, Kyoto is even worse than Tokyo.

I stayed occasionally with Donald Keene, of whom I had seen a great deal during the Harvard year. During the fifties I saw him less frequently, when he was in Tokyo or I was in Kyoto. He had a beautiful little place overlooking a green valley in the eastern hills of Kyoto. The valley is no longer green. The Shinkansen, commonly called the Bullet Express, passes directly below. The house has been moved to the campus of Dōshisha University. My little house in Koishikawa was Keene's place in Tokyo in the early years after I bought it. Then he got to know the Shimanakas of Chūō Kōron and stayed with them. For this I was sorry. I enjoyed having him.

More often I stayed with my old friend Hara, Takahashi Osamu's brother-in-law. He moved to Kyoto, a place for potters, shortly after our summers on the beach. He married a Kyoto girl and built himself, with his own hands, a house, also in the eastern hills, within walking distance of Keene's. It stood on temple grounds, on the slope leading up to the municipal cemetery. Mrs. Okumura, Keene's landlady, used to say that it was a slope up which every Kyoto person passed, sooner or later. The house reverted to the temple when Hara and his family emigrated to the United States and, some years later, his mother returned to her native Chiba. He spent his last years in Virginia, an easy drive from Washington. I still miss him. I think his departure from Kyoto may have had something to do with the waning of my interest in the place. There is this in my diary, for May 8, 1965, after the departure: "Mingled in with my sleepiness all day has been, for reasons I cannot identify, a scarcely bearable nostalgia—for Colorado when I was young, for Kyoto when Hara was still there (how grievously I failed to appreciate him), for Honolulu twenty years ago, for this, for that." A trouble with Hara was that he was too good natured. Without knowing it a person would take advantage of him.

The fifties were the years when I did most of my traveling in Japan. I covered the country fairly thoroughly, though there are still famous places, including some spectacular mountain ranges, to which I have not been.

People, most of them Japanese, are always asking what Japanese place I like best. The honest answer, Tokyo, is often a disappointing answer, and so I have other answers at hand. Osaka is not among them. That too would be disappointing. Conversely, neither is Kyoto, which is probably the answer most likely to please. I say that my favorite provincial cities are Nagasaki and Kanazawa. The latter is not as honest an answer as the former. Kanazawa, though it came safely through the war, has been busy destroying itself ever since. Nagasaki has been better at holding on to its past. Not much survives from the Tokugawa centuries, when it was Japan's one narrow window on the world, but much does from the late nineteenth century, one of the most pleasing periods, for me, in Japanese history.

My genuine favorites among the provincial cities are northern ones, Sendai, Hirosaki, Morioka. Indeed I am fond of the whole northern region. The best-looking Japanese, in my view, are northerners. But Tokyo has its way in everything, and the day is at hand when they will be like Tokyo people, altogether more sullen and sneering, especially the young ones.

I was never among those foreign persons who so immersed themselves in Japan that they severed relations with the foreign set. Tokyo was, in those years, full of friendly and amusing people of European, including American, stock. For me the most amusing and interesting, aside from the Jesuits, were bureaucrats of one kind and another. The foreign set was actually several sets, bureaucratic, commercial, religious, and more. The bureaucratic set included diplomats, representatives of cultural agencies, and spooks (as we called the people of The Agency, whom we could easily identify, though they had covers).

There were the most delightful parties at the British embassy, where, through more than one night, no one all across the very handsome grounds can have caught a wink of sleep. My best friend in that embassy once said that he was going to have to choose between partying and working. He actually does seem to have made the choice, in favor of working, but, happily, this did not happen until he had left Tokyo. It was through the cultural agencies that I met people of huge international fame, such as Igor Stravinsky, Arthur Koestler, and Margot Fonteyn. The last once said, in my hearing, with regard to traditional Japanese dance, that moving so slowly must certainly require great discipline, but was not, really, her cup of tea.

Another fairly regular visitor to my Koishikawa home was Gregory Henderson, a Korean specialist in the Foreign Service. He was studying Korean at Berkeley the year the four of us were studying Japanese at Harvard. He held several posts at the American embassy in Seoul, the last of them as cultural attaché. His widow, Maria von Magnus Henderson, known to all of us as Maia, is a Berliner and a sculptor. They put together a splendid collection of Korean ceramics, now in the Fogg Museum at Harvard. I do not know whether it was Gregory's influence or a general liking for the Korea of those years that made me prefer Korean ceramics to Japanese.

I was a guest of the Hendersons in Seoul more frequently than Gregory was a guest of mine in Tokyo. I first went to Korea in 1959, and quite fell in love with the place. I went frequently in the two decades or so that followed, staying with the Hendersons whenever possible. Like my fondness for Kyoto, my fondness for Seoul has waned, though I do not doubt that the temples in the provinces are still lovely.

The sere, brown beauty of the Korean landscape made me feel at home.

The people seemed richly humorous, as the Japanese were not by any stretch of the imagination. They bubbled with laughter, and they were so open, even criticizing the dictator of the day, Syngman Rhee. (I have since come to think that the appearance of openness was largely illusory. My first visit came at a time when I was much put out by the Japanese and their apparent willingness to allow the bunch of lunatics known as the *interi* to lead them about by the nose.)

In the 1950s, Seoul was a delightful city, still in large measure a sea of Korean roofs, tiled in the old manner, far stronger and more fibrous than the Japanese roofs. Today it is a city of hotels, automobiles, and frightful traffic jams. Tokyo has an excellent rapid-transit system, which Seoul does not. It is hard to deny that the Japanese have been better than the Koreans at building a huge city.

The countryside too has changed. Rather ugly houses in a somewhat modern style prevail, and the thatched roof has virtually disappeared. The old Korean farmhouse had a most wondrous thatched roof. It had infinite flexibility, and could cover any space. It would wander off in this direction and that in search of new spaces to cover, and whatever shape it finally took was beautiful. I am sure there are still very beautiful places, if one is willing to wander through hills and mountains to find them.

My best Korean friends were mostly official sorts, associated not with the Korean government but with the embassies. The Korean I most admired, however, lived apart from such institutions. This was Chang Chun-ha, publisher of the monthly magazine *Sasangge,* which means something like *World of Ideas.* It stood for what I think of as liberal ideas, democracy and tolerance and the like, in a country plagued by dictators. It continued to do so until Chang, thinking that something more direct was called for, went into politics and was elected to the National Assembly.

He did not in the slightest fit the Japanese stereotype of a Korean: noisy, quarrelsome, and reeking of garlic. Though friendly, he was very soft-spoken, and he had huge dignity. His Japanese was not good, because he had spent much of his adult life in China, but he did not mind using it. I think perhaps he had a Chinese sort of personality. I thought of him as the Confucian superior man. He went on receiving me even after association with foreigners had probably become a political liability.

This from a diary entry for the 1968 stay in Korea in the course of which I learned of Kawabata's Nobel Prize: "I ventured to call Chang Chun-ha, who is now an opposition member of the National Assembly, and was startled to find myself invited to lunch, which was Korean, and very lavish, in a place behind the embassy. I expected him to be silent or else to talk bitterly of the corrupt ruling party, but he is too complex and interesting a man to be easily predicted. Of corruption he said only, upon my urging, that things are no better than they ought to be, only better organized than they used to be. The matters he is concerned about are the continuing imbalance between urban and rural living, with nothing being done, he says, to help the farmer, and defense."

A few months later I saw Chang in Tokyo. "Down to the Prince Hotel in midafternoon to see Chang Chun-ha, who occupies an eleventh-floor room looking out upon the base of Tokyo Tower, which, from such a perspective, is ugly and menacing. He is on his way back to Seoul from a trip through Southeast Asia. You certainly do get a different view of things from Korean opposition MPs than from Japanese opposition MPs. He is against a quick peace in Vietnam because he thinks that, as things stand, the country would be in the hands of the communists in three months. This is because the government is almost completely alienated from the people. Almost no one will report on the activities of the guerrillas. He fears that the same thing may happen in Korea, and continues to be worried about the farm situation. He also worries about Okinawa, which he wants us to hang on to."

On November 29, 1975, there is this sad entry: "Ishihara [of the Japan Culture Forum] said one thing that made me sit up and listen, with horror: that Chang Chun-ha was killed in a mountain-climbing accident last month. He fell over a cliff on one of the mountains north of Seoul. When such a thing happens to such a man, it seems far likelier that someone pushed him or that he jumped than that he slipped. He was a remarkable man for whom everything went wrong. I suppose the summation must be that he was a failure."

I have not read or heard of further inquiries into his death.

In the mid-fifties, I had exhausted the fellowship circuit. I started teaching at Sophia University and otherwise eked out a living by part-time jobs, such as that with the Congress for Cultural Freedom, and by free-lance writing. Sophia was a pleasant and interesting place, but it did not, in those years, pay very well. Father Roggendorf used to say that, unable to live in the style for which it was meant and which a hierarchic society such as that of Japan demanded, it relied on "Frings benefits." This was a reference to the cardinal archbishop of Cologne, who subsidized Sophia generously.

For several years, down to 1962, I wrote a weekly column for the English edition of the *Yomiuri Shimbun.* On May 16, 1962, I announced that the column would appear no more, because I was going home. These are the concluding sentences of the last column: "The Japanese are just like other people. They work hard to support their—but no. They are not like other people. They are infinitely more clannish, insular, parochial, and one owes it to one's self-respect to preserve a feeling of outrage at the insularity. To have the sense of outrage go dull is to lose the will to communicate; and that, I think, is death. So I am going home."

I have not really changed my mind, though I would not I think express myself in so highly wrought a fashion today. I was fed up. The passage is, I am sure the most widely quoted one from the scattered miscellany which I might call my writings, and the reason is clear. It is in a sense prophetic. It looks ahead to the big debate between those who are called the revisionists (also the Japan bashers) and those whose clearest designation is probably "the Chrysanthemum Club." This expression refers to their willingness to accept Japanese orthodoxy. One of the most fundamental points in the debate has to do with whether the Japanese are like the rest of us. The revisionists hold that they are not, and that it is vain to hope that they will become so at any time in the near future. The others hold that if the Japanese occasionally seem a bit peculiar, they are just going through a stage and soon will be like the rest of us. Clearly I was a revisionist ahead of my time a third of a century ago, and I still am.

I was deeply upset by the anti-treaty disturbances of 1960. I should perhaps have listened more carefully to the calm counsel of people such as Takeyama Michio and allowed myself to be persuaded that the worst was past. I did not. I did not think I could stay on much longer in a country where opinion seemed to be shaped by intellectuals so utterly out of touch with reality. I resolved that when a good opportunity for academic employment on the other side of the Pacific came along, I would accept it.

There had been several such opportunities during the fifties. I had turned them away because I still found Japan fascinating, even if maddening. The passage quoted above gives adequate expression to the feelings that came to be mine as a result of that high summer of 1960. Early in 1962, I was asked to substitute for a Stanford professor on special assignment in Japan. I accepted.

I did not mean by those ringing words in the *Yomiuri* that I would have nothing further to do with Japan. I meant that I would not again have residence in Japan and would not again work there. All of my entry permits since have been valid for no longer than six months as a "cultural entrant."

The time had come to depart, and I am grateful for having had almost a quarter of a century in three good American universities after returning to the United States. If I had stayed on in Japan, I might presently have found myself teaching in one of the myriad English-language schools. I have made numbers of important decisions impulsively, and they have generally proved to be good ones. I waited quite a while for the Stanford invitation to come, but I made the resolution to give up residence in Japan impulsively, during the summer of discontent, and stayed faithful to it.

The disturbances of 1960 were not the only reason. I was fed up with being a foreigner, and there can be few places where a foreigner is more foreign. The aftermath of the centuries of seclusion lingers on, so much so that one sometimes wonders, half jokingly, whether the main object of Japanese foreign policy might not be a return to seclusion. The Japanese language, as no other language with which I am familiar, is constantly making distinctions between insiders and outsiders, which for our purposes can be taken to mean natives and aliens. In such circumstances, things that should not matter at all do come to matter, and the accumulation rankles and festers.

I have come to think, in the years since, that it is better to be a foreigner in Japan than to be a Japanese in Japan. The foreigner is not encumbered by the strait jacket of rituals and obligations which the middle-class Japanese—the "salaryman"—is compelled to wear. I did not think so a third of a century ago, however.

I must now revisit the fifties to comment on my relations with other famous authors.

FIVE

FRIENDLY RELATIONS

THE YEAR 1954 NOW SEEMS CRUCIAL, a crossroads, and it is right that the two expressions share a common etymology. It now seems clear that in 1954 the tide began to turn against the peaceful progressives. It was also the year in which I was approached by Harold Strauss of Alfred Knopf to translate modern Japanese fiction. In my personal life, it was the year in which I bought the only house I have owned. Along towards the summer solstice of the year I had been alive precisely a third of a century.

I do not remember that I considered the year crucial. I was probably on the beach in Katakai, pleasantly summering, when I passed the third of a century mark, and I doubt that I gave it a thought. I did not yet realize the significance of Fukuda Tsuneari's attack on the peaceful progressives. Nor did I foresee that much of the following years would be given over to Strauss's publishing program. So it may not have seemed a crucial year, except perhaps in the matter of lodgings; but it was.

Aside from Saeki Shōichi from the Sasebo days, and diplomats and politicians from the DipSec days, Kawabata Yasunari, later to be the first Japanese Nobel laureate in literature, was the first eminent Japanese I met. Saeki is now a famous critic. Our friendship is of doubtful antiquity. It is possible, as I have said above, that we met in Sasebo, where we were both concerned with the problem of getting the Japanese armed forces repatriated from the continent.

Nor can I give the precise details of my meeting with Kawabata. It was at a dinner party or reception, I am sure, probably given by some embassy or diplomat. I am sure as well that it was shortly after I left DipSec. We talked about a novel of his (*Maihime,* or *The Dancer*) that was then being serialized in a newspaper. Serialization began late in 1950 and ended early in 1951. I thought then and still think that it is not a good novel. I did not say so, of course, and it gave us something to talk about. Finding something to talk to Kawabata about was never easy, and it was very daunting until I learned to follow his example and be content with nothing at all. A lady once came up, at a later party, and asked what the two of us were meditating upon. We must indeed have looked as if we were sunk in meditative profundities. For all I know, Kawabata may have been.

He was a sparrowlike man with extraordinary eyes, large and piercing. The silence and the eyes were conspicuous on that first meeting, and they continued to be. In my diary entry about his death I remark that when I was taken to view the remains it was the first time that I had ever seen him with his eyes closed. The absence of the eyes changed the face utterly. Strangely, in death, it became a more approachable face. The eyes had seemed to delve to the very core of a person, though presently I got used to them. I suppose the important thing was coming to see that neither the silence nor the eyes indicated animosity.

Mishima Yukio, more famous as a writer but with no grand international prizes, once told me of an evening with Kawabata. They were at some gathering of an international sort. Kawabata had been silent, and the picture of boredom. The two left together. Mishima remarked upon what a pity it was that Kawabata had to put up with such affairs. "Oh, it was fascinating," Kawabata had replied. I sought to hide my surprise, for to show it would have suggested that I suspected Mishima of fibbing. I had had identically the same experience, and it must have happened more than twice, an apparently morose and unhappy Kawabata indicating delight at events that were the cause of apparent malaise.

In 1954 I had a letter from Harold Strauss, the chief editor at Alfred Knopf in New York. He wished to know whether I would be interested in translating modern Japanese fiction for Knopf. In the years following, I was to hear a great deal of "The Program," as Strauss called it. The program was Strauss's creation, and to it he devoted most of the last active years of his life. As a result, he became the person most responsible for bringing the riches of modern Japanese fiction to the attention of America and Europe. I rather think that I got on better with Strauss than did Donald Keene, who has little to say about him in *On Familiar Terms.* I think the reason may have been that I was a Westerner, whereas Keene and Strauss were both New Yorkers. Keene more than once remarked on Strauss's "arrogance." There was that about him, undeniably, but it was tolerable, given the highly laudable work he was doing.

We never quarreled, and on the whole he listened to my advice and followed it. He handed down the law on only one occasion that I remember. He asked when I proposed to submit my translation of Mishima's last novel. Never, I replied, because I did not like it. He became a tower of rage. We had had a gentleman's agreement, he said, that I would do it, and speedily. On only one occasion had I thought him to be dishonest, and even then I was not sure. So I was certain that I had agreed to do the translation speedily, and had quite forgotten about it. I did do it, as speedily as the circumstances of the time permitted. It is not among the translations of which I am proud. I have long held that a good translation emerges only when the translator has a high regard for the original work.

The instance of possible dishonesty has to do with Kawabata. I had published in a Japanese magazine a partial translation of *The Sound of the Mountain,* arguably Kawabata's best novel. I asked Strauss if he might be interested in publishing a complete translation.

"Oh, Ed, he's so *precious,*" said Strauss, with a particular New York emphasis on the last word.

This was some years before Kawabata won the Nobel Prize. When he did win it, Strauss was very much interested in the novel. He denied ever having made the remark about preciosity. But he did make it. The dejection with which I walked westwards across Manhattan from the Knopf offices is too vivid to have been imagined. It is always possible that he quietly forgot.

Strauss's arrogance did not go as far as bullying. Generally I had my way. He was not obsessed with best sellers. As long as The Program as a whole was in the black, he did not mind if a little red ink blotched this and that work along the way. Although I share no Knopf secrets in that regard, I suspect that Mishima and Murasaki Shikibu, the greatest classical Japanese writer of prose fiction, did more than anyone else to keep it in the black, and so to keep it going.

Strauss might not have come to me had he not seen early translations of mine, and had he not lost his first translator. He had already published one novel by a living writer, a popular sort of writer. The translation was more than adequate, but, alas, the translator committed suicide shortly after its appearance. Strauss made clear that, having had a moderately successful debut, The Program need no longer worry about such things as popularity and approachability. Provided I was found up to the work, the choice of the next translation would largely be up to me.

My translation of the *Kagerō Nikki* had already been brought out, under the original title, by the Asiatic Society of Japan (which, bless it, has never bowed to the dictates of political correctness to change the first word to "Asian"). Later it was published commercially as *The Gossamer Years,* an allusion to the very famous passage from which the original title comes. My first sallies into translating modern Japanese were two little stories published in the inaugural issue of *Encounter.* What I think to be the earliest of the three dozen letters I have from Kawabata informs me that he has obtained permission to publish the translations from the widow of the author Dazai Osamu. The letter is dated August 24, and the postmark establishes the year to be 1953. The address is Katakai, where I was happily summering on the beach. Kawabata never failed to do what I asked of him in such matters as translation rights. I think he probably held it to be among his duties as president of the Japanese PEN to do what he could to promote translation even when it went against his own interests. I was not aware of the possibility at the time, but I have since come to think that to do favors for rival authors, not all of whom he can have liked, must sometimes have been difficult, requiring an uncommon amount of charity. It is well known that Dazai and Kawabata had never been not on the best of terms.

Since the choice of the Dazai stories was entirely my own, I must have liked them better in 1953 than I do now. (Dazai was the writer news of whose suicide, or murder, reached the *President Wilson* when it was bearing me from San Francisco to Yokohama and all those other places in the summer of 1948.) His early writings are informed with a wry humor that I still find very attractive. The late writings seem altogether too full of self-gratification and self-pity.

My next endeavor in translating modern Japanese was more considerable: Kawabata's *The Izu Dancer.* This is the work, published in 1926, which established Kawabata's position in the literary world. Though often called a short story, it is really that most inconvenient of lengths, the novella—too long for most magazines and too short to keep the covers of a book apart. Abridgment was needed.

I of course asked Kawabata's permission. I have a pleasant letter from him dated October 20, 1954, granting the permission. In *On Familiar Terms* Donald Keene describes a similar letter, having to do with an anthology of Japanese literature on which he was then at work. My letter seems to be the simpler of the two. Kawabata says that I may do as I wish with the story, and that it may be used both in the Keene anthology and in the *Perspective* which the versatile James Laughlin, poet, critic, and publisher, was then doing for the *Atlantic.* Laughlin did a series of *Atlantic* supplements, all under the same blanket title, on various countries, and was then at work on one for Japan. As Keene describes his letter, Kawabata set several conditions. In mine he set none. The translation does not appear in the Keene anthology, which, however, includes a shorter Kawabata story, also translated by me.

When I undertook to do *Snow Country,* my first book-length Kawabata translation, Keene said it was altogether too insubstantial a work to endure translation. He may well have been right. Some think the translation a success and some do not. More to the point is that the same thing could have been said of *The Izu Dancer.* I have no recollection that Keene ever seriously considered it for his anthology.

I have regrets for the abridgments, on two grounds. The first is that I now think them badly done. The main story is a sweet little idyll about an unhappy Tokyo high-school boy, clearly Kawabata, who journeys on foot and initially in solitude, north to south, the length of the Izu Peninsula, a few miles southwest of Tokyo. He strikes up company with a family of itinerant performers, among them the young girl of the title. As a result of their company, and especially hers, he returns to Tokyo dissolved in tears but much revived. I cut all traces of ugliness, of which there are striking ones, and everything that seemed to me to approach the sentimental. I now think I should have been more evenhanded, cutting from the main narrative as well, until I had things down to size. Thus I would have preserved the delicate balance which I now think makes the story succeed.

The second cause for regrets is that the reader was not informed of what had been done. I think that there is nothing wrong with abridgments provided the reader is clearly informed that they have been made. I do not remember that I ever suggested to Laughlin that this be done. My sense of the ethics of translation was not then, perhaps, as highly developed as it might have been.

I was very grateful for the chance later to publish a complete translation. It is in *The Oxford Book of Japanese Short Stories* (1997), and I was astonished to find it not the longest piece in the anthology.

The story of my earliest professional relations with Kawabata has been a digression from the story of my relations with Strauss, who had nothing to do with the Dazai translations or the earliest Kawabata translations. I must now leave the Kawabata story for a time to continue with Strauss. The first work we chose for The Program was not by Kawabata but by Tanizaki Jun'ichirō. An end to digression having been announced, it must continue a little more, because, as was the case with Kawabata, I had already translated a bit of Tanizaki before I was summoned by Strauss to be a part of The Program.

I translated part of a famous essay called "In Praise of Shadows" in 1954 for the inaugural issue of *Japan Quarterly.* I imbedded excerpts from the Tanizaki text in summary and commentary of my own. It was presumptuous of me, I now see, to think that my commentary could supplement the words of the great master. I was by no means sure, however, that I liked the whole of the essay. Some of it seems a little silly. There is an anthem of praise to a bowl of soup, for instance, that makes me think of nothing so much as "Soup of the evening, beautiful soup." One of my best students, Thomas Harper, later completed the translation, and the two sets of translations were amalgamated and published in 1977 without my original commentary.

"In Praise of Shadows" was written during the years, from the late thirties into the early forties, in which the action of *The Makioka Sisters* occurs. The best of it is very good. It has become the most famous and persuasive statement of the austere, medieval system of Japanese aesthetics. Not the only such system, it is probably the one which the world has come to think most Japanese. It prefers the withdrawn, the dusky, the monochrome, to the bright and cheerful, although there is plenty of this last in Japanese culture too. The polychrome system, as we may call it, is even older and just as important. The Kabuki, the plebeian drama of the great merchant cities under the Tokugawa shoguns, is highly colored, sometimes dazzlingly. There is evidence in *The Tale of Genji,* hard to accept today, that the Japanese court thought Korean taste rather drab and colorless. I may say that I myself prefer the bright tradition to the somber one, but it is the latter that we are talking about at the moment.

There is without question an element of pretense in the Tanizaki essay. Tanizaki's own dwellings, such of them as I saw, were not at all submerged in shadows. They were bright and lively, looking out over (and not at all out of harmony with) one of the raunchiest resorts in Japan. I do not mean to suggest that they were in poor taste. Nothing Mrs. Tanizaki had a hand in was in poor taste. They were not shadowy, however, nor did they seem to have any particularly antiquarian intent.

Mrs. Tanizaki told of something that happened while one of their numerous residences was under construction. Tanizaki asked the architect to come around for consultation. He would be happy to do so, said the architect, but he did not think it necessary. He had studied "In Praise of Shadows" carefully, and knew exactly what Tanizaki wanted.

"Oh no!" said Tanizaki. "Don't build me that kind of house!"

If it is posturing, however, it is like the posturing of a good actor. It is very successful. It goes beyond Tanizaki's tastes to tell the world, in memorable language, with striking imagery, something the world should know about.

I did not initially do well with The Program. Having told Strauss that I would be happy to translate for him, I suggested that we think of Tanizaki. This is because I agreed with Keene to an extent. I thought Kawabata and Tanizaki the best of living writers, and I thought Tanizaki the more robust of the two, the more likely to emerge in reasonably healthy shape from the ordeal of translation. It is a clumsy meat-axe kind of process, constantly demanding that something be thrown away, and the necessary sacrifices could be more reasonably asked of Tanizaki than of Kawabata. Strauss was agreeable. He asked for a sample translation.

I chose my passage unwisely. My thought was that we would plunge immediately into the long work, *Sasameyuki,* that is generally considered Tanizaki's postwar masterpiece. It turned out to be the second Tanizaki work in the program. Strauss and I had a devil of a time with the title. The Japanese title demanded a noun and an adjective. The noun was easy enough: "snow." The qualifying adjective was impossibly difficult. A very delicate fall of snow was asked for, to be applicable to the affairs of the heroine (we may say, though the matter is arguable), a retiring Osaka beauty. We could think of nothing that was not either ambiguous or sentimental. Finally, at Strauss's suggestion, it became *The Makioka Sisters.*

The passage I selected to translate was an unwise one for a simple reason: it contains dialect. A little experience would probably have shown me the folly of the choice. I now think that translation is a succession of soluble problems, which should be addressed because they are soluble, and problems which can be dismissed, and therefore are no problems at all, because they are insoluble. Dialect falls in the latter category. Strauss found the conversation in my translation stilted. Of course it was, I retorted. I was attempting to convey the feel of the dialect, and for this standard English would not do.

He was not convinced. I conceded him his point and had another try, this time of a straighter passage, so to speak. This time he was pleased. He thought, however, that *The Makioka Sisters* was a bit heavy to be our first Tanizaki. For my part, I was chary of experimental works, and Tanizaki was a very experimental writer. He liked experimenting with traditional forms, or non-forms. In pre-modern Japanese prose the discursive essay is as important as the tale or narrative (or, in one great instance, the novel). I wanted something more clearly recognizable as a novel. It may be that I felt inclined to accept Strauss's reasons for making the first work in The Program a somewhat popular one. In any event I did not want quite yet to undertake indoctrinating readers in something outside accepted conventions.

So we hit upon a novel from a few years after the Tokyo-Yokohama earthquake of 1923. The word "novel" is here very important. Modern Japanese literature has been dominated by confession that scarcely seems fiction at all. I wanted a novel that would be recognized by my audience as a novel, centered upon believable character. Tanizaki was not a very confessional sort of writer, but much of what he calls fiction hovers on the border between essay and fiction. I wanted something that was undeniably and successfully fiction.

A great many people, including a great many writers, left Tokyo and Yokohama after the disaster. Tanizaki had been living in Yokohama. He took refuge in the Osaka region. Unlike most of the rest of them, he did not go back. The novel has to do with the inability of the hero to make up his mind. Will he get a divorce? Will he not get a divorce? Will he return to a more traditional way of living? Will he not? He does not know, and neither do we, quite, at the end of the novel, though the suggestion has been strong from the outset that the former choice will prevail in each of the big dilemmas. I find it harder all the time, however, to believe that Tanizaki was drawn to Osaka because it is more traditional than Tokyo. In this regard I have changed, for I clearly oppose a traditional Osaka to a modernizing Tokyo in my introduction to the translation. I now think one of the chief charms of Osaka, of which I am very fond, to be its lusty, unapologetic modernism.

I had fun selecting a title, and the result, *Some Prefer Nettles,* brought me as near as I am likely to get to somebody's famous quotations. The rendering of *tade kuu mushi mo sukizuki* in Kenkyusha, the big Japanese-American dictionary is "Every man to his taste . . . /Tastes differ . . . /There is no accounting for tastes . . . /Some prefer nettles." The first three words (*tade kuu mushi*) are the Japanese title. Numbers of people claim to have been with me when inspiration came and I announced the title of my new translation. My recollection is different, but they may be right, for recollection is an untrustworthy tool. Mine has me at my desk with a thesaurus at one hand and a botanical dictionary at the other. "'Nettles' is the word for me," I said to myself, and the rest was easy.

It is not a completely accurate translation. Probably the best translation for *tade* would be "persicaria," but that did not seem very good for a title. The Japanese expression covers a variety of weeds, among which is not the nettle. The variety accounts for the proverb from which the title derives. Some worms prefer one kind of *tade,* some another. Indeed, having a pleasantly bitter taste, some are eaten by human beings as well as worms. But the English title goes on seeming to me a good one, and within the bounds of the permissible.

I do not remember that anyone has ever taken exception to the title, nor have people said of the translation, as they have said of some of my other translations, that it is not a good one. The contents of the original novel, however, have aroused strong feelings. Some have been directed at the inconclusiveness of the conclusion. I can think of far more inconclusive Japanese novels, however, which have not aroused similar hostility. It may be that the others are more ethereal, and so fit the stereotype of the exquisite Japanese. For me, the problem of the inconclusive novel is not difficult. It is a Japanese thing which is to be taken or left. The Japanese are not Aristotelians. If a novel has a beginning and a middle, it can stop just about anywhere that the author feels like stopping. Of the Aristotelian states, the ending is the one that does not matter to the Japanese.

But something else was at stake in the matter of *Some Prefer Nettles.* It was feminism, then in its infancy. Something about the novel caused the hackles of the devout feminist to rise. "Why on earth did you pick this one?" began a report by a woman student at one of my three American universities. She was a gifted student and it was a good report, and I gave it an A. I would have thought the feminist complaint, which this proved to be, as easy to answer as the complaint about the inconclusive ending, but it was not. I pointed out that the women in the novel were consistently stronger than the men. "What else could a man do?" I concluded. She was not convinced. Women were chattel in the novel, and this was not permissible. It was probably a reasonably good account of the lot of womanhood in those days, I persisted. She still was not convinced. Aroused feminists are not easy to convince. But we remained good friends.

One could not go to a better man for introductions to Tanizaki than Shimanaka Hōji of Chūō Kōron. Well-established Japanese writers are often rather promiscuous in their relations with publishers. They wander from one to another. Tanizaki, however, was reasonably faithful to Chūō Kōron. So to Shimanaka I went. He was very kind and helpful and one of his employees, Takisawa Hiroo, was, if anything, even kinder. Takisawa forwent a Sunday holiday to accompany me to Atami, at the northeastern corner of the Izu Peninsula, where Tanizaki spent his summers. He still spent the more clement seasons in Kyoto. He never actually lived in Osaka, to which so much of *Some Prefer Nettles* is an anthem of praise.

It was a hot Sabbath in 1953. A hot day along coastal Japan is not comfortable for one whose hide has evolved from several thousand years in northern Europe. I was sweaty and sticky and itchy. I had no notion what I would say to this man who had been of godlike stature ever since I began reading modern Japanese literature. But there we were, after a taxi ride from Atami Station northward to a headland overlooking the sea. There was the great man, and there, an unexpected presence, was his wife, his third wife, Matsuko, the second of the Makioka sisters.

I think that Mrs. Tanizaki was present at every interview I had with Tanizaki, and a most remarkable presence she was, too. Hers is the image that immediately comes into my mind when I hear the word "elegant." She was a very beautiful woman, utterly Osaka, a demonstration if ever one was needed that Tokyo and Osaka differ subtly, and that Osaka need never ask Tokyo for advice in matters of elegance. Her presence made things so easy. I never had to think of anything witty to say. She always had something first, always in the Osaka dialect, which I found delightful. I did occasionally think of something feebly witty, and she was the audience every wit desires. It is a terrible admission to make, but I was sadder when she died than when the great man died.

I think I would probably have got on perfectly well with Tanizaki even had Mrs. Tanizaki not been present. It might have been harder to think of things to say, however. I would describe Tanizaki as a pleasantly plump old gentleman with a touch of the childlike about him. We had all been trained, by Japanese criticism, not always of the highest quality, to think Tanizaki a "satanic" sort of writer. This view derives from his earliest writing, full of the weird and the grotesque, masochism and sadism. Japanese criticism has a way of affixing a label early in an author's career and never allowing it to be removed.

I was prepared to grant that there were devils in the early Tanizaki, but not that the early Tanizaki is important (it is my view that had he died in the earthquake he would not be remembered, and that he came into his own only after the earthquake), or that the devils that beset him were very devilish. They were rather cheerful imps. The important point is that, seated there before him, I did not think him at all satanic, or devilish, or whatever. I was pleased to learn, in a 1962 letter addressed to me at Stanford, where I had begun teaching, that he too hated the expression "satanism."

There was always another presence, a cat. This was most fortunate. Tanizaki was a cat lover and I am one too. I have a charming cartoon which appeared not long ago in a big newspaper. The cartoonist is Wada Makoto, a very gifted man. Tanizaki and I, each kneeling on a cushion, are talking over cups of tea. Mrs. Tanizaki is not present, but a cat, a fat short-haired cat, just the kind I like best, is leaping through the air between us. Tanizaki is very recognizably Tanizaki, and I am recognizably I, but I think the cat must be fictitious. Tanizaki preferred long-hairs. I never saw anything else in any of his dwellings, which were always on the coast southwest of Tokyo. I never visited his Kyoto house, on the Kamo River. For this I am regretful, because, never having seen it, I am not really a Tanizaki insider. Insiders talk endlessly of the Kyoto place, known as the House of the Murmuring Waters.

I do not remember that we talked much business that day. The interview was mostly ceremonial. Business matters were up to Shimanaka and the Chūō Kōron lawyer. I had no difficulty obtaining their agreement to the Knopf contract, but I was startled to receive a bill from the lawyer. I had not asked for his services, I said, and did not propose to pay for them.

In this I now think, though I was not alive to the possibility at the time, that I violated Japanese convention. A lawyer is often held to be engaged not in litigation but in mediation. Both of the parties on whose behalf mediation occurs are expected to pay him. (I was startled and outraged to learn later that this is also true of real-estate agents.) I did not pay and heard nothing more of the matter. If there were injured feelings I was not made aware of them. The lawyer could probably have threatened to take me to court, but he did not.

The longest and most elaborate of the two dozen messages I had from Tanizaki—cards, letters, a telegram—congratulates me upon completing the *Some Prefer Nettles* translation. It is dated May 25, 1954, and addressed to the little Koishikawa house. It is in brush on a single length of Japanese paper. Some of his letters were in brush, some in pen. Probably the ones he thought most important were in brush. He was not the celebrated calligrapher Kawabata was. This may have been because he was less quirkish. He wrote a strong, no-nonsense hand, easier to read by far than the celebrated Kawabata hand. Other signs that he took the letter seriously are that it was sent special delivery and that it contains no marks of punctuation, though there is an occasional paragraph break. The envelope bears a Kyoto postmark.

Very promptly indeed, it acknowledges a letter I had written on May 22 announcing that the translation is finished. He means to read it, he says, though he cannot be sure that he will be alive to all the niceties, and he must beg leave to keep the copy for a time, since he has pressing work to take care of. He invites me to visit him, either in Kyoto or in Atami, to which he will be returning in June.

It does not, to be sure, add up to a great deal. It is little more than a stringing along of convenances. It is carefully composed, however, and his pleasure at having been translated seems unfeigned. I was hugely honored at having so scrupulously composed a message from so eminent a writer. The approval of his author is important in keeping a translator at it. I later had evidence that he did read the translation, and with considerable care. In his young years he had a spell of infatuation with English literature, the fin-de-siécle kind. I would have expected it all to have vanished long since. I never heard him speak English, but he seems to have gone on reading it with some facility.

The translation was a critical success and sold reasonably well. Not surprisingly, most of the sales were in big coastal cities and university towns. The Program was well launched. It was time for Strauss and me to think of another offering. Strauss's main condition was that we choose a living author. From the outset he had looked toward a Nobel Prize, and Nobel Prizes went to the dead very infrequently. As to literary quality, he left that to me, though he assumed it would be high. And he did not want to do another Tanizaki novel immediately. He wished to have several novelists in his stable, so to speak, and it would be well to introduce a second (there seemed to be no thought of returning to the popular novelist who had inaugurated The Program) before it had come to seem that there was to be only one.

This fitted in well with my own thoughts, and so I suggested that the time had come to introduce the second of the two whom I held to be the most eminent among living Japanese novelists: Kawabata Yasunari. Strauss had learned some Japanese and done some reading, and he recognized Kawabata's worth. I recommended *Snow Country.* It would not be easy, I said, and the translation might be a failure. Too much depended upon too little (which was essentially Keene's position). Do your best, said Strauss. The translation came out in 1956. I first saw a copy when I was back in Colorado after my mother's death. Between 1954 and 1959 I worked alternately on Tanizaki and Kawabata, and translated two books by each. I then translated no more Tanizaki, largely because Strauss was not yet friendly to short fiction, and the only other Tanizaki works I liked well enough to translate were short. I translated two more books by Kawabata and Mishima's last novel, published posthumously. So during the Strauss years, perhaps half the Japanese fiction Knopf published was in my translation.

Among good modern writers, Kawabata is by no means the most inconsistent. He has his ups and downs, but others have more extreme ones. He seems among the most indecisive, however. The reader sometimes has great trouble knowing whether and when a Kawabata novel is finished. Apparently Kawabata did too. He left many a novel unfinished, and finished many a novel at a point that seems no finish at all. More disconcertingly, he sometimes resumed work on a novel that the whole world had thought finished.

I choose *Snow Country* because it seemed, among the Kawabata novels for which I had a high regard, the one most likely to be finished. I am not sure that it is my favorite among Kawabata writings, but it is among my favorites. Its textual history is complex. In 1935 a short piece, essentially though not in every detail the opening passages of what was to be the novel, appeared in a magazine. Several other installments in several other magazines followed. In 1937, with additional material, he brought all these pieces together in a single volume, evidently as a complete novel, for the first time bearing the title *Snow Country.* So matters stood through the war years. In 1947 he started writing again, and in 1948 there appeared the version of *Snow Country* that I translated. Given the book's history, I could not be sure there would not be more. I felt reasonably safe, however, and if yet another *Snow Country* appeared, people would understand. Indeed, I did later translate a Kawabata novel which I thought to be finished but which proved not to be. No one gloated and no one jeered. People who cared about Kawabata were familiar with his habits.

As I have already indicated, not everyone likes the *Snow Country* translation. It is my favorite among my modern translations, not because I think it best, but because I most enjoyed doing it. Translation is a bore when it is easily done. Contrary to generalizations about translating from Japanese, some things are more difficult than others. Many things are difficult to translate, but not everything is. *Snow Country* was very difficult. I have already given the reason: so little does so much. A slight shift in word usage on the part of one of the speakers will change things utterly. It can be a little like Ivy Compton-Burnett.

I had found almost nothing in *Some Prefer Nettles* that puzzled me. Tanizaki wrote clear, rational sentences. I do not, certainly, wish to suggest that I disapprove of such sentences; but translating them is not very interesting. There was little I felt inclined to ask Tanizaki about. So, rather than bother him with trivia, I asked him nothing. There was much that puzzled me in *Snow Country.* So, initially, I sought to consult with Kawabata. He was pleasant, but of no help at all. "Do you not, my esteemed master, find this a rather impenetrable passage?" He would dutifully scrutinize the passage, and answer: "Yes." Nothing more. The sensible thing was to stop asking.

Early in 1979 my Benedictine friend Father Neal Henry Lawrence, whom I have known since DipSec days, sent me an article from a Catholic magazine, *The Fleur-de-lis Review,* published by Shirayuri Women's University. "A bit of a botanical muddle here," I said smugly. *Shirayuri* means "white lily," and the heraldic bearing of the kings of France is surely an iris. Investigation established that Shirayuri knew more about the matter than I did. There are several theories as to what the bearing represents, and one of them is a cluster of lilies.

I glanced at the article, written by a gentleman named Meguro Masashi. One of the things that come and can be tossed away, I said to myself. As I was about to toss it away something said to me that I should give it a look. I did, found it interesting, and kept it. The subject is the rendering of the verb *omou,* "to think," in three of my Kawabata translations. It says a good deal about why I found Kawabata interesting to translate. The verb *omou* and equivalents are complex words in any language. It may be particularly so in Japanese, in which it has such meanings as "to yearn for" and "to remember," not to be found, I think, in English.

I was not aware of anything like elegant variation when I was at work on the translations, but the variety is astonishing. *Omou* is rendered by twenty-nine verbs, the most common of them "think," by eight adjectival locutions preceded by "be" ("be afraid" and the like), by six auxiliary verbs ("shall"), by two adverbs ("possibly" and "perhaps"), by an interrogative statement, and (nineteen instances) by nothing at all. I do not feel apologetic about the nineteen. In one brief instance the original, *The Sound of the Mountain,* says literally: "It might be thought that the moonlit night was deep." The translation says: "There was a vast depth to the moonlit night." Is that not enough? Possibly the translation errs in the direction of saying too much.

Among my reasons for making a gesture in the direction of the wastebasket was that I was often reproved for things which seemed to me not to matter at all. I no longer think that the intent of the article was to reprove. The gentleman had come upon something interesting, and he went to great trouble in putting together his tabulations.

Tanizaki is always being compared to Murasaki Shikibu, probably because he translated her great work, *The Tale of Genji,* three times. The two do have similarities, perhaps most striking among them a liking for endless sentences. But in some profound respects, Kawabata was closer to her than was Tanizaki. For one, Kawabata and Murasaki were both people of few words. Both remedied the paucity of words by employing all-purpose words. In both cases, this is among the reasons for the endless fascination—which may seem to contradict my statement that I was not aware of the wealth of variations on *omou.* Subliminally, I must have been—else I would not have been so interested.

A case of bacillary dysentery sent me to an isolation hospital just when the end of the translation was in sight. (I asked the doctor what the source might be, that I could avoid it in the future. Most likely draft beer, he said, the season being summer. *That* I did not propose to avoid, said I. And indeed I have not avoided it, and I have had no bouts with dysentery since.) I was very sick for maybe four or five days, and then I was all right again. Even after I felt all right I was kept on at the hospital, the ailment being communicable, requiring isolation until the danger of transmission had passed. The nurse assigned especially to me was as sweet as she could be. She just loved her work, she said, because she loved seeing sick people go away well. There must be an occasional sick person who did not go away thus, I objected. She did not want to talk about that.

But mostly I remember the convalescent days as a time of happy concentration. Aside from callers, and people, both native and alien, were very kind about calling, I had only the translation to occupy me. So I kept at it beyond what, in more usual circumstances, I would have called its conclusion. In a state of almost mystical intensity I would search for exactly the right word or phrase. I felt, or thought I felt, a little like Flaubert. Perhaps I alone am aware that it was this translation on which I worked hardest. It has probably called up more dissatisfaction than any of my other translations. I do not care. I know how hard I worked, and because I worked so hard I am particularly fond of it.

The opening lines of the *Snow Country* which I translated are not those of the first magazine installment. Kawabata put them there when he first published the work under the title it now bears. This was very canny of him. They constitute probably the most famous passage in the whole body of modern Japanese literature, and had he left them buried further down in the work it is doubtful that they would have had the same impact. They have been the most thoroughly scrutinized lines in any of my translations. Most of the scrutinizers have been Japanese. Given the esteem in which the passage is held, this is not, perhaps, so very curious. Nowhere else in the world, I suspect, are translations from their literature, given the attention they receive in Japan. Americans, at least, care not at all.

I give as a piece of advice to aspiring translators: "Be careful about opening and closing passages." These are the passages people will notice and find fault with. I think if I had formulated the principle earlier, I would have translated the beginning of *Snow Country* more literally. A train comes out of a long tunnel that passes the border between two provinces, and it is the snow country. Outside the train windows "the bottom of the night" lies white. My translation, according to unfriendly scrutinizers, is guilty of two serious delinquencies: I did not state that the mountain range through which the long tunnel passes is the provincial boundary; and I failed to include Kawabata's trope.

I do not even now think the matter of the boundary worth worrying about, but I think they are right about the bottom of the night. It is a striking image and the chief reason for the great fame of the passage, and it should be there. My reason for omitting it seems to me now wholly inadequate. I did not like having "night" and "white" in such intimate juxtaposition.

I made amends later, when the translation was published in a limited edition. "Night" and "white" are there side by side. The trouble is that the edition, brought out by the Limited Editions Club in New York, is expensive, and few people have seen it.

Scrutinizers also compile lists of mistakes, sometimes elaborately classified lists: trivial mistakes, considerable mistakes, outright howlers, that sort of thing. None of the mistakes on any of the lists sent to me has included anything that falls unquestionably in the howler category. I have a letter from Tanizaki saying that he is passing my *Some Prefer Nettles* on for the scrutiny of a friend who is an English professor, and another letter arranging a meeting between me and the professor. I thought this just a touch insulting, but did not say so. Tanizaki seemed to think it a natural part of our relationship and my education. The professor did not turn up anything that much bothered me.

I think that we who translate from Japanese into English have on the whole done better by our originals than have those translators who work in the opposite direction. The worst blunder I can think of in translation from Japanese into English is Ivan Morris's, in a sad, lovely story by Hayashi Fumiko called "Tokyo" in the Keene anthology. The story is set immediately after the war. The heroine, a war widow and a peddler of tea, has an affair with a truck driver, who dies in an accident. We are introduced to the driver's lodgings. On the inside of his door he has a card-size pinup, of what Morris calls "the fifty bells of Yamada."

Now this is a celebrated and beautiful actress of film and stage, Yamada Isuzu. Her given name, the second element, is written with the characters for "fifty bells." I was the first person to point out the mistake to Morris. He looked at the page in silence for a moment, then said: "A howler." In silence I agreed.

It seems very strange that no one along the way, translator to editor and proofreader and reviewer, questioned the fifty bells. Truck drivers the world over tend to be robust, earthy people. Why would a Japanese truck driver have chosen a picture of fifty bells for his pinup (and each of the fifty, given the size of the pinup, so tiny as to be discernible only with the help of a magnifying glass)? In those days the Japanese were looked upon as delicate and ethereal. They were not a few years earlier and they probably are not now. Perhaps everyone along the line, editors and the rest, caught overtones of Zen in the fifty bells. I recently looked at the twentieth printing or so of the anthology. The fifty bells are still there.

But this is more amusing than serious. For the serious howler, one should look at translations into Japanese: at the Japanese title, for instance, of Jean Genet's *Nôtre dame des fleurs.* It is *Hana no Nôtre Dame,* which calls to mind a big cathedral in cherry-blossom time. Another instance the reader may wish to look at is described in a little article of mine which appeared in the English edition of the *Yomiuri Shimbun* for February 1, 1962. It is carried in the collection *This Country, Japan* (1979). The title is: "In Pursuit of English, or Who is That Lady on your Carving Board?" Among other things, it tells of a translation from English into Japanese which I had had the mixed pleasure of going over (for generous pay).

In the limited edition I made amends in another regard that had come to bother me. In the introduction to the Knopf edition, I likened Kawabata's method of composition to that of a haiku poet. It is true that he habitually started out with a fragment, an account perhaps of something or someone he had seen on a train or a street. If it seemed to work he would add to it, and presently he would have what might be called a novel. So it certainly was with *Snow Country.* The haiku comparison has come to seem so obvious as to approach the trite, however. I now prefer to liken the Kawabata method to *renga* linked verse. This accommodates the fragmentary, episodic quality, and it also accommodates the inconclusiveness of the conclusion—and even after all his attempts, it remains very inconclusive.

Reviewers have objected to the peculiar imagery. "Leeches, Mr. Seidensticker?" said one of them. "*Leeches?*" Yes, it is peculiar, but it is a literal translation, and it is peculiar in the Japanese too. Kawabata more than once likens the smooth, moist lips of his heroine to a pair of leeches. There was, I decided, nothing I could do about the simile. If Kawabata thought leeches beautiful, very well, he thought leeches beautiful, and it was not for me to reform him.

There were other instances in which I chose literal translation as the best way of conveying something subtle and obscure, and perhaps untranslatable. I thought that a moment's thought on the part of the intelligent reader would see him or her past the difficulty, and I thought it very forbearing of Strauss not to complain. An unfortunate thing about editors is that they often demand clarity in a translation when there is none in the original. This means, of course, that something is taken away. And from such difficulties came much of the pleasure of translating the work, and in them is the essence of Kawabata.

I had forgotten that I cut certain repetitious passages from the *Snow Country* translation until I recently came across a letter from Kawabata giving me permission to do so. They were, he said, a result of the eccentric circumstances of the original publication, in various magazines at irregular intervals. He was aware of the problem when he brought them together in a book, but did nothing about it.

I saw more of Kawabata than of Tanizaki. I am sure that Tanizaki would have received me courteously if I had gone calling frequently, but Atami, and later Yugawara, where he died, were not an easy day's excursion from Tokyo. Tanizaki did not often come to Tokyo, and when he did he always had many things to do. Kawabata was nearer, a short distance from the Great Buddha in Kamakura, and often came to the city. I saw him often, in both places. I also saw him once in San Francisco during my Stanford years. He had just arrived by plane from Tokyo. The first thing he wanted to do was go to a Japanese restaurant.

Early in 1957, when the snows were deep, Kawabata took three of us, the Strausses, Harold and his wife Millie, and me through the long tunnel and on to Yuzawa, in Niigata Prefecture or the old province of Echigo, to observe the filming of a movie version of *Snow Country,* which is set in Yuzawa. The snows and the tunnels through them were most marvelous, and the Takahan Inn, setting for most of the novel, was still exactly as it had been when Kawabata went visiting a score of years before. It is that way no more, though fragments of the old inn are still to be found among all the improvements.

In the course of the excursion I received the nearest thing to a reprimand that I ever had from Kawabata. The director, the cast, including the extremely famous Kishi Keiko, whom I was to meet again at the Nobel observances in Stockholm in 1968, and the four of us all gathered for dinner. The sake flowed without encumbrance, and I waxed somewhat garrulous. I did not, I observed, think that the novel had in it the makings of a movie.

"The movie will be better than the novel," said Kawabata (I think "snapped" might better characterize his manner, but in this I may be imagining things).

Nothing more was said on the subject. I did not sleep well that night. I feared I had alienated him; but there was no aftermath. The next morning it was as if he had forgotten the incident. Perhaps he had.

He was right, of course, that I should not have said what I did, but in the deeper matter of aesthetic judgments, if we may assume that he meant what he said, I was right. The movie is not a good one. If the novel is not very dramatic, the movie is melodramatic. I went to the gala opening in Tokyo and wrote a review in which I said what I thought. The review was not printed. Kawabata's writing has been much favored by moviemakers. *The Izu Dancer* has been remade endlessly, we might say, for the end is not yet in sight. Not one of these movies seems to me really successful. The reason is generally the same. In the endeavor to introduce drama into a novel of which the dramatic is not the most striking quality, moviemakers lay it on with a shovel.

Kawabata had a superb art collection, mostly paintings and ceramics, Chinese and Japanese. Several pieces are National Treasures. The family managed to keep the collection together after his death by turning it into a museum. It is not one of the massive collections of the world, but in quality it is among the best. On a limited budget, Kawabata maintained his collection at a level that many a prince of industry with an unlimited budget has been unable to imitate. Clearly he had a very discerning eye for such things. He was good about letting me delve into the collection. I am one of the more accomplished people of the world at knocking things over and probably should have forborne, but ceramics are what I like best, and ceramic masterpieces have an especial feel to them. Getting to know this is a part of one's education. Opportunities are not frequent.

At the opening of the museum I struck up a conversation with a famous Tokyo art dealer. I learned that Kawabata was not quick about paying his bills. He would take a masterpiece home on approval, and that would be the end of the matter until the dealer contrived to make inquiries, through suitable intermediaries.

"I suppose he forgets," said I.

The dealer had a different explanation: "He's from Osaka."

So now it was back to Tanizaki for Strauss and me. Strauss later added a younger writer, Mishima Yukio, younger by a quarter of a century than Kawabata, and a Kawabata protégée, to his roster of authors. But until I felt constrained to translate Mishima's last novel, completed just before his death in 1970, I did only Tanizaki and Kawabata for Strauss. This was entirely as I wished it to be. We agreed that moving back and forth between the two was a good idea. We did not wish either to be forgotten because of long absence from the bookshops.

The Makioka Sisters is probably Tanizaki's most famous novel. It sold very well when it was first published in full, shortly after the war. It had a bad time during the war. Two installments were published early in 1943 in *Chūō Kōron,* then presided over by Shimanaka Hōji's father. At that point it was banned, the contents held to be of little relevance to the national crisis. Tanizaki kept on writing.

I could think of plenty of reasons to translate it, chief among them the concluding statement, which I will quote presently. I could think of plenty of reasons not to do it. I do not much like autobiographic fiction. *The Makioka Sisters* may be considered autobiographic, even though Tanizaki himself does not figure importantly in it. His last wife, Matsuko, is central. Her maiden name was Morita, and the four Morita sisters are the four Makioka sisters. It is more than a chronicle of their affairs, but in its general outlines it is faithful to fact.

It is a very long book, and the action is on the whole far from bold and striking, though there are famous scenes, such as the firefly hunt about a third of the way from the end. The censors may have been wrong to suppress it, but they were right in thinking that it rather stood apart from the crisis. The principal narrative has to do with the efforts of the Makiokas to find a husband for their third daughter, Yukiko, Morita Shigeko in real life. Donald Keene offered a discouraging piece of intelligence. Arthur Waley did not like it. This gave pause. The name Waley was synonymous with good taste and literary sensibility.

Then there was something that took me back to my initial difficulties with Strauss and Knopf, when Strauss had first suggested that I might participate in The Program. Much of the conversation was in the Osaka dialect. I thought, though without confidence, that I might find devices for distinguishing between Osaka speech and standard Japanese, or Tokyo speech. I did come upon devices and sought to put them to use, but they may be said to have failed utterly. No one seems even to have noticed their presence. What finally made the difference was a strong feeling that someone was sure to translate so famous a work some day. I would as soon be the person. So I got to work, and the translation came out in 1957.

My favorite story of its reception by a waiting world was from Glenn

Baxter, then on the staff of the Harvard Yenching Institute. He said that he overheard this exchange between two ladies in the Harvard Coop:

First lady: "Who are the Makioka sisters anyway?"

Second lady: "I don't know. Something like the Maryknoll Fathers, I suppose."

Tanizaki read the translation, and again handed it over to an English professing friend, that lists of mistakes might be drawn up. Again, nothing that the friend came upon bothered me greatly. In a letter dated October 19 of some year, Tanizaki says that he has been reading the *Makioka Sisters* translation and likes it better than that of *Some Prefer Nettles.* Although he does not exactly say so, Tanizaki seems to have been upset by the reviews. In a letter dated November 16, and again I must assume the year to be 1957, he says: "Mr. Strauss has sent me many clippings from America about *Makioka Sisters.* One could not say that they are excessively friendly. That from the *New York Herald Tribune* of October 13 seems especially harsh, but I would now agree that the work is too diffuse and rambling. Indeed there are many points that I agree with. The statement that something must have been lost in translation is a great disservice to you."

Tanizaki uses the English title, dropping the definite article. The last sentence is certainly very kind, and there is truth in it. I do not think that much if anything is lost in translation, except of course dialect, and I certainly think that less is lost in translating Tanizaki than in translating Kawabata. I hold this verse, composed by a friend and fellow translator, to be the case:

It's the same the whole world over.
It's a bloody crying shame.
The author gets the credit.
The translator gets the blame.

To my mind the *New Yorker* review, by Anthony West, was the worst. He called it a work which pioneered a new genre, the medical novel. It is true that there are a great many doses and injections, but to say that they are the whole of the work is to miss the point completely. I doubt that West was much interested in the point. He was interested in being witty, and wit and truth are often at odds with each other. I suggested to Strauss that he protest. He replied that any review in the *New Yorker* is a good review. This seemed most professional of him. The translation is still in print, and has been among the steadiest sellers in The Program.

At about this time Strauss put me to work gathering testimonials to Tanizaki from other famous writers. He was looking toward a Nobel Prize. I should have been aware that some of the people I asked very much wanted the prize for themselves. Mishima certainly did, and Kawabata was widely thought to be, with Tanizaki, the strongest candidate. Some have said that his failure to get it when Kawabata did, in 1968, in effect killed Mishima. I do not myself think so, but that he wanted it was certainly very true, and helps a good deal to explain his cosmopolitanism during those years. We will never know whether Tanizaki or Kawabata would have won the prize had the former still been living in 1968, but that the latter was very pleased to get it is clear. So it was obtuse and even cruel of me to ask for testimonials from such men. I should have told Strauss to take his business elsewhere. Everyone I asked complied in a most gracious manner.

I like Mishima's remarks best. I sent translations to Strauss and kept the originals. I had doubts about Mishima as a novelist, but thought him a first-rate critic. I once told him that he should give up novel writing and devote himself to criticism, at which he would be the best man around. This made him very angry. Or so I am told. He never indicated his anger to me. He was an impressionistic sort of critic, relying on vivid imagery. He once characterized Kawabata's writing as that of the lonely wanderer, and said that central to Tanizaki's writing was good food.

Here, in part, is what he said of Tanizaki for Knopf: "If the writings of Tanizaki were erased from modern Japanese literature, it would be like a flower garden without flower—or, if we choose to emphasize the sensual quality of his writing, like a zoo without animals. Applying fabrication to natural sensuality, he produced many a masterpiece unsurpassed both in grace and in cruelty. None was more versatile than he in giving a new turn to the Japanese classics. He apprehended the decadence of the Western fin de siècle in terms of pre-modern Japanese aestheticism, and combined Western realism with the inquiry into the human spirit characteristic of *The Tale of Genji* and its times. He is at the same time an aesthete and a powerful realist. His heroines are incarnations of an elevated eroticism."

I am not sure that this last remark is true of Sachiko and Yukiko, both of whom are rather staid; but that is all right. Many of Tanizaki's heroines are as Mishima says they are. I am inclined to think that the chilly Swedes were warmed by Mishima's remarks, and by Tanizaki. Whether he would have won the prize had he lived until 1968 is anyone's guess. I think the chances good, since he was a sturdier writer than Kawabata, and came across better in translation.

I translated no more Tanizaki after *The Makioka Sisters.* I could see nothing I wanted to translate except short fiction. I told Tanizaki so, and had in return a letter saying that he quite understood and that I should do exactly as I wished. Why not, it will be asked, translate short fiction? Well, because Strauss had said that he did not publish short fiction. He was a great one for saying that he would not do something and then doing it—which is better than the reverse. Having found a new Tanizaki man, Howard Hibbett, he not long afterwards commissioned a collection of short and medium-length fiction.

When I left Japan in 1962 to begin a teaching career in the United States, the Tanizakis were very kind. They telegraphed regrets from Atami at being unable to see me off.

In a letter dated June 20 Tanizaki says: "I have heard from Koyama Itoko that you will be returning to America in August. She says that you have come to dislike Japan. When we meet you must tell me your reasons. I am not, these days, very happy with Japan myself. If I were younger and stronger I would have thoughts of taking refuge in a foreign country.

"I am pleased to hear that you will visit us before your departure. I hope that your work at Stanford University will be good for you and good for America."

(Koyama Itoko has been mentioned in chapter four. She was a novelist, and among the sturdier and braver ones in resisting the "progressives.")

I asked Tanizaki for a bit of his calligraphy suitable for hanging on a parlor wall. He responded with an original *waka,* a thirty-one-syllable poem. Actually it contains an extra syllable, acceptable because the last two vowels of the most important word in the second line can be elided. It is on one of those rectangular pieces of cardboard, sometimes decorated and sometimes not, for a ceremonial sketch or inscription.

Furusato wa
Inakazamurai ni
Arasarete
Mukashi no Edo no
Omokage mo naku

Laid waste, my city, by rustic samurai.
No trace remains of Edo as it was.

In 1977 Mrs. Tanizaki published a very beautiful book, a collection of Tanizaki's short poems in an edition of a hundred fifty copies. Quite aside from the contents, the book itself, published in Osaka, is beautiful. The *waka* translated above is in it. The date of composition given by Mrs. Tanizaki is that on which the *shikishi* was dispatched to me. So we may think that the poem was written expressly for the occasion. I do choose to think so, and it is therefore among my genuinely prized possessions. I will give it to the Museum of Modern Japanese Literature in Tokyo, where the provenance is more likely to be remembered than if it were to fall into the hands of a dealer.

I last saw Tanizaki early in September 1964. He had built himself a house in Yugawara, a bit nearer Tokyo than Atami, where he had for some years passed his winters. Though voluble in his distaste for his native city, Tokyo—this in fact had become a part of his image—he had given up residence in the Kyoto-Osaka district and was edging back towards Tokyo.

Two other Americans were present on the Yugawara occasion, Howard Hibbett and Donald Keene. I have heard it said that Tanizaki never smiled for the cameras, and it is true that he was much given to scowling at them. But there is at least one exception: a photograph of the four of us side by side on a Yugawara sofa. We are all amused at something, and Tanizaki himself is having the biggest laugh of all. My favorite picture of him, it has had some currency, appearing in several collections of his works. I have no notion what struck us all as so funny, but venture to hope that it was something I myself had said. I am the least open in my amusement, merely smiling, and it may be that I am showing artistic restraint after my coup.

I returned to California a few days later, and was not again in Tokyo until June of the following year. Late in July, at Yugawara, a few days after his seventy-ninth birthday, Tanizaki died. The obituaries said the cause was acute nephritis. Since he fell ill on the day after his birthday party, it may be that rumors were right, and he died from overeating; and that Mishima was altogether too right about the importance of good food in his life and writing.

On crutches, for I had broken an ankle, I attended both the wake and the funeral. At the funeral, I saw assembled for the first time the four Makioka sisters, or Morita sisters. To my mind, the second and third Morita sisters were more like their corresponding Makioka sisters than was the youngest. The oldest does not figure much in the narrative. Spiritually distant from the others, she presently becomes physically distant as well by moving to Tokyo. The youngest is the family troublemaker. I may confess that the real-life counterpart did not seem to me interesting enough for the role.

The family is not as conspicuous in my account of the funeral as are a couple of movie stars. "Takamine Hideko put on a real act, strangled weeping and all that, when she offered up her flowers. If I felt like the principal ham yesterday evening [by virtue of my crutches], I certainly had every right to feel displaced today. Kyō Machiko, who I am sure was the more grief-stricken of the two, was quiet and composed. Nothing was said, the worst thing about Japanese funerals, of the last illness."

Which may support my suspicion that it was from overeating. Takamine (she is now retired) was a supremely good actress and one of my favorites, but, like so many of them, she could occasionally be accused of over-acting. She and I have apartments in the same building in Honolulu.

Mrs. Tanizaki, almost two decades younger than Tanizaki, survived him by some three decades. I saw her numbers of times after his death. She was still beautiful in her eighties. There are such people. I did not visit her as she lay dying. People told me that she did not want me to see what a fright she had become. I have twenty-one letters and cards from her. Her letters are pleasanter to look at than his. She was an accomplished calligrapher, and on the whole a legible one as well. Most of the letters are written with brush on beautifully decorated Japanese paper.

I called on Mrs. Tanizaki in Yugawara in mid-August, a fortnight after Tanizaki's death, and came away wiser. "She told me that the last lines of *Sasameyuki [The Makioka Sisters]*, of which critics have made so much, had nothing whatsoever to do with the philosophy of the master. They are there because it actually happened that way. Indeed it is extraordinary what tiny details in the book are there because they actually happened. The powder puff, the obi, the cat, the blushing officer—everything."

Here is the last line, actually only a dozen or so words: "Her diarrhea continued through the day, and was a problem on the train to Tokyo."

The line is certainly very famous, and the critics have gobbled it up.

Like many Japanese, Tanizaki has two graves. (Some have even more.) Cremation being universal in the large cities, the ashes, as we would call them, or bones, as the Japanese call them, can be divided. The principal one, where now Mrs. Tanizaki and Mrs. Watanabe rest as well, is at the Hōnen-in, a Buddhist temple in the eastern hills of Kyoto. A portion of the ashes is with those of his parents at a temple in Tokyo.

I attended services at the Hōnen-in on the second anniversary of his death.

"The placid charm of the ancient capital.... As we were proceeding south on Higashiyamadōri, in search of Hara's mother, our streetcar ran into a truck. Never have I seen this happen in Tokyo. The truck sidled over onto the streetcar track, about to make a turn onto Gojōdōri, and the streetcar calmly crunched into it. One would have trouble distributing the right and the wrong, but my sympathies were all with the truck driver. The streetcar man was a shrill, self-righteous little bastard, with the worst kind of Kyoto whine, and the truck driver was a country boy—the truck had a Kagawa license. Kyoto people are not nice people. I think so then and I thought so still....

"First we had prayers, gloomy, cacophonous things of which Sei Shōnagon [of *The Pillow Book,* of the Heian Period] would not have approved at all. Certainly she would not have approved of the priests. They were uniformly ill endowed, not in a way ascetic or saintly, but merely vulgar....

"The announcements were all in a whisper, and my legs were hurting me too much—'twas all *tatami* [straw mats] of course—for me to concentrate on the words. Then Nishikawa Koyuki did [the dance] 'Snow.' The memories were too much for Mrs. Tanizaki. She gave herself up to tears. (Takamine was sniffling too, but Mrs. T's tears struck me as real.) Then Inoue Yachiyo did 'Aoi.' She is a very compelling dancer. You sense that her origins are in Nō and not in the pleasure quarters, you forget that she is an old and rather ugly woman. All is youth and passion. As for 'Snow,' to me it was a jug of syrup.

"Then, as darkness crept through the palms and maples from the carp pond, we were served elegant refreshments from the Hyōtei, with geisha, from Pontochō, I gathered, to pour for us. The room, an enormous one some slight distance from the main hall, was lighted by candles only. It was a scene in praise of shadows. And cicadas shrilled all the while.

"And so here I am at the station, waiting for another Radiant Express to take me back to Tokyo."

The last sentence of the first paragraph quoted above, from my diary, is with very slight modification from one of my favorite poets, Edward Lear. The next to the last sentence of the next to last paragraph is a reference to Tanizaki's most famous essay, "In Praise of Shadows," already mentioned.

It is curious that there is nothing in my diary about the incident that day which is most vivid in memory. I was snubbed by a famous Kyoto geisha, a favorite of Tanizaki's. I was introduced to her by Shimanaka Hōji of Chūō Kōron, and she sniffed and turned away. The sniff was the only sign of recognition I had from her. One might expect the women of "water business," as it is called, with reference to its dependence on undependable popularity, to be ingratiating. The sniff was directed impartially at Shimanaka and me, but it is hard not to believe that most if not all of it was for me. She would have no reason to sniff at him, but I was the blue-eyed outsider. Mohammed Ali and a great many others have said that the Japanese are without racial prejudice. They are wrong.

One more book by Kawabata, and I withdrew for a while from The Program. Strauss said that he did not want to do short books by Tanizaki, and I could find no long ones that I wanted to do. I would as soon have done more Kawabata, but Strauss at that time still found him precious. So there seemed no alternative to withdrawing.

I had deep regrets. The Program may have been good for modern Japanese literature, but it was good for me too. It gave me a sense of doing something that mattered, and but for it I might never have known Tanizaki and would not have known Kawabata as well. I think it a good thing that I went back to the United States in 1962. If it had not been for the modicum of repute that The Program brought me, I would probably not have been able to begin my American career at so distinguished a university as Stanford.

The second Kawabata novel was *Thousand Cranes.* The obvious choice was between it and *The Sound of the Mountain.* The two of them, fragment by fragment, were coming out at the same time. I liked and continue to like *The Sound of the Mountain* and think it the better of the two. I chose the other because it could with more plausibility be considered complete. He had, it was true, already added a bit to it, but the bit did not seem to figure for much, and I went ahead. In a way I was right. The new *Thousand Cranes* was still incomplete at his death. He must have been among the world's more prolific creators of unfinished novels.

But in a more important way I was wrong. For all the inconclusiveness of the ending to *The Sound of the Mountain,* Kawabata never redid it. I think that if I had known that Strauss and I would be parting company, I would have translated it while he was still receptive. Instead, it is the novel I did after the Nobel Prize had made him receptive once more.

Thousand Cranes centers on chanoyu, which word my favorite English-language dictionary informs me has become a part of the language, thereby relieving us of such absurdities as "tea ceremony." My trouble is that I do not really know what it signifies, and am therefore left with an uneasy feeling that it does not signify much of anything at all. It is a nasty story, full of quasi-incestuous relationships. I have sometimes thought it worthy of Mishima, who was very good at nasty stories.

Kawabata once said that his purpose was to take the prettiness out of chanoyu. One feels that the founders of chanoyu would approve. They were creative people, who probably did more than any others to establish the aesthetics of the monochrome and the austere. Down through the Tokugawa centuries (to the mid-nineteenth century) chanoyu was a very masculine endeavor. Now it is altogether maidenly and without a shred of individuality. Debunking is a laudable endeavor, but it does not offer huge promise for him who sits down to write a novel. Nor does it seem to characterize adequately what Kawabata was up to. What, then, was he up to? I am not sure. Enigmas can sometimes be not profound but puzzling in a useless sort of way, and not everything Kawabata did was superior. *The Sound of the Mountain,* inconclusive conclusion and all, is a better novel.

I have said earlier that I quickly learned the futility of asking Kawabata to explain his writing, and stopped doing it. I must have done it at least once more. I have a letter from him dated March 15. Again there is no envelope, and I cannot be sure of the year. It must be 1958 or 1959. I seem to have asked for an explanation of the title, "Double Star," of the last section of *Thousand Cranes* in the version I translated. There is no explanation of it in the text. I was not, he said, to read deep meaning into it. "Of course it would seem to be some astronomical term, but I used it only because of my feeling for the words." Perhaps we have here a small hint that it is possible to worry too much about what the work as a whole signifies.

I did not stop translating Kawabata as I stopped translating Tanizaki. I did parts of *The Sound of the Mountain* for *Japan Quarterly* during the years before the Nobel Prize, and in 1969 Kodansha brought out a collection of short Kawabata fiction under the title of the longest of them, *House of the Sleeping Beauties.* The Japanese title is merely *Sleeping Beauty,* but this did not seem wholly adequate for a language in which the connotations are so universal and specific. All three of the pieces in the collection seem to me first-rate Kawabata. All are rather perverse, but the perverseness does not seem, as in *Thousand Cranes,* less than to the point. Mishima had high praise for the title story, not the translation but the original, and his judgment was generally sound.

My Kodansha editor, Nicholas Ingleton, came around one day looking a little troubled. What troubled him was a spasm of fidelity, as a translator, that had come over me. There were numerous botanical terms in the book, including the names of several varieties of pine. I had provided Latin names for them in footnotes.

"It's very nice," he said, "But do we really need all these pinuses?"

The letters from Kawabata are not as warm as the letters from Tanizaki. This need not surprise or disappoint us. He was not a man given to expressing himself with warmth. The earliest letter that I can precisely date is from March 1953, having to do with the Dazai translations that appeared in *Encounter.* He acted as intermediary in getting the permission of Dazai's widow. "It is a source of great happiness to us," he said, "that Japanese works should appear in England." We need not worry too much about the fact that "us" is not clearly defined. Probably it means something like "Japan" or "the Japanese literary world."

I will leave my later relations with Kawabata, including the glad matter of the Nobel Prize and the sad matter of his death and how it came about, to chapter seven.

I knew Mishima Yukio before I knew Tanizaki. I met him, through the good offices of Herbert Passin, very shortly after I left DipSec, though I cannot give the exact date and was not then keeping a diary regularly. I already knew his writing. I had read the autobiographic *Confessions of a Mask.* I do not much like autobiographic fiction, but this was autobiographic fiction with a difference. Several differences actually, but one of them stood out, a singular eroticism. Japanese autobiographic fiction tends to be rather prim and unrevealing when it comes to the sex life of the authors. I liked the openness. Here was a writer who really did seem to reveal all. And the all, too, had a difference. It was strongly homoerotic. There is plenty of homoeroticism in Japan, but the Japanese are not much given to confessing such tendencies. They keep their closet doors firmly closed.

It may be cruel to say that so prolific a writer reached his peak so early in his life, but *Confessions of a Mask* is arguably the best thing Mishima wrote. I would not have minded translating it, had someone else not appropriated it first. Though I did translate short stories, and his short fiction may on the whole be better than his novels, I did not much admire the novels and did not translate any of them until circumstances required me to do the very last, *The Decay of the Angel,* published posthumously. He cannot but have known about my feelings, and may have punished me for them by not inviting me to his wedding. Ivan Morris, who had translated one of the novels, was invited and made a speech. I would have gone to his funeral uninvited had I not been beyond the ocean.

We had our little differences, but on the whole, I think, got on well. He had one foible that bothered me. He laughed too much. People who laugh at everything, and he laughed constantly and loudly, seem not to be really amused by anything. Yet he was a witty and amusing man. His imitation of an "education mama" recommending the works of Mishima Yukio as a means of enriching the lives and strengthening the probity of little ones was very funny indeed.

I am convinced that he was homosexual, though not exclusively so. Eminent critics have either denied the possibility or ignored it. To do either of these things seems to me to throw away one of the most valuable keys towards understanding his life and death. He also had a "square" side to him. His marriage seems to have been happy, and produced a daughter and a son. We might perhaps describe him as ambidextrous. I would not wish to suggest that I find this deplorable. Many of us show similar tendencies. My point is that homosexuality was significant, in his life, his writings, and his death. His death preceded Kawabata's by a year and a half, and there may have been a relationship between the two.

He rather frequently took me to dinner, always at an expensive Tokyo restaurant, generally in the Ginza district. I never took him to dinner. I more than once tried, but he was very good at paying the bill before I had a chance at it. When a man of eminence wants to be the host in Tokyo and the restaurant knows who he is, there is no gainsaying him. I never saw Mishima in the United States, where I might have had my way. He spent most of his time in New York, whose "decadent exuberance," as he characterized it, fascinated him. During the years between my return to the United States and his death, I lived in the Far West or Middle West.

I also visited his house in the far south of Tokyo, with some frequency. It was a strange house. There was not a trace of the Japanese in the visiting rooms. All was European, and I had a sense that Spain predominated. Passing through a formal courtyard, one was immediately in a grand hallway with stairs leading up to a parlor. This seemed like an anteroom. One wished to see what lay beyond. In fact nothing but the bedrooms and Mishima's study did, or perhaps these, or some of them, were in the adjoining building. I have no notion what style the bedrooms were in. I have seen pictures of the study, which seems to be essentially Japanese and looks, as studies will, cluttered. I once remarked to a fellow visitor (another of those Osakans) on what seemed to me the eccentric nature of the visiting, or public, rooms. "Exactly like Mishima himself," he said, in good English, although I had addressed him in Japanese and it was a Japanese-language gathering. "There's less than meets the eye." I was last at the house for Mrs. Mishima's funeral and see no likelihood that I will ever visit it again.

I have only seven written messages from Mishima, including the remarks on Tanizaki that I have quoted above. None can be dated from as early as the fifties. Three are from the year of his death. I knew him almost as long as I knew Kawabata. Clearly we were not as close. The fact that we had no business relations, by which I mean the fact that I translated none of his novels while he was living, doubtless had something to do with the matter. Arrangements for the short-story translations were taken care of by *Japan Quarterly*, in which they were published.

I learned later, from a mutual friend, that Mishima was infuriated by abridgments in the longest of the three stories I translated for *Japan Quarterly*, "Death in Midsummer," long enough, perhaps, to be called a novella. I have felt guilty about the passages I deleted from my first Kawabata translation, *The Izu Dancer.* Though necessary, they were, I think, badly done. It is not so with "Death in Midsummer." I think that it is a better story without the deleted passages, which seem to me strained and pretentious. Mishima said nothing to me about his anger. Indeed I can think of no hostile word he ever directed at me, though he had many unfriendly things to say about his countrymen. Another reason for my want of remorse is that the quarterly had undertaken to get all necessary permissions. I would have thought that permission to make cuts would surely be among these.

I have left a thing unmentioned about Koyama Itoko, the novelist who was such a source of strength and comfort when the progressives were having their day. She was a canny literary critic. In a card sent from Karuizawa, where she spent her summers, she had this to say about *Spring Snow*, the first volume of Mishima's final tetralogy: "The style is so florid and highly decorated as to take away from one's sense of authenticity. It is all too clever. And do we not hear too much about how beautiful the young couple are?"

I agree less with her view of Kawabata, whom she did not admire, but can usually see her point. In a letter addressed to Stanford shortly after my arrival there, she says in effect that I might not like him as much if I were Japanese. She cites a telling example, in which the sound of a tea kettle is likened to a wind in pine trees. To a Japanese, she said, it is so common as to be trite. In an essay on Kawabata I had said that that is the point at which the novel should have ended. Hearing the sound of the tea kettle, the hero decides that the time has come to return to Tokyo with no intention of visiting his mountain geisha again. The charge of exoticism was frequently made when Kawabata won the Nobel Prize. I much resented it then because of course it belittled the event, but clearly there was an element of it in the announcement of the award by the Swedish Academy, and there may have been an element of it in my admiration for *Snow Country.* Going through a volume of Nobel speeches after Kawabata won his prize, I was interested and diverted to observe that the reasons given for the award in his citation were almost opposite those offered in the case of Rabindranath Tagore, an early Nobel laureate in literature and the only other Asian laureate. In 1968 the Swedes wished their Asians to be very Asian. In 1912 they welcomed affinities with Christianity.

As I think about the matter, I am made to conclude that almost every eminent writer I knew had uncomplimentary things to say about Mishima's writing. The exception was Tanizaki, but he was worse than uncomplimentary. He was completely silent. I do not remember that he ever had a word to say on the subject. In many cases pettiness and jealousy may explain the unfriendliness, but this is hard to imagine in the case of Kawabata, Mishima's recognized patron in the literary world.

Here is a part of my diary entry for May 26, 1964. The setting is initially Palo Alto, and, as will be seen, it moves to San Francisco. "It is, as Jack Kerr [my old Honolulu friend] said in a note that came this morning, the season of migrant birds, 'honking as they pass,' though this last of course could scarcely be said of Kawabata, who has a most wonderful capacity for silence. Presently he was down here, escorted by a Mitsubishi person, and silently we made our way about the campus, and silently we sat in my house as evening came on, and silently we made our way back up to San Francisco, there to have something to eat and drink in the Chōchō on Kearney Street. Silently—and yet what an air of excitement the man is able to create. As we sat in the Chōchō and all sorts of people recognized us, the consul general among them, I had again the feeling, so common in Tokyo, of being at the very center of things.

"Well, it was not all silence. I did pick up a remark from time to time.... That he does not admire Mishima's most recent work any more than I do, but considers the plays perhaps a little superior to the novels.... He is on his way to Oslo, to be in silent attendance upon the PEN congress."

The Chōchō is, or was, a Japanese restaurant, the name meaning "butterfly" (Madame Butterfly is Chōchō Fujin). It is strange, but I was at the time acquiring a certain admiration for Mishima's writing, not of great magnitude but more considerable than before. He had entered the strongly nationalist phase of his last years. I find the content of the nationalistic works repugnant, but there is a strength in them suggesting an honesty difficult to detect earlier.

One often hears that disappointment at his failure to win the Nobel Prize accounts in large measure for the late-blooming Mishima nationalism. It is much to his credit that his nationalism emerged several years *before* Kawabata won the prize.

As for the restaurant, Japanese just off the plane from Japan always wanted first of all to go to a Japanese restaurant. Americans are said to take their Hilton culture with them wherever they go. In this pursuit the Japanese are even more ardent.

Probably my chief regret, looking back over the fifties, is that I never met Nagai Kafū, the writer of whom I was probably fondest among them all. This does not mean that I think or thought him the best among them all. Affection and admiration are not the same thing. I saw him more than once in Asakusa, almost the only part of Tokyo he visited during his last years, but never ventured to go up and address him. I knew that I could get an introduction from Shimanaka Hōji whenever I wanted one. Chūō Kōron was his publisher, as it was Tanizaki's. Then, suddenly, in the florid fullness of the spring of 1959, he died, alone, in the night. He and Tanizaki both died at seventy-nine, but Kafū was nearer his eightieth birthday.

I have mentioned the Tanizaki *shikishi* as being among my dearest treasures. Three other pieces that fall in the category are hanging scrolls inscribed in Kafū's hand with haiku of his composition. Two have little paintings, also by Kafū. The third is only the haiku. The two were given to me by Kawabata, the third by Mrs. Tanizaki after Tanizaki died. Having told me that I could have any two pages except one that was a Kafū self-portrait, Kawabata dismembered a Kafū sketchbook to give them to me. I had them mounted as wall hangings by a famous Kyoto craftsman recommended by Mrs. Tanizaki. The third is exactly as Mrs. Tanizaki gave it to me, complete with an inscription on the box in Tanizaki's hand verifying the important fact that it is by Kafū Sensei, "Kafū my teacher." They are dear treasures indeed, and all of them will, like the *shikishi*, go to the Museum of Modern Japanese Literature.

As the inscription on the box makes clear, the two men were very close. Kafū was seven years the elder. A famous essay by him established Tanizaki as a writer. Both of them had trouble with the censors during the war, and both fell silent, to emerge at the end of it trailing clouds of glory.

Kafū published his diary. Considered by some to be his most important work, it is also considered by some to be a very large novel, with Kafū taking upon himself the novelist's privilege of not telling it exactly as it was. That Kafū redid his diary for publication is well known. The extent of the redoing is a secret Kafū took to his grave. We will probably never know. In its published form it is a strongly pacifist document. His hatred of the Nazis and their Japanese epigones is abundantly clear. Was all of it added to get into the good graces of the pacifists who now ran the world? We can do little more than look at probabilities. I think that some of it may have been added, but that all of it was is highly improbable. There is too much. The anti-Nazi element is entirely in keeping with Kafū's gallomania, and for him (and a great many others) the Japanese militarists were tin Nazis.

There is no point in redoing what I have already done well enough. I will take the liberty of quoting myself. What I said of Kafū in other times and places, I still hold to be true.

Shortly after his death I wrote an article about him which might be called an obituary and which appeared in the English *Yomiuri* for May 9, 1959. "While a few of Kafū's . . . colleagues are still with us the Meiji period is still with us; they are the men of Meiji, messy, confused, brave, and energetic. And on the other hand, the Meiji period seems so extremely far away. . . . So near and so far, the Meiji period is the focus for the nostalgia which, in many ways, a liking for Tokyo amounts to. . . .

"With Kafū's death it seems to recede another sudden enormous step into the distance. . . .

"Kafū continued to write through the war years. A number of stories that could not be published then have appeared since. The best of them is about Asakusa dancers. It verges on the indecent—indeed there is a downright pornographic version, though I do not know whether or not it is authentic—and hides nothing of Asakusa sordidness, but there is a wistful evocation of changing Asakusa surfaces that is most effective, and makes one sorry to see the hero move away— to the western suburbs, of all places—at the end of the book. . . .

"It is not for his social criticism or his naturalistic reporting, but for exactly this, that Kafū will be remembered, for his lyrical evocation of the moods of Tokyo. He will probably never be as adequately translated as less deserving writers. He is too much a part of the city, and therefore lacks what we call universality. One has to know something of the city to guess what losses that tree among the ruins symbolizes. Not likely to find his translator, Kafū is perhaps the best reason one can think of for learning Japanese."

I did in fact have a go at translating Kafū. *Kafū the Scribbler,* published by Stanford in 1965, is half biography and half translation. Towards the end of the biographical section I have a go at redoing a citation from the Japanese government.

"His citation for the Cultural Decoration said: 'His many works replete with a warmly elegant poetic spirit, with an elevated form of social criticism, and with a penetrating appreciation of reality; his pioneering researches in Edo literature; his many achievements in bringing foreign literature to Japan; in all these respects he has left behind mammoth footprints.'

"A bit florid, but as accurate as most citations. Had someone with less of a penchant for rhetoric written it, it might have gone something like this: 'A querulous, self-righteous man whose social criticism rarely rose above the level of personal complaining, and whose grasp of the complex reality that is the human spirit was less than adequate; but a man, withal, whose love for his city and its traditions never wavered, and who expressed that love in prose worthy of the great classical Japanese essayists.'"

The following are the opening sentences of my preface to *Low City, High City,* published by Knopf in 1983, a cultural history of the city from the Meiji Restoration, when it became Tokyo, "the Eastern Capital," down to the great earthquake of 1923: "When young, I did not dedicate books. Dedications seemed overblown and showy. It is too late to begin, but if this book carried a dedication, it would be to the memory of Nagai Kafū.

"Though he was not such a good novelist, he has come to seem better and better at what he was good at. He was his best in brief lyrical passages and not in sustained narrative and dramatic ones. He is the novelist whose views of the world's most consistently interesting city accord most closely with my own. He has been my guide and companion as I have explored and dreamed and meditated upon the city."

It will be seen that I have known and admired and indeed loved Kafū (albeit I never met him) for rather a long while. I cannot say that my affection for him has been as durable as was his affection for Tokyo, since I was already in my thirties when I started reading him, and he knew Tokyo from infancy. I think I can say, however, that my steadfastness has been comparable to his. I would not change my appraisal of him from nearly forty years ago. He was not among the greatest of modern writers, but he was a writer one had to love if one loved Tokyo.

I loved exploring the city, always on foot, and he really was my guide and companion. Often when I set out, my bourne would be a place I had come upon in his diary or one of his essays, the temple a little to the north and west of the Yoshiwara, for instance, just at the limits of the Meiji city, where the ashes of so many Yoshiwara courtesans repose.

Sometimes I had other companions. On one memorable occasion I was with my old friend Nakamura Eiko and her mother and a friend of theirs. (Eiko was the victim of Osborn's practical joke about Mr. B. and Jesus Christ.) It will be seen that she was born east of the river in the region I found so comfortable and provocative of nostalgia. The family lived there until the bombings of 1945 drove them to the western suburbs. The entry is from late in the summer of 1965.

"The afternoon was a delight—the appointment with the Nakamuras and Mrs. Watanabe that I attempted prematurely to keep two weeks ago. We had sushi in Tsukiji [east of Ginza, site of the original Tokyo foreign settlement] and then went east of the river to Honjo, to explore the land where they lived before the war. Here was the family sake shop, there was the ditch, and all over that way was mosquito-infested swamp. It did not sound all that attractive, and yet, as in Kafū, the disappearance of swamp and mosquitoes was made to seem like a real loss. It was their first, or perhaps for one of them second, visit since the war, and the search for something familiar besides the elementary school Eiko went to was very touching. There did not seem to be a single family left from the old days, anyone they wanted to look up.

"And yet, strangely, a certain air alien to the part of town I live in [I was then in hilly Koshikawa] does survive. We went to look at the Ryūgenji, commonly known as the *hagi* temple [*hagi is Lespedeza bicolor,* often called bush clover] over beyond the ditch, where once there was an embankment. Now there is a concrete wall. It is really very beautiful, something one would not expect to come upon in all the hot asphalt. The buildings, postwar, are concrete, but simple and without the fuss of most concrete temple architecture, and the grounds are all *hagi,* a field of it, riffling in the late-summer breeze. The most conspicuous man-made object, aside from the temple buildings, is a common tomb for the *muenbutsu,* the bondless ones, studded with little stone grave statues from as early as Genroku [a span of about a decade and a half from the seventeenth century into the eighteenth].

"Then there is Myōkensama [another temple]. . . . The principal object in *its* yard is what appears to be the common grave of a band of *yakuza* [gangsters] in residence from the river as far east as Funabashi [in Chiba Prefecture]. Together to the end. I wonder if any of their skins have been preserved."

Muenbutsu are departed spirits without survivors to tend to graves and make offerings. The last sentence is a reference to the Tokyo University Medical Museum, a chamber of horrors with elaborately tattooed skins on its walls, and on its shelves such treasures as the brain of the famous novelist Natsume Sōseki.

Kafū lived briefly in the plebeian flatlands, which I call the Low City, but he lived most of his life in the wealthy, hilly parts of the city, until 1945, when he moved to Chiba Prefecture, where he died. I have never lived in the Low City, as that term ought properly to be understood, but perhaps I have been more consistently plebeian than Kafū, since my Tokyo abode, except for a brief period in 1969, has been in the north, considered to be a bad address by those who live in the south and west. For most of the years between the two disasters, that of 1923 and that of 1945, Kafū lived in Azabu, one of the wealthiest parts of the city, very high bourgeois indeed, though it is becoming less and less residential.

"As that term ought properly to be understood," I have said, but the significance keeps changing. It ought to refer to the flatlands to the east of the hills, at the edge of which the palace stands. I like to call this the Low City. Now it seems to refer to anything north and east of the palace. This is a definition with which I will not argue, although the purist in me rejects it. I do like the east and north better than the south and west, and so did Kafū.

It is getting harder and harder to see why. In the years just after the war, an afterglow of Edo and Meiji lingered on. For an outsider like myself, it was most apparent in the street life, and the streets were liveliest in the clement seasons, spring and fall, and in steaming summer. Kafū has a beautiful essay on the pleasures of the Tokyo summer. For all the fact that the summer is much the worst season, soupily hot in coastal Japan, it did have its pleasures. On a warm, clear evening (as clear goes in the Tokyo summer) in the Low City everyone turned out. The street that ran through a neighborhood became its community center; and there was community, as there was not in the hilly High City to the west. The lower orders who lived in the Low City were mostly of northern and eastern origins, and one felt that they brought the seasons of their villages with them, and their sense of community as well. One had to search long and often fruitlessly for anything of the sort in the High City.

In my diary entry for April 12, 1974, I describe a walk east of the River Sumida, which runs through the heart of the Low City. It concludes thus: "I munched upon an ear of corn at just about the point where old Ragetsu must have boarded his ferry, slightly drunk, and I thought how strange that when I first came to Mukōjima by myself, when the New Year kites were flying in 1949, I felt insecure and apprehensive, lest someone come up and molest me. Now it is among the places where I feel most serene and secure."

Mukōjima is a district east of the river opposite Asakusa. Ragetsu, the poetically inclined uncle of the hero, crosses the river at the beginning of "The River Sumida," one of Kafū's most beautiful stories, published in 1909. It seems entirely proper that I should think of Kafū in a moment of serene happiness at a place we both loved. If we had met I would have had so many things to talk to him about that I would not have known where to begin. I cannot of course speak for him.

Now the Low City is utterly changed. There is no street life any more, except on a rare festival night, and festivals continue to be livelier in the Low City than in the High City. Quite aside from the fact that I am not the walker I was, there is less and less incentive to go walking. Many influences can be blamed for the change, and chief among them is probably television. Everyone has it, and so everyone is inside on a summer evening watching baseball. A half century ago everyone would have had to consult the grapevine or the morning newspaper. As I try to keep alive memories of how things were, Kafū is a dearer companion than ever.

He is the great example of the companion I never met. There are examples of something like the opposite, people with whom I felt on companionable terms and found that I was not. The fact is worth recording because it tells something about Japanese society, a society that continues to perplex even after more than half a century of pounding away at the edges of it. The really perplexing thing is not that a friendship should run up on the rocks, but that a person, or at any rate this person, rarely finds out about the nature of the rocks. Something went wrong, and what was it? I do not know, I cannot say.

For me the striking example of a friend who all of a sudden turned out not to be is Yoshida Ken-ichi, the son of Shigeru, the prime minister. Ken-ichi was an eminence in his own right, neither political nor diplomatic, but literary. He was a respected essayist and critic, and he made a rather endearing thing of the bad terms he was on with his father and his sister, the latter a power behind the power of their father.

Ken-ichi spoke and wrote excellent if quirkish English, Shigeru having been ambassador to the United Kingdom. We used mostly English when we were together. I have a rule of thumb with regard to which language is to be used, Japanese or English. If my Japanese is better than the English of the Japanese with whom I am speaking, and I may in all modesty say that it often enough is, then we will speak Japanese. In the reverse case we will speak English. It is I think a good rule, though I am not always able to put it into practice. There is a kind of Japanese who cannot speak English and will not speak Japanese. If the intent is to make communication impossible, it works. In the Ken-ichi instance, there was no question that the language should be English.

He was a splendid companion for an evening on the town. He liked and knew his drink and his food, and would have only the best of either. I was very sorry when it became apparent that there would be no more evenings. He wrote a recommendation for Tanizaki, in the days when Harold Strauss was seeking such recommendations and I was doing what I could to get them for him. In Ken-ichi's covering letter is an invitation to join him in finishing off a cask of sake of which he was particularly proud. It contains an excellent example of the quirkishness: "I should very much like to have another of those gatherings over the sake, of which nearly half a barrel or more still remains." The expression "nearly half a barrel or more" is surely richly ambiguous.

The recommendation itself was the only one I got in English. It is a very good recommendation. Here are the opening sentences: "Junichirō Tanizaki is one of the acknowledged masters among Japanese novelists of today. He has the distinction of having tried his hand at most forms of the novel, modern, historical, imaginative and realistic; and achieving an originality of style in each."

One evening, for no reason that I could detect, he said substantially this: "There is a kind of American who is the most urbane, witty, and generally charming person in the world; but you are not it."

And who, I asked, was or were the American or Americans in question. I knew perfectly well whom he meant. He meant Donald Keene. I asked because I wanted to see whether he would give me an honest answer. All I got was the tense, high-pitched laugh which an English lady likened, most aptly, and I would not have thought of the simile myself, to the self-starter in an automobile.

I would as soon have forgotten the remark but, given these sentiments, I did not wish to impose my company on him. I would, I told myself, wait for him to call, and I would be very pleased if he did. He did not. Occasionally we exchanged nods and the tersest of greetings at large literary gatherings, but I never spent another evening with him. We finished the half, or more, barrel of sake before the break occurred. I never learned what caused him to make so gratuitously unkind a remark. If I were to learn that it did not seem so to him, I would not be changed in my view that Japanese can be peculiar. I did not go to his funeral. Neither, I am told, did his sister.

There may be just a touch of malice in my diary entry for December 8, 1967. "Old Yoshida" is Ken-ichi's father, Shigeru, the former prime minister. "Over to the library to read a few newspapers. Old Yoshida's state funeral. He managed to be the center of controversy down to the end. There are those who think the whole institution of the state funeral to be unconstitutional; and, ironically, it seems to have been Yoshida himself who vetoed the suggestion that the dowager empress be given a state funeral. Ken-ichi is sitting there, pleased as a pussycat, with the ashes in his lap."

Quite aware that listing all the eminences one has known can become the pompous thing of name-dropping, I will not list all the other literary eminences who were kind and friendly in those years. Another two or three and I will be finished. I am grateful to them all, and I think that with brief mention of the two or three I will have listed the ones to whom I am most grateful. Others will make their appearance in later years, though not so many of them, for I was no longer in residence among them.

During the fifties I translated a couple of longish stories, novellas they might be called, by Inoue Yasushi. After the first of these he invited me to dinner. It was an elegant and I am sure shockingly expensive dinner, Tokyo having the most expensive restaurants in the world, and afterwards we went to an elegant and I am sure shockingly expensive bar in Ginza, the sort of place I would not dream of going to in circumstances in which I might have to pay the bill. During the years after I had returned to the United States and was in Tokyo only during the summer, I always telephoned him, and the same thing happened again.

I did not telephone him because I wanted an elegant and expensive dinner. I telephoned him because I wanted to see him. He was a scholar and a gentleman, and there is nothing trite about the characterization in his case. He really was. He had begun his career as an art reporter for a large newspaper, and he knew his stuff. He knew everything there was to know about Central Asia, and about the Japanese in America and—well, as they say, you name it. From him I learned something I have since established as true, that many Japanese-Americans are more Japanese than the Japanese.

Only one thing stood between us. I am sure that he did not know of it, for it was my secret. I did not like to talk about the Nobel Prize. The subject was always coming up. Before Tanizaki, Mishima, and Kawabata died, they were the favored candidates for prizes. Then it was Inoue. Year after year there would be a rumor that another Japanese was to get it, and year after year Inoue would be kept on the alert, waiting for the camera bulbs to start popping. He had by then become dean of the literary world, and what more obvious candidate for the prize could there be?

My secret was that I was sure he would not get it. Talks with literary Swedes in Stockholm and in Tokyo had persuaded me that, for their taste, he was too much a writer after a formula. I knew what they meant, and may confess that I did not myself have great regard for his fiction, and especially the historical fiction, which is most highly regarded in Japan. It is mostly history with a splash here and there of fiction. I did not reveal my secret to anyone. I could have been mistaken, which would have been embarrassing, and I would not have wished to spoil the fun for the reporters and cameramen. Though it would have been nice if he had won the prize, hopes were from the outset unreal.

A little about the Muramatsus, brother and sister, Takeshi and Hideko, and I will be finished. Both were close to Mishima. Hideko was his protégée and gave one of the eulogies at his funeral. Though she writes poetry that is highly regarded, she is better known as an actress. Mishima, some of whose best writing was for the theater, gave her good parts. I met Takeshi through Mishima, and Hideko through her brother.

Takeshi was the most conservative Japanese I have known, if we leave aside the ranting sort of conservative. He was no ranter. He was a very cool sort of person, and he had arrived at his position coolly, from a dislike of communism. He was the only Japanese I ever heard present a reasoned defense of Franco. A communist Spain, he said, would have been worse than Franco's Spain. If he approved of Hitler for similar reasons, he kept his thoughts to himself. He disliked my habit of voting for Democratic presidential candidates. His expressions of disapproval were mild, but I suspect that the disapproval itself was strong.

He was an extremely erudite man. He wrote long books, impressive for the learning subsumed in them, that were sometimes literary and sometimes cultural and historical. He did all the research himself. He did not, he said, trust paid researchers. I never asked him a question he did not have an answer to, impromptu, and it was always an answer based on a wealth of fact. I asked him once about the troublesome era-names by which Japanese history is fragmented. I wished to know in what circumstances one era name was changed for another. The pattern seemed erratic. He gave me an answer so detailed that I wished I had brought a tape recorder. I cannot remember a third of it.

He was not always right. He denied Mishima's homosexuality. I have given my own views in this regard. But he usually was, and his command of the facts was awesome. I suppose that except for those closest to him there were no facts, only feelings and intuitions, with regard to Mishima. It may be too that Takeshi said what he did out of loyalty towards Mishima. Homosexuality has a not dishonorable place in Japanese martial history, but today, quite possibly in imitation of the West, it is not socially acceptable.

I visited Takeshi as he lay dying, in a cancer sanitarium way out in the wilds of Chiba. He was unable to speak, but he clearly recognized me, and something in his eyes said that he would love to have a good long talk.

His sister is known professionally as Muramatsu Eiko, and her real name is Muramatsu Hideko, and the strange thing is that both given names are written with the same Chinese characters. Among quite a few annoyances which the Japanese language perpetrates is the fact that it is often impossible to know how a place name or a personal name is pronounced. Is it Hideko or is it Eiko?—and it could also be Fusako. Go and ask her. To which the uninitiated often replies: well, for goodness sake, I thought you knew Japanese. In vain one explains that many Japanese proper nouns can be pronounced more than one way, and there is nothing to do but consult a dictionary in the case of eminences, or ask someone who knows, such as the person himself or herself, in the case of lesser ones. (The story is told of an assassinated prime minister whose son was asked by reporters for a definitive reading of his elusive given name. "We always called him Papa," was the answer.)

There was a strong family resemblance between the siblings. Yet I thought her very good-looking and him not at all that way. He had a pleasant and intelligent face, if a somewhat sleepy one, but I would not have called him handsome. It was all very mysterious. I was never able to solve the mystery to my satisfaction.

She was a good actress. I use the past tense because she is now mostly to be seen on television, and I do not own a television set. I liked her best in a one-act stage role, as an insane woman in one of Mishima Yukio's Nō plays. She alternated in the role with Bandō Tamasaburō, probably the most popular of female impersonaters in the Kabuki theater. I saw them both, and liked her better than him, which is very high praise. (Fukuda Tsuneari, of whom much has been said above, was the director. She said that he forbade her, and presumably Tamasaburō, to use classic poses.)

She is a devout Catholic, a not at all common species in Japan. Through her I got to know the cardinal archbishop of Tokyo, an unassuming man whose pleasantly old-fashioned manner might make one think (it is not true) that he had come to town recently from some remote province. I would be hard put, if we include one-night stands, to say what was the most delightful dinner party I ever attended, but when it comes to multiple dinner parties at irregular but not infrequent intervals, hers were the best. They were small parties and we were all good friends, and there was no fussing about having the right division by gender, or about what language to speak. The language was Japanese.

The two Muramatsus would always be there, and Hideko's husband, Nannichi Tsuneo, and Father Roggendorf, and sometimes Saeki Shōichi, the aforementioned eminent critic whom I may or may not have met in Sasebo just after the war but whom I have definitely known for forty years and more. Saeki and I do not always agree about literature—he knows and cares more about American literature than I do, and about Mishima Yukio as well—but we generally agree about social and political matters. Unlike so many Japanese intellectuals (and American professors) he is no ideologue.

Nannichi, like Takeshi, died much too soon, of the same ailment, cancer. His ashes repose in St. Mary's Cathedral, where the cardinal has his seat, and near where Hideko still lives. He had one endearing little peculiarity. He played the cello very well, and could even manage a Bach unaccompanied suite. One evening I remarked, and I think it was rather a silly remark, that it is easier to hide one's inadequacies while playing Bach than while playing Mozart. It is easier to fake, I said, because things are not quite so much out in the open. He took up his cello and played a strain from one of the accompanied cello suites. Then he pushed it towards me: "Now show me, please, how it is possible to fake that one."

It need surprise no one that my answer was silence.

Those dinner parties were warm and intimate, the food and the conversation were superior, and it did not seem to matter at all that the good father and I were not Japanese. There are not many Japanese gatherings of which this can be said.

Probably my relations with the Japanese literary and intellectual world were their most cordial towards the end of the sixties, when Kawabata received the Nobel Prize. The fifties, however, for all the rough spots, were more interesting.

Towards the end of the decade I paid my first visit to Europe, to attend a conference organized in Basel by the Congress for Cultural Freedom. I did not know when I departed Tokyo that it would be, but it was, the end of my formal association with Sophia University. When I returned to Tokyo in December, 1959, by way of south and southeast Asia, I did not ask, because I really did not want a positive answer, whether Sophia University had further need of my services, and Sophia uttered no word suggesting that it did. So, without dismissal or resignation, I was no longer on its staff, though I continued to be on friendly terms with the Jesuits. A few years earlier I would have said that I expected to end my years in Tokyo. I was becoming less sure all the time that I wished to do so. I was beginning to feel that I could not take much more of the progressive culture-mongers.

There were bad moments in Europe. The one that remains strongest in memory was in Munich. I had thought of spending a couple of days there, but was rudely treated at an information counter and so immediately boarded a train for Venice. One would not have expected to be thus treated in jolly Munich, and I am sure that the incident tells us nothing about Munich or Germany. These things happen.

On the whole I loved Europe and asked myself why I had waited until I was almost forty to visit it. I think the part of the trip that brought the greatest pleasure was a drive along the coast of Sicily with dear old friends from DipSec days, Tom and Julie Murfin. Tom had just been posted to Palermo as consul general and they were busily engaged in moving from temporary quarters into a big house just outside the city. They dropped everything to take me on the drive. In the course of it I saw my first Grecian temple. To say that I was stunned does not adequately describe my feelings. My next stop was Athens, where of course I saw the Acropolis. It was anticlimax. I think it is probably common experience that the first Grecian temple one sees is the most beautiful thing one has ever seen.

But there was an utterly trivial happening in Paris that still brings a tingling of pleasure. I was standing on a street corner, feeling and doubtless looking puzzled. "*Vous cherchez, monsieur?*" asked a lady. The Metro, I replied. She pointed and said not another word, but I can still see her. She was beautiful and she was charming. It was a day when the French, or so it was said, were not being kind to Americans, but no one in Paris was as unkind as the lady in jolly Munich.

People from the Congress were very attentive on the way back to Tokyo. Every place I stopped was new—until the last place, Hong Kong. In the parliamentary building in New Delhi I bowed to Nehru and his daughter, both of them uncommonly good-looking people, and they bowed back. There is a thing about having had a diplomatic career, even a brief one: a person has friends and acquaintances all over the world. In Hong Kong I stayed with Tom and Sue Ainsworth, one of three couples at whose weddings I have been best man. I had been to Hong Kong before, but visited Macao for the first time. In those days it was a lovely town, no more than a town, a bit of the Mediterranean world dropped down on the other side of the world. I hope the Chinese will be good to it.

I found the tumultuous summer of 1960, when anti-American demonstrations rendered the center of the city inoperable, deeply disturbing. I resolved that when an opportunity came to return with dignity to the United States I would not let it pass. The opportunity came in 1962. I did not, however, want to go.

Tokyo was such a lively and interesting and amusing city, much more so then, to my mind, than it is now. It was and is a youthful city. Young people pour in from the provinces. I have blamed television for the disappearance of street life. It might also be blamed for the fact that the young have changed. They used to be bouncing and eager and, well, young. They were always striking up conversations, usually in English, for they wished to practice their English. Today they are haughty and world weary. There were such amusing little brushes. A tiny scattering from my diary will suggest what they were like:

"I was assailed, in the course of my musings [the setting is Shinobazu Pond, in Ueno Park] by perhaps a dozen eager learners. One young gentleman said: 'My name is Mr. Owaki. I want to go where you go.'"

"I found myself on the wrong train, getting off not at Myōgadani but at Ueno; and so, as usual, I had a stroll around the lake. . . . A young man sat down beside me and, smiling, said: 'Yankee, go back to Shinjuku.'" Shinjuku, some distance west of the palace, is much favored by young foreigners.

"I was having a beer in some nameless place when a lad with a sturdy northern face sat down beside me, and said that his name was Kaitō, and that he wished to show me the six toes on his left foot. So he took off his left shoe and sock, and he did indeed have six. They seemed very important to him."

I was sure that nothing of the sort would happen in Palo Alto. In Tokyo eager students of English were always young and they were of both sexes; the young men were more amusing on the whole than were the young women. I suspect the reason was that Japanese women are on the whole better at languages, and so the men tried harder.

In any event, I knew that the time to leave had come.

SIX

THE GOLDEN AND NOT-SO-GOLDEN WEST

ON A WARM AUGUST EVENING IN 1962, a Norwegian freighter bore me from the Yokohama docks down Tokyo Bay and then turned eastwards towards the Golden West. We would next make land at Los Angeles.

Had someone asked me ten years earlier whether I meant to live again in the United States, I would almost certainly have said no. I liked Tokyo very much. Indeed, I had already fallen into the habit of saying in response to questions about why I liked Japan: "I don't like Japan. I like Tokyo." I did not doubt that I would live out my days there. Something had always come along to keep me from starvation. And then came the "progressive" intellectuals.

I have already spoken of the farewell gifts, priceless to me and valuable as well to the rest of the world and all its purveyors of collectibles, which I received that summer, from Kawabata, Tanizaki, Hirabayashi Taiko, and others. The days and nights were dotted as well with splendid farewell parties, most of them given by Japanese. They were uniformly lavish and interesting, and I learned a thing or two from them.

I had it as the opinion of an eminent literary critic, at a party given by Mishima, that the Japanese writers whom I most admired, such as Tanizaki, were not held in the highest esteem by the Japanese because the Japanese are suspicious, among men of letters, of the genuine professional. It is true that the man who was before the war known as "the god of the novel," Shiga Naoya, was to me a superb writer of short stories but a man whose more ambitious works seem scarcely novels at all. Tanizaki has come into his own since the war, and it is just possible that we who introduced modern Japanese literature to America and Europe may have had something to do with the matter.

I will quote from my diary account (July 11, 1962) of a farewell party at which I acquired a bit of knowledge about Tanizaki not, I think, to be found in studies and reference works. "In the evening, errands in Roppongi . . . and on to the Akabane for another real whang of a farewell party, the Bunka Forum's. Most impressive." I then give the guest list, which reads like a roster of eminent non-progressives, Mrs. Hirabayashi, Father Roggendorf, many others. "Admirable people all—enough to make me think that it has not perhaps been a complete waste—that maybe something is underway that I may have had just a little to do with getting started. . . . I scarcely remember what was in [the speeches], save that it is Amamiya's view that Tanizaki's exceptionally small penis (A. has been in the bath with him) explains a great deal about him."

The Bunka Forum was the Tokyo branch of the Congress for Cultural Freedom. Amamiya Yōzō was an important journalist. He held high positions on *Chūō Kōron* and the *Yomiuri.*

More than one cynical foreigner has been heard to say that the Japanese give these marvelous parties to make it difficult for the guest of honor to come back. They certainly had the effect of giving me second thoughts about going, thoughts which the parties themselves made it impossible to execute.

The very best party was given not by Japanese but by a pair of foreigners, Peter Robinson and Robert Fisher. The former is an Australian journalist now in Sydney; the latter is an American publisher of travel books. They took an Ueno theater for the night, a stage theater, not a movie one. The pits were cleared of chairs and jammed with guests, and performers from the variety halls, paper-cutters and the like, entertained us. Paper-cutters cut impromptu representations from paper with most extraordinary skill. Someone asked for a representation of "Yankee go home," and the result was a cutting of a "demo," short for "demonstration," meaning rally, which I still have. I still have as well the banner that hung in front of the theater. It was one of the best parties I have ever been at, and it was all mine.

Memory has not failed me with regard to the day of my departure. It is vivid, but of course no account from thirty-six years later can ring as true as the words set down that day. Here are some of them, though not all: "Ishihara saw me to the ship, too sleepy to have yet a sense of finality. Sakaguchi was already there; and after a beer and some small talk they departed, for the sailing was not, as the Dodwell idiots in Tokyo had told me, at sunset, but at eleven. They drove off down the dock and left me to come back aboard alone, and it suddenly struck me. I felt utterly desolate, as people feel when the funeral is over and the house is empty. I went into my cabin and stood looking at myself in the mirror for a time, incredulous that I should have allowed this to happen.

"Then, wanting so much to go back to Tokyo that I could scarcely restrain myself, I went for a walk along the docks, which, however, proved to be as desolate as I. I was back aboard ship staring at a dim Fuji in the sunset and thinking that I could not possibly face my fellow passengers at dinner, when Tom and Julie Murfin, dear people, appeared. They were on their way to Tokyo, and, upon learning that I had forgotten my typewriter, insisted that I go with them—their driver would see me back, and they would go back by train. The driver, a Yokohama man, did what no Tokyo man would have done, went smack through the center of the city, and so I saw the Ginza and Kōrakuen crowds once more, and returned with my typewriter, too tired to feel more than merely melancholy. I was reading the evening papers . . . when the tugs started bleating ominously; and as we moved down the bay in the moonlight I drank."

Ishihara Hōki was the director of the Japan Culture Forum. Sakaguchi Kin-ichi was a drinking companion of some years standing, the chief photographer for a slickish women's magazine, who was killed in an automobile accident not many years later. The Kōrakuen, on the site of a Tokugawa family estate, still preserves a part of the old grounds, but is mostly a big amusement center, including a bicycle-racing track that is a point on which the minds of gamblers converge, and a baseball stadium on which the minds of most of Tokyo converge, for it is home grounds for the gigantically popular Tokyo Giants. The Murfins were the couple who took me on the unforgettable drive around Sicily in 1959. Consul general in Palermo at the time, Tom had returned to Japan as consul general in Yokohama. (We no longer have a consulate, general or of another kind, in Yokohama. It should have been kept for old times' sake and for public relations, Yokohama having been the site of the first American diplomatic post in Japan.)

For reasons which now escape me, if ever I had any, I say nothing in my diary of the most intense spasm of regret, when we passed the very beautiful weekend retreat on the Chiba shore of the bay of some dear American friends, Herbert and Maggy Burrows, he with The Agency, she a journalist. It is pleasant to add that good weekends were yet to come, in later summers. "A beautiful day, Fuji visible for a time in the morning, just above the Defense Academy, where, says Herbert, 'they think of ways to run away when the Russians come—that's why they're so conveniently located to the shipping lanes.'" This is from my diary entry for July 7, 1963. The academy is on the opposite coast of the bay, in Yokosuka, a navy city.

I do not remember that we in Colorado, although there was gold in our hills, ever referred to our abode as the Golden West. The student newspaper in my years at the University of Colorado was *The Silver and Gold,* and silver and gold (nearer gray and yellow) were the university colors; the Golden West lay beyond the mountains, beside the Golden Gate. Los Angeles was not there, exactly, but, being on the coast, it would do. My memories of it, from its first Olympic summer, 1932, and the war years, were pleasant.

I could not say that my regrets at leaving Japan had vanished by the time we reached Los Angeles, but they were much diminished. The ship's company, passengers and crew, was a jolly lot. I am still in correspondence with an English couple, Clare and John Bryant, who were approaching the end of a honeymoon trip around the world. I have not seen them these three and a half decades, but I feel close to them. They are now divorced. She lives on the Isle of Man, he near London. The Isle of Man is one of the places I keep saying I must visit and probably never will. They tend to be remote places, Patagonia, Greenland, the south coast of the Arabian peninsula.

We did presently reach Los Angeles, with no stops between Yokohama and it. The plan was that my brother would meet me there and we would drive up to Palo Alto. The only problem was how long we would stay in Los Angeles.

When we went to Los Angeles for the 1932 Olympics I immediately fell in love with the city and stayed in that condition through the summer. My brother had spells of homesickness and, I think, would have happily turned around without leaving the railway station. Now, thirty years later, our positions were reversed. He loved thundering down the freeways, with which Los Angeles was in those days as abundantly provided as any city in the world. I think they gave him feelings of power. I kept wanting to go away and he kept wanting to stay. We did the sensible thing, compromised, staying not as long as he wished and longer than I wished. Los Angeles goes on feeling to me like a city in which I could not possibly live. I could, of course, if I had to, but it felt then and feels now far more alien than Tokyo.

Here is part of a diary entry (August 29, 1962) after a look at the city: "The dead heart, and the women, were my chief impressions—the hard, dyed women, like nothing so much as the male prostitutes of Tokyo.

"And Pershing Square. I do not think that even in Calcutta was I ever quite so filled with a simple, primitive urge to flee. Or to take a bath. Diseased. How could anyone from Vermont or Wisconsin think Pershing Square better? . . . .

"Of Los Angeles it can be said, however, that the flowers are very beautiful. . . . And the freeways really are grand, that is the only word for them. Great, cruel sweeps and swirls of concrete plunge and soar along, and forget the un-city that made them. They may be murder, but then so were the extremes of the Gothic cathedral. The Los Angeles way of reaching for God." I was to be similarly disappointed with Union Square in the heart of San Francisco. Once elegant, it now was seedy. It was not as bad as Pershing Square, however.

We stayed with an old family friend from Colorado. People were always moving to southern California from Colorado when they could no longer stand Colorado winters. In his apartment I got a good taste of mid-American kitsch, long forgotten. There is plenty of Japanese kitsch, but it is different, more pictorial and less verbal. On the kitchen wall was a poem doubtless brought from Colorado by his deceased wife.

God bless my little kitchen,
I love its every nook,
And bless me as I do my work,
Wash pots and pans and cook.

"Old John, scrubbing away at the cook," I remark in my diary.

John died, suddenly and alone, on Christmas not many years afterwards, and I acquired a morbid and interesting piece of information: insurance companies will not pay up for a sudden, solitary death on Christmas until they can establish that the cause was not suicide. The probability of suicide is high, it seems, in such deaths.

It was not as if we were in Los Angeles for a long time, but it felt like a long time to me. On the fourth day my brother loaded my baggage and me into his automobile and we set out northwards. I suspect I could not have prevailed upon him to leave Los Angeles so soon had he not known that he would have lovely freeways to thunder up all the way to Palo Alto.

I have remarked upon how the golden hills and purple mountains of California seemed like paradise after the pine barrens of the North Carolina coast. There was in 1962 no such striking contrast to set California off, but the drive was a beautiful one. California goes on being beautiful in spite of everything, probably because there are parts of it that no developer could sell even if he developed them. The Santa Lucia Mountains, north of San Luis Obispo, did as much as any place could possibly have done to persuade me that I had not made a monstrous mistake in leaving Tokyo. They were the Golden West, even if there was no gold in them.

The first thing I learned about Palo Alto was that you could not buy a martini there. You could *drink* one if a kind hostess provided it, but you could not buy one. Not long afterwards, I learned that a five-minute drive from our hotel on University Avenue would have taken us beyond the city limits and back into martini land, but I did not know it at the time, and of course my brother, no more familiar than I with Palo Alto ways, did not know it either. Maybe a hotel clerk would have committed a crime had he provided us with this dissolute information? Silence prevailed, in any event.

So my feelings at the end of the long journey were similar to my feelings at the beginning. The world seemed a bleak place. It went on seeming that way through most of the first of my American academic years. I made friends, and my colleagues were congenial, but I was bored. I do not blame Palo Alto for the fact that I was unhappy there. It was and goes on being a very pretty town. I would probably have been bored in most American places after the huge bustle and stew of Tokyo. I quickly persuaded myself that boredom is the worst of all conditions. Being the first of my American residences, Palo Alto was the most boring. I was heard frequently to remark, during that first winter, that I would far rather be in a dangerous place. This might be interpreted as suggesting that Tokyo was and is a dangerous place. It is not, although, as my evenings with Koestler demonstrated, one can have a rather pleasant feeling that danger lurks not far away.

I found a great deal to complain about. Friends and colleagues listened patiently, and I do not doubt that I became something of a bore myself. One of them said that it was true: Palo Alto had something to offer to people interested in gardening, riding horseback, and disciplining children, but not much for anyone else. The wife of that same colleague said, years later, when all three of us were safely out of Palo Alto: "We all agreed with you, but we couldn't say so."

Much of my complaining was reserved for the privacy of my thoughts and my diary, and I can see now, and probably could see then, that much of it was unfair. Some of my students were pretty bad. I have my diary to remind me of one of them.

"A master's translation informs me, among other things, that Shimazaki Tōson's affair with his niece was 'from the standpoint of eugenics . . . immoral and prohibited.' Also that he 'willfully maintained his sanity,' and that incest was a pretty nasty thing to be guilty of 'considering his situation.' This from a master's candidate—it sort of gives you the feeling that California is a half-civilized place, if that much." (April 6, 1964)

Shimazaki Tōson was a very famous, and I think very bad, novelist of the early twentieth century. The most famous episode in his life was the eugenically unsound liaison with his niece.

In another entry I note that Pat Brown, our governor, has one day recently informed us that California leads the nation in all manner of endeavors, including education. "Wish someone would invite me to a backward state," I add.

I cannot but have known that this was unfair. Some of the students were, to be sure, disappointing, but the best of them were very good, much farther along in their studies of the language than I was at their age. Several of them are professors at this and that good university now, approaching retirement age, if there is such a thing any more at their several places of employment.

Occasionally I had comforting evidence that I was not alone in my dissatisfaction with California. Thus there was the automobile I saw heading eastwards across one of the bay bridges and bearing this legend on its bumper: "Good-bye California and all your goddamned geraniums."

The town itself was much as I remembered it from drives with my Yokohama aunt and uncle, who in the years after the war were living in Marin County, across the Golden Gate from the San Francisco Peninsula, on which Palo Alto reposes. They chose that very year to move back to Colorado. This I thought cruel of them. I was fond of them and of Marin

County, and an occasional weekend there would have made Palo Alto easier to take.

The lands around Palo Alto had changed greatly. Once a sea of flowering fruit trees, they were now bedroom tracts for the large cities on the fringes of the bay. One of the larger cities, San Jose, was a particularly keen disappointment. It had a been pleasant little Mexico town when first I saw it. From my boyhood I had been strongly drawn to Mexican things. I had loved Santa Fe, also very Mexican, and one of the smallest state capitals the land over. When I took up residence in Palo Alto, San Jose was by way of becoming what it is now, a city larger than the mother city, San Francisco, and not a city at all, but an endless tract of featureless suburbia. My first trip to Europe persuaded me that among the things I liked about Mexico and the Mexicans was that they were of an older world than we.

Stanford kept calling itself the Harvard of the West, as did many another Western university. I kept telling it that it should call itself, rather, the Princeton of the West. I had no evidence whatever that it listened. The two universities, Stanford and Princeton, have much in common. Both are most filthily rich, and both are at an unfortunate distance from a large city. Another similarity may be that each is more pleased with itself than it has any right to be. San Francisco, like Stanford, is not as good as it thinks it is. In those days, before it had acquired the Brundage Collection, it did not have an art museum as good as that of Honolulu, a city only a fraction its size. I used to enjoy being asked, as the newcomer is constantly asked, whether I did not think it a most uncommonly beautiful city. The expression on people's faces when I replied that I thought Chicago a more beautiful city was worth remembering. My meaning (and I would happily explain it if the inquirer did not rush off in consternation at being faced with a lunatic) was that the beauty of San Francisco was made by God, and the beauty of Michigan Avenue in Chicago was made by man.

Palo Alto is a very quiet place. It has plenty of vehicle noise but is without the buzz of society. Faculty housing has one pretty garden after another, and seems virtually uninhabited. Once on a visit to Christchurch, on the South Island of New Zealand, I was with a party guided by a lady who insisted relentlessly on the Britishness of everything. I finally said that it all looked pretty much like California to me. The remark did not please her, but it worked. She insisted no further.

It is perhaps fitting, given the quietness, that the two most memorable times during my Palo Alto years were times of utter silence. One was when the Giants beat the Dodgers in playoffs for the National League pennant. The silence was far more intense than during the Cuban missile crisis, when we could not with any confidence say that we would still be alive a moment hence. Then it was broken by a monstrous blare of automobile horns, and even the few of us who were not provided with television knew what had happened. The other was the morning, for it was morning on the Pacific Coast, when Kennedy was assassinated. It is said that everyone alive and past infancy that day still remembers where he or she was when the news came. I certainly do. I was about to commence a witty lecture on a light work of classical Japanese prose. I went ahead with the lecture but suppressed the wit. Afterwards I was let know by students, California students being a frank lot, that it had been in poor taste of me not to dismiss the class. Despite the fact that Stanford is proud of being a "national" university, most of its students are, or were then, healthy, good-looking Californians. One of the pleasures was seeing them all decked out in cardinal red on a football day.

Among the troubles with that first California academic year were my living arrangements. I had a two-room apartment across El Camino Real from the Stanford campus (The Farm, it is called, in pleasing contrast to the Harvard of the East and its Yard). It was a drab, dark place, and darkness in sunny California is next to inexcusable. An old friend of the family who was then in a retirement home in the Portola Valley, between Palo Alto and the coast, caught the spirit nicely when she first stepped inside. "I'd cut my throat," she said, "if I had to live in a place like this." I think she exaggerated, but she had a point.

The real trouble was not with the apartment but with the small back yard on which it faced. There was room in this for a one-car garage and a tree, and virtually nothing else. The tree was a coast redwood, generally considered among the more majestic of God's creations. I came to hate it intensely. If I had had an axe at hand I might have gone out one drunken night and chopped it down. Dark, dirty, pushy, it was everything a tree ought not to be. One of Ronald Reagan's more memorable remarks, was addressed to the Sierra Club, or some such institution, tenaciously engaged in battle to save the redwoods. "If you've seen one of them," Reagan is said to have said, "you've seen them all." I was not often inclined, even conditionally, to agree with him, but I wished to see no more redwoods after living nine months with that one.

I have just used the expression "drunken night." I did not do so in a casual, off-hand fashion. It indicates an unhappy truth, that during my Palo Alto years I started drinking heavily. I had felt no inhibitions about drink during the Tokyo years, and many a delightful party at the house of this and that diplomatic or bureaucratic friend had been fairly drunken. The crucial word here is "party." I drank only on social occasions. In California, quite aware of the danger, I started drinking alone.

Actually I started aboard the Norwegian freighter. I left Yokohama with an ample liquor closet, farewell presents from kind friends who knew I would need bolstering. I had consumed all of it long before California was in sight. I came to think that the effective part of a Stanford week narrowed to a single day, Wednesday. On Monday and Tuesday I was still recovering from the preceding weekend, and on Thursday and Friday I was getting ready for the next one. It was an unhappy situation, one not easy to remedy. It may have had little to do with the return to my native land. It may be that bad Tokyo habits simply became worse. As to that I cannot say. What I can say is that I would not wish again to be so prodigal in my expenditure of time.

I do not know, but think it possible, that it was owing to drink that I had such odd dreams during my Stanford years. Thus there was a series of what I may call réveille dreams, which, as they persisted, I found so interesting that I started noting them down. They would occur just at the hour when I should be rising, and in each of them, under a different name, I would be ordered to do so. Here are some of them:

"Anthony Pule, you get out of bed this minute."

"Alfred A. Lee, you get out of bed this moment."

"Ezra Breakwater, you get out of bed this instant."

"Noel van Bundle, you get up this very instant."

"Get up this moment, Dour Wrigley." (A couple of nights after this one I dreamed that I was Pandit Nehru's successor, and that my name was Pundit Dwinge.)

"Lola Twohogs, get up this instant."

"Millie Monadnock, you get out of bed this very moment, and I mean it."

I do not put much store by dreams, either as devices for analysis or as devices for prediction. They tell me whether I was happy or sad at the moment of the dream, and that I seem to be more imaginative when sleeping than when waking. Some may find the fact that the dreams are androgynous to be of deep significance.

There was a scattering of what I might call bookish dreams:

"I dreamed that I was shaving with a runcible spoon. It was taking a long time but working very well."

"I dreamed that my Aunt Adelaide never reads the first half of a book." This is my Yokohama aunt, who was by then back in Colorado Springs.

"I dreamed I was sent a novel to review. It was a single volume, six thousand pages long."

Some of my favorite dreams, which fall into no category, are, I think, the better kind of nonsense, with their own mad reason.

"I dreamed I offered Tex Weatherby fifteen million for his property. 'Dollars or yen?' he asked. 'Dollars,' said I. 'Then I won't sell,' said he." Meredith Weatherby was the founder of the Weatherhill Publishing Company. Everyone called him Tex in the DipSec days, for he was from Waco, as deep in the heart as you can get. I went on using the nickname, although in his later years he came to dislike it. The dollar was then several hundred times as valuable as the yen.

"I dreamed last night that Cousin Peg and I were motoring in the northern part of the San Luis Valley (the locale could not have been clearer and more specific) and were in a terrible state. I had fallen into a bed of roses and she had fallen off of a bar stool." Elizabeth Dillon Boyer, here called Cousin Peg, is one of my favorite cousins. The San Luis Valley, in south central Colorado, is the source of the Rio Grande.

"I dreamed I had a long lecture from my Aunt Mary Brustman on the dangers of beating an egg. It fights back." Mary Brustman Dillon, the widow of my mother's youngest brother, is another favorite. In her nineties, she lives in Denver.

And have I, in recounting these dreams, revealed dread secrets? I really cannot believe so.

I returned to Colorado at Christmas and again in the spring. It is strange to report, after all the complaining I myself had done in those seasons, that I thought Coloradans great complainers. It may simply be that one is not annoyed by one's own complaining. A difference, however, is that I complained about specific things, such as the boredom, whereas my relatives in Colorado were always complaining about "them." Since Castle Rock was then a farming and ranching village, and farmers and ranchers are among the most pampered elements in American society, it was difficult to see that "them" could be The Government. Yet in a vague, most imprecise way, it did seem to be. The Government was responsible for everything that is wrong with the world. This is a common theme not only in Castle Rock but all through the agrarian West.

There were interesting times and beautiful times in Colorado. These were my first visits since I commenced keeping a diary, as opposed to a journal. In the latter, for most of the fifties, Colorado scarcely figures at all.

"Dinner at the Clarkes' and back early to the arid, unsheltered plot that used to be home. It will be early to bed, too, for the effects of last night are suddenly apparent; but I do not know what good bed will do if that little dog, firmly rooted by the furnace, goes on barking all night. His hearing has left him, says Willie [my brother], and he hears coyote voices from the past."

"While they [my brother and a cousin] had some target practice, I, having little affinity for guns, wandered about the place. A very lovely day, meadow larks singing, now and then a ping from the gun—but the fundamental quality of my native soil comes as a new surprise each time, its stillness. The still heart of the continent. Honey bees, meadow larks, a soughing in the evergreens sleeping out behind the house, and, more than anything, stillness." (March 22, 1963)

"We drove over to Kiowa. The country was very quiet and beautiful, black pines rising from golden ground, an effect almost of lushness, not characteristic of Colorado. And then we came out of the pines, and the plains lay before us, so radiant as to require squinting.

"Though cloudy in the morning, it turned out to be a glorious day again, the sort of day when you want to get out and roll around. And such a clamor of meadow larks. And Uncle Dick found his first robin." (March 23, 1963)

The Clarkes were Uncle Dick and his daughter Mary. An uncle-in-law, he was the husband of Aunt Lucy, one of my grandmother's sisters. When he died in the summer of 1965, a half-dozen days after Tanizaki, and word reached me in Tokyo, I wrote in my diary: "And so ends the generation of the pioneers. . . . Who now is left to remember driving cattle down Sixteenth Street in Denver?" I think I probably meant Seventeenth Street, at the bottom of which, beside the Platte, is Union Station, but it does not matter a great deal.

I was surprised, as I was getting ready to go back out to Tokyo in June, at being asked to teach at Stanford a second year. I would not have thought my performance during the first year even mildly successful. Nor would

I have thought my colleagues forbearing enough to put up with another year of complaining. I accepted without hesitation. I think I wanted to have my mind made up for me. Another year at Stanford could well mean staying permanently.

I may have sketched too grim a picture of that first year. I was bored, but not miserably unhappy. I had good friends, some old, some new. I had congenial colleagues. I had numbers of very good students. And, though my lodgings may not have been ideal, I worked in a beautiful place, far more beautiful than Tokyo.

With one of the old friends, Charles Hamilton, then a librarian at the University of California in Berkeley, I explored northern California and found most of it beautiful. The northern coast, beyond San Francisco, has a savage beauty, and the gold country, in the Sierra foothills, where so much savagery occurred, has a beauty gentle beyond compare. We both liked exploring cemeteries. The cemeteries of the gold country are sad and interesting. "Isn't it strange," Charles remarked as we were gazing at the tombstone of a maiden who had died young, way back in the middle of the last century, "that you assume she was beautiful." We looked forward to the stones in the Chinese cemetery, and found none. The remains that once lay beneath them were long ago taken back to China.

My first year in Palo Alto was the last in which I had an automobile of my own. I am very un-American in preferring to avoid automobiles when possible. I do not really know why I dislike them, although I put them in the category of gadgets, and I dislike gadgets. An Irish cousin visiting Colorado some sixty years ago remarked that he was allergic to gadgets. Though a stripling, I knew exactly what he meant. My definition of a gadget is: anything I have to learn to use. A can opener is a gadget, but a straw for sipping cider is not.

I had several automobiles during the early Tokyo years. The streets belonged to us Americans, and it could be rather fun barreling down Ginza even as my brother barreled down the Los Angeles freeways. The Japanese soon began having money for automobiles, however, and bad things clearly lay ahead. I sold my last automobile in the summer of 1952, as I was about to board a ship for San Francisco.

The California automobile was not really mine. A friend, Thomas Carlyle Smith, the eminent historian of Japan, let me have the use of it because he was going to be away that year. I will always think that that automobile took a liking to me. As instructed, I left it in the driveway of their house up in the golden hills. It never ran again. And I never again drove anything but a rented automobile, or the briefly borrowed automobile of a friend or relative. It is possible to get by without an automobile even in California. Public transportation may be skimpy, but if you know how to use it you can. Of course it is always good to have friends around, to turn to in a pinch. I think if I had to I could survive without an automobile even in Los Angeles.

Upon my return from Tokyo in the fall of 1963 I found an apartment on the other side of El Camino Real, in a better part of town, a district known as College Terrace because its streets bear the names of colleges and universities. It lay along El Camino, across from the Stanford campus.

The neighborhood may have been better, but the apartment was no great improvement except for the fact that no redwood glowered down upon it. In a few weeks my good friends Alfred and Maribel Kilmartin, he a navy captain, did what one hopes good friends will do, found me a far better abode, a few doors from them on Amherst Street, way up at the top of the terrace. The next streets down are Bowdoin and Columbia. One has little trouble establishing the principle that operated in the naming of the streets. My residence during the remainder of my sojourn in Palo Alto was 2010 Amherst Street. I moved into 2010 on the day of the Kennedy funeral.

My new home was (and still is) a dear little place, a dream cottage like the one at the end of *Bleak House,* with an overgrown garden that I turned to taming. Except when the weather was bad, I tried to be out gardening during the most beautiful hour of the day, the twilight hour, when the hills above Amherst Street were gleaming gold, and I felt that I was indeed in the Golden West. It may be remembered that I was the family gardener back in Colorado. Perhaps I have a greenish sort of thumb. My garden became one of the best up and down Amherst Street, which is lined with beautiful houses and gardens, just possibly as good as anything in Christchurch.

Maribel, now a widow, still lives at 2100 Amherst. She was born and reared in Tokyo, and has, I think, a somewhat romantic view of it. I tell her she had not been there long enough as an adult, that you have to know Tokyo and Japan well to start finding distasteful aspects. She but smiles. I have crossed California east to west and west to east many times since I ceased being a resident. When I can make only one stop, as is usually the case, I stop in San Francisco. My chief reason is to see how Maribel is doing.

The Kilmartins made Palo Alto a better place than it had been before I met them. So did the Sansoms, Katharine and George, more properly Sir George and Lady Sansom. He was the eminent British historian of Japan, perhaps the last in the brilliant line of amateur British scholars, who had other things to occupy them during the working hours. Sir George has been mentioned above as one of the persons I wished to emulate. Because he suffered from a respiratory ailment, perhaps asthma or emphysema (I never asked for details) and was more comfortable in a dry climate, they passed the sunny seasons in Palo Alto, and the winter, when northern California is often rainy, in Tucson. I had met them once, on a brief stay in Palo Alto during my Tokyo years. Now I got to know them well. Sir George held a position at the university. Katharine states in her memoir, *Sir George Sansom and Japan,* that he was an Honorary Consulting Professor.

If one is to be thoroughly scrupulous about addresses, they lived not in Palo Alto, California, but in Stanford, California. The two are different entities. They had a beautiful house and perhaps an even more beautiful garden on Stanford land, across Junipero Serra Drive from the main Stanford campus. The house had been put up for them by an Australian who owed his very considerable wealth, from mining in southeast Asia, to information Sir George had acquired during the war. I thought it utterly like Sir George to give to someone else information for the grounding of what might have been his own fortune. He was a generous man, a modest man, an erudite man, an urbane and humorous man, the embodiment of everything that makes for a gentleman. The garden was Katharine's. She had the English genius for gardening and she had the hills of northern California for a background.

I think that between my arrival at Stanford and Sir George's death, I probably saw more of them than any other persons on the Stanford faculty or staff. I went to see them at least once a week, at first by means of the borrowed automobile that refused to move a wheelspan after being returned to its driveway, and afterwards on the bicycle that became my chief means of transportation.

Sometimes, when Katharine needed me, I would go up and serve as her bartender. I was an inept bartender, but I managed. The clientele tended strongly towards whiskey-and-water types, and when someone wanted something more complicated I would motion towards the bottles and suggest that he or she could do better than I. At one cocktail party it became apparent that I had partaken too freely of my own wares. Katharine suggested gently that I have a rest. I called the next day to apologize. "Oh, we loved you," said she.

They early insisted that I call them by their first names. This is not easy when one is confronted with a Knight Commander of the Most Distinguished Order of St. Michael and St. George (a Knight Grand Cross of the Order of the British Empire to boot) and his lady, but I presently forced myself to acquire the habit, and during most of my residence in Palo Alto they were Katharine and George. Sir George liked to say of his knighthoods that he was much prouder of being elected to membership in whatever the British organization of fly fishermen is called.

I can think of only two people from whom I heard unfriendly words about Sir George: Jess Bell, then chief editor at the Stanford University Press, and Helen Craig McCullough, a colleague on the Japanese faculty at Stanford, and later a professor at the University of California in Berkeley. Jess, a genial fellow, said that he had known two genuine savages during his years as an editor. One was Sir George. Apparently the editing of Sir George's history of Japan was nightmarish. He would not tell me the other, but said that it was a Stanford professor well known to me and thought by the world to be a perfect gentleman. One evening on a drive back to Palo Alto from Berkeley, Helen, in an uncharacteristically sharp mood, said that Sir George was no scholar. She had been his research assistant.

From Sir George, I had harsh words about three people: Helen, another professor at Stanford, and Sir Robert Craigie, the last British ambassador under whom he served in Tokyo. He said of Helen that she had erudition but no culture. I could not agree. She read voraciously and she read good things, and such people do not end up uncultured. There may have been something in her uncompromisingly Californian manner (she was a native of the somewhat backward far north of the state) that put him off, and then too she had been his research assistant. Like the relationship between lawyer and client, and between husband and wife, that between writer and assistant is a privileged one. Of the other professor, the remark was the sort of witticism one smiles at and neither agrees nor disagrees with. He said that the person thought literature something to write articles about.

When Sir George spoke of "the pipsqueak," we knew whom he meant. He never used a remotely similar epithet for anyone but Sir Robert. It seems clear from Katharine's memoir that the hostility was returned. Essentially it was incompatibility between knowledge and ignorance. Sir Robert had had no experience of the Far East when he was posted to Tokyo. Sir George probably knew more about Japan than any other living being, including several tens of millions of Japanese. Their differences were also specific, having to do with policy. Sir Robert thought that there was a moderate faction among the Japanese elite that could be used to keep Japan from going the way of Germany. Sir George thought that if such a faction existed, it was small and powerless. Sir George of course was right. It was not without reason that Sir Robert was thought by many to be a Neville Chamberlain among diplomats.

Sir Robert was not Sir George's only problem during his last posting in Tokyo. There was Japan itself, which had become a most unpleasant place. "Life here is absolutely intolerable," he wrote to Katharine, then in New York, in August 1940. And a few lines later: "The curs are yelping! I've never known anything like this atmosphere. There are no standards of behavior left, everything you do is right if you can get away with it. We have a crisis every day, sometimes two or three! And pinpricks are innumerable. I begin to think the best thing would be complete evacuation of all British from the Far East down to Singapore. I almost feel that people who have only bombs to fear are almost lucky!"

Despite these huge provocations, Sir George was utterly fair-minded in his views of Japan, more so, I had to admit, than I was, and I had had only the progressive intellies to exasperate me.

Sir George's low-keyed humor was rather wonderful. I loved the story of his shipwreck. He was on a Japanese ship making port in Korea. Safely inside the harbor mouth, the ship failed to turn in the direction of the dock at which it was to berth. It went on straight ahead towards a beach, and on and on, and presently ran up on the beach. "And that," said Sir George, "was my shipwreck."

Then there was the story of his conversation with Churchill. At some large gathering he found the great man beside him. He asked if he might venture to mention some problems he thought they were certain to face with regard to China. "Oh, China's all right, China's all right," said Churchill, pushing on to find more agreeable company.

In my diary for November 24, 1964, I tell of a visit to the Sansoms with my colleague, Robert Brower, the expert on early Japanese poetry. "She was bright and talkative, and he from time to time was almost puckish. In California you don't need a license to shoot quails in season, he said, but if you shoot them out of season they take it away. Bob thought the remark quite accidental, but somehow the twinkle in the eye made me think we had a brief reappearance, perhaps the last, of the old Sir George."

And it may indeed have been the last. They left shortly afterwards on the journey to Arizona from which he did not return.

Katharine early announced that I was to stay permanently in California. To make the prospect a pleasing one, she set about finding friends for me. She introduced me to rich and interesting people up and down the peninsula, and it is one of the wealthier parts of the United States. Only one of the friendships she sought to plant took root, with Ruth Lilienthal, who had a big and beautiful house in the hills above the San Francisco airport. The house was full of valuable modern art and the garden was especially beautiful in spring, when the primroses were in bloom. People who knew that her maiden name was Haas and who knew something about California also knew that she was rich, for the Haases control the hugely successful Levi Strauss enterprises.

Admiration approaches awe in my diary account of my first Lilienthal dinner party.

"Fortunately everyone wanted to talk about Greece, and so we did not have to talk about Japan. The women seemed superior to the men, and Mrs. L. towered over everyone, a truly splendid lady whose warmth seems a factor of her affluence. I had not realized the proportions of this last until I noted that I was sitting under a Braque, while across the way, glowing like stained glass, was a Rouault, and out in the hall, a Kokoschka. After knowing her, how can one ever again believe stories about the vulgarity of the moneyed American?"

I spent a number of weekends with her, I could not give the exact count, although they all have to be in my diary. She would always go down to get us a bedtime snack on Saturday night and I would go with her, and the small lady working among the pots and pans of the vast kitchen was a sight to remember. She had plenty of servants to call upon for the work, but she preferred to do it herself.

She was already a widow when I knew her. Her husband was named Philip and she had a nephew-in-law who was also named Philip and was for a number of years director of the University of California Press in Berkeley. Handsome, rich, successful, he would have seemed to have the best things in life; and he killed himself. I thought him rather like E. A.

Robinson's Richard Corey. "There is a blight upon the family," Ruth once said, referring not to the Haases but to the Lilienthals. I did not ask her to elaborate.

Here is a part of my diary entry for February 28, 1970, several years after I had departed California for Michigan: "A long telephone call from California in the evening. Ruth Lilienthal and Katharine Sansom, the latter back from Honolulu. They were about to set out in the liquid California twilight for Woodside, and were reminded of me. Why? Because they were going to the Village Pub. And why did the Pub remind them of me? Well, it was there that I was so shaken when Katharine poured her tomato juice into the lampshade."

Woodside is a very pretty and very rich town in the hills between the bay and the ocean. It is where Shirley Temple Black lives and where she ran for Congress in 1966. Like most Jews in the congressional district (bless them), Ruth had little use for Shirley. Before the 1966 election, she remarked: "I have to tell people that George Murphy is my senator and Ronald Reagan is my governor. If I have to tell them that Shirley Temple is my congresswoman, I'm going to move." Shirley lost, and Ruth was still living in San Mateo County, the district, when she died.

Sir George died in Tucson in the spring of 1965, a year before I myself left Palo Alto. There were no funeral or memorial services. I offered to go to Tucson and help when the news came, but Katharine said it would not be necessary, because her son was coming from England. The ashes were "laid" (the word Katharine uses in her memoir) in a valley which, she said, reminded her of her native Yorkshire. I do not doubt that she described her feelings about the place honestly, but it is hard to believe that anything even in the Brontë country has quite the harsh beauty of the Arizona desert. Before returning to England, she gave me the bow of a medieval Japanese warrior, given to Sir George to be used as a walking stick by Hasegawa Nyozekan, an eminent journalist and commentator who was a decade or so older than Sir George and outlived him by a few years. Hasegawa did not get on well with the prewar militarists but was much honored after the war. The famous bow sits, with an appearance of eager alertness, beside my door in Honolulu. I occasionally walk it.

Here is a part of my diary entry for March 26, 1965: "Up to Lady Sansom's with Brower in the evening. She wished us to go over the last of Sir George's books (as in that Chinese poem loved by Kafū, there were not many left) and take what we thought we might find useful. I felt utterly shameless as I took in autographed book after autographed book. . . . None, perhaps significantly, from Waley. Maybe when Lady S. is out of her daze—she seemed to be in even more of one than last time—and settled down I will return them to her." A few days later I report that she has left us for England.

I was then at work on a study of perhaps my favorite modern Japanese writer, Nagai Kafū. A translation of the Chinese poem is to be found on page 271 of the study, *Kafū the Scribbler.* I did write to her about the works when she had her place in London, but she replied that they were mine to do with as I wished. The most notable of them, such as a signed copy of the autobiography of Yoshida Shigeru, are now in the Museum of Modern Japanese Literature in Tokyo.

Then there are numbers of letters written by Sir George and to him. Among the latter is one which I hold next to priceless. Being from Sir Charles Eliot to Sir George about Sir Ernest Satow, it is in the great line of British scholar-diplomats. Sir Ernest (the family name is not Japanese, as it might well be, but Swedish) was the oldest of the three, Sir George the youngest. Both of the older men headed Japanese diplomatic missions in Tokyo, the former as minister, the latter as ambassador. The letter was sent from the Nara Hotel, and is dated December 21, 1929. The opening paragraphs are about Sir Ernest.

"I am flattered by the Asiatic Society's request to write an obituary of Satow, but do not see my way to comply, because I don't know enough about the subject and have not time to get it up. The first time I set foot in these regions as a tourist was in 1906 & it was about then that Satow retired from Peking. My ideas about the changes which he saw and the part which he played in them are very vague and also I am not competent to write about his literary career, to which the Society will naturally attach importance. I only know that Parlett once said to me that whatever subject be treated of, he made it dull. That would not make a good quotation in a memoir & it does not encourage me to study his work.

"Only once did I have a personal interview with him. It was in 1893 (I think) when I had come from Tangier & he was going there. He was sitting in a large room at a London hotel surrounded by doleful elderly women dressed in black. All that I can remember is that he looked like a polygamist who had lost all his harem in an epidemic and was exchanging condolences with his mothers in law."

I have heard more than one theory as to why Sir George, without question the man in the service best qualified for the post, did not become ambassador in Tokyo. It is said, for instance, that the fact that he had a clandestine Japanese family was held against him. This is hard to believe, since such staid and successful diplomats as Sir Ernest Satow also had such families. The fact that he and Katharine were slow in getting ceremonial blessing for their union has also been offered as a possibility. There may be something in it.

The best explanation may be that given by Frank Ashton-Gwaskin, a Foreign Office eminence who wrote fiction about Japan under the pen-name John Paris and who was a long-time friend of Sir George's. He blamed it all on bureaucratic bungling. Sir Robert Craigie may have been responsible in part and indirectly. An inability to work with him persuaded Sir George to resign from the service when still in his late fifties.

Sir George does not seem to be as well remembered as he should be. Shortly after his death I recorded in my diary: "The British Permanent Secretary for Foreign Affairs . . . told Don [Brown] that when someone suggested to the Foreign Office—the Japanese one this time—that there should be some sort of memorial service for Sir George, the reaction was a complete blank—no one knew who he was. Just another odd foreign name."

Don Brown was what they call a fund of knowledge. An American, he was a journalist in Tokyo before the war and a bureaucrat after the war. He was also an avid bibliophile. His collection of materials on Japan in European languages was bought by the city of Yokohama and reposes in the old British consulate.

The progressive intellectuals continued through my Stanford years to be pestilential. Here is evidence from the late Stanford years. "I went down to Clarence's for a beer, and read some Japanese newspapers. Got all annoyed at the intellies again, for their Thomistic methods, their way of moving backwards from their conclusions (that China is not warlike, for instance). But I suppose that intellies are much the same the world over." Though I do not remark upon the fact, this is akin to my misgivings about John King Fairbank at Harvard. He could find ways to excuse the Chinese, whatever they did.

Here is a little item from the summer of 1966, showing how things still were among the intellies when I had finished with Palo Alto and was moving to Ann Arbor. I had moved my possessions to Ann Arbor and would move myself a bit later, and was summering in Tokyo, as I always did. "Early in the afternoon I met [the eminent literary critic] Saeki Shōichi at the Imperial Hotel. After a couple of beers there in the Garden Bar, we went to Nihombashi for sushi. He is having a journalistic debate with some idiot who says that *Citizen Kane* is banned in the United States—too anti-establishment." The date of the last entry is July 5, which calls to mind Ambassador Reischauer, my teacher at Harvard in 1947. There had been no reception the day before, because he did away with Independence Day receptions. I could see that he had good reasons for doing so, and yet I was sorry. I loved going to the embassy on the Fourth. The smell of gardenias brings remembrances of them from long ago. The garden of the ambassador's residence was full of gardenias. They seem to have gone away, I do not know why. I suppose that some ambassador or ambassador's wife did not like them.

I think I was probably a steadier frequenter of the embassy during the Reischauer years than any others. My diary is dotted with references to embassy and ambassador. He was a Kennedy appointee and served through the Kennedy thousand days and most of the first two years of Johnson's full term. He was very kind, frequently inviting me and people like me to the embassy.

Yet a sour note runs through the entries. I liked him, but was by no means sure that I liked his performance as ambassador. It had been rather that way at Harvard. I liked him and he was kind to me, but I could not honestly share his views about Japan. He exaggerated the importance of what is known today as Taishō democracy, of the years after the First World War, and a result was that he excused, or so I thought, too many Japanese aberrations. A big example was their indifference to reciprocity in international matters. They wanted things of us that they were not prepared to give in return, such as (a matter once of more importance to me personally than it is now) the right to pursue a career in a state university. They were not, in a word, prepared to abide by the golden rule. A major inadequacy in the Reischauer approach was his indifference to economics, which were during his tenure emerging as the most important matter in Japanese-Americans relations.

Reischauer has been sanctified by the Japanese. His house in suburban Boston has been turned into a shrine to which busloads of Japanese pilgrims are taken. I do not suppose it can be set down as a rigid principle that it is not good for ambassadors to be hugely popular in the countries to which they are accredited. Yet I thought and think that it was not good in the Reischauer instance. I thought at Harvard that he was too permissive towards the Japanese, and I thought it all the way through the Reischauer years at the embassy.

"Johnson is said—this Owen did not overhear—to have remarked to Miki somewhere along the way that the Japanese should be paying half of Reischauer's salary." Owen Zurhellen, my good friend from the war years, was then in the political section of the embassy. He was too honest to pretend to have heard something he did not hear, but the anecdote rings true. Johnson is of course L.B.J., and it was the sort of thing (he had a tart sense of humor) he would have said. Miki Takeo, later prime minister, was at the time one of the two or three most important members of the cabinet, the Minister of International Trade and Industry. It is a little difficult here to know exactly what I mean by "important." In a sense, not even the prime minister is of much importance. It has been something like traditional for politicians to do little by way of curtailing the authority of bureaucrats.

Here is another pithy bit of information received from Owen about happenings far above me. "To the Okura to meet Wendell Woodbury. . . . We drank in his room until Owen, fresh from interpreting for Rusk, joined us. . . . The best little anecdote had to do with Fujiyama and Rusk. The former came forth with the usual burblings about the Asian mind and how Americans do not understand it. 'Well, after all, Asian problems are caused by Asians,' said the latter."

Wendell Woodbury was another good friend high up in the Foreign Service. He was an Iowa boy and an economist who made his way into the Foreign Service via Harvard. In addition to erudition and intelligence he seemed to me to have in ample measure Middle American common sense. Fujiyama Aiichirō was the foreign minister. He was a very rich man and he wanted desperately to be prime minister. He never made it, thereby giving evidence that not even in Japanese politics is money everything.

A diary entry from fairly early in the Reischauer years says most of what I would wish to say about the Reischauer embassy. "Wendell is extremely bitter about his position in the embassy—says he is tired of being a second-class citizen, and wants to get out and never come back. The difficulty seems to be twofold: that there is an 'in-group' of language officers, and that they are not interested in economic affairs, which W. thinks, probably rightly, the most important affairs we have with Japan these days."

I am a little suspicious of the entry, which seems to put Owen Zurhellen in the enemy camp, when we both had the highest regard for him. I suspect I may be putting words into Woodbury's mouth, because they make explicit an uneasiness that had been growing within me, and for which, perhaps unwittingly, I may have been looking for expert support. They grew from earlier days, from my suspicions during the Harvard year of Reischauer's sanguine view of Japan. We were lurching towards a trade deficit with Japan, and late in the Reischauer years it came, and it has never gone away.

I was sure that it would be a very long time in going away, if ever it did. I think that my fundamental ignorance of economics may have had much to do with the conviction, for many an economist was saying that a shift in the exchange rate would send the deficit on its way. And there was another thing: an awareness of the way the Japanese had of undertaking to do something and then subtly shifting the nature of the something even as they were in process of fulfilling the undertaking. I would be inclined to call it not dishonesty but an instinct for survival more highly developed than that of most of us.

Essentially it was instinct on my own part, or intuition, or something of the sort, that made my premonitions so urgent as to require action. When, in the seventies, the dollar was devalued against the yen, and presently floated, I converted most of my dollar resources to yen. People sometimes ask how I manage to spend so much time in Japan with the hideously high prices and the hideously low dollar. The answer is that once the dollar started slipping against the yen, I was sure it would not easily stop. Though pocket money comes in from this and that source from time to time, I still live on the money I converted then. Bad home economics, no doubt, for it means eating into a bottom that will presently disappear, but it has certainly made life in Tokyo easier. And there is always the possibility that I will disappear first. The point to be made here, however, or repeated, is that I was in deep agreement with Woodbury. A very black cloud, the American deficit in foreign trade, was coming over the horizon, and Reischauer seemed unaware of it.

"In the *New York Times,* a story of how Eddie and Haru are having all sorts of speaking engagements cancelled because of their involvement in the American imperialistic adventures in Vietnam. One does not wish to gloat over their discomfiture—but is it not rather as one had said? It is quite possible to have a dialogue with the Japanese Left when there is not much of anything to talk about; but just let something of substance come up and whammo, there it is, interrupted discourse all over again."

This diary excerpt is from fairly late in the Reischauer years and in my Stanford years as well. The matter of the dialogue with the Left is a reference to a famous article that seems to have a good deal to do with Reischauer's becoming ambassador. It appeared in *Foreign Affairs,* averring that communication had been interrupted between responsible Americans and the Japanese Left, and caught the attention of the Kennedys. Reischauer believed the aim of resuming communication was desirable and realistic, insofar as it concerns such matters as relations with the peaceful socialist world. I thought that it was not.

Here is an entry from the summer of 1967, after my departure from Palo Alto and removal to Ann Arbor, and perhaps a year and a half after the end of the Reischauer tenure in the Tokyo embassy. "Owen very amusing on the subject of the Yoshida-Reischauer interview. Much of what Yoshida said had to be cut, for he called everyone a dunce—used the word *baka* fourteen times. R. would say something nice about the Japanese. 'It is very kind of you to say so,' Yoshida would reply, 'but God help us if they believe you.' Among the nations of the world, it is [Yoshida's] view, the British rank first in stupidity, and the Japanese second. Owen thinks that Johnson will be nothing like the public figure Reischauer has been, but that he will be a success among the press, largely because of his ability to speak with authority of China."

(Johnson is U. Alexis Johnson, Reischauer's successor as ambassador. A Japanese-language officer, he was, at the end of his career, the senior officer in the American Foreign Service. Yoshida Shigeru was before the war the Japanese ambassador in London, and several times after the war served as prime minister. I would be surprised if Yoshida intended to include Sir George Sansom in his generalization about the English. They were not far from the same age, Yoshida being five years Sansom's senior, and were good friends. If he was thinking of British appeasers such as Craigie, Sir George would have agreed with him.)

The entry just quoted also contains an amusing and interesting little episode of a sort I can seldom resist passing on: "Along towards midnight . . . as I stood watching the lotus pads, a pair of policemen came up and demanded that I show my passport. I had none to show. So they took me to the station, where I was examined, physically and verbally. . . . It went on for perhaps a half hour, and the decision was a benevolent one: if they could take me home and see my passport, that would be that. So I had a free ride in a police car. It was as leisurely a ride as I have ever had in Tokyo, far from the rush of a taxi driver. I kept thinking we were holding up traffic, and looking for a police car."

The lotuses were doubtless at Shinobazu Pond in Ueno. I often left rapid transit there and took a cab or bus the rest of the way home. The pond was and is the most famous place in the city for admiring the lotuses of high summer.

I liked Reischauer, and he was very kind.

Here is an instance, of more importance to me than to him, in which we agreed. It was one of those nine-day media wonders. The date is September 14, 1964. "Then to Chūō Kōron to take my leave of various people and the embassy to do the same. . . . I was surprised to learn that the ambassador agrees with me in my disappointment with the Olympic committee." The Tokyo Olympics began not quite a month later. A month or so earlier I learned that a young man born in Hiroshima on the day of the bombing had been chosen to run the Olympic torch into the stadium. I mentioned to an important journalist, Hasegawa Saiji, president of the Jiji Press, that I thought the choice in poor taste. I still do. There can be few people besides me who still remember.

Hasegawa informed other journalists, and I was interviewed widely and appeared widely in the media. One newspaper said that I was hysterical, and pointed out that the United States was not the only country in the Olympics. It is a thing we forgetful Americans are constantly being reminded of, that we are not the only country in this thing and that thing. The most sizeable treatment was in *Weekly Shinchō*, brought out by the big publishing house whose name is the second word. It was fair and even friendly. It made me suspect that the editors were inclined to agree with me. I may be accused, with justice, of making a mountain of a molehill, but may say in my defense that I had no notion so much would be made of my remarks to Hasegawa, and that the equivalent of the Olympic runner would have been a person born in Honolulu on the day of the Pearl Harbor bombing (he would by then have been a little old for such capers) and designated to bring the flame into the Los Angeles or Atlanta Olympic Stadium.

One more diary entry, and Reischauer can be left to eternity, busloads of tourists, etc. It is from some years after he ceased to be ambassador. He was still very active in the media. "At noon, at the bag lunch at Lane, we were shown Ed Reischauer's television drama. . . . Certainly it had some good moments . . . but it kept striking false notes. . . . The treatment of the student problem and the siege of Yasuda Castle approached the dishonest. Each side left the other side with room for maintaining its dignity, says he. Faugh, say I. The police and the students themselves may be left with some amount of dignity, but not the university."

Lane Hall is on the campus of the University of Michigan, to which I moved from Stanford in 1966. Yasuda Castle is a popular designation for the main administration building of Tokyo University, occupied by radical students who were driven out by the police in 1969.

The reduction of Yasuda Castle, early in 1969, may be seen to mark the beginning of the end for the student uprising. There had been an earlier beginning, however, in December, 1968, when Sophia University broke the taboo against summoning the police. It had until then been the policy of the police not to enter the grounds of a university until summoned, and that of the universities not to summon.

The origins of the American student uprising were in the Vietnam War. Those of the Japanese were in the treaty disturbances of 1960, which were the remote cause of my return to the United States in 1962. When that tumultuous summer was over, the communists for the most part returned to business, and the non-communist Left, frequently calling itself Maoist, broke into factions that started fighting one another and, when an opportunity was at hand, taking over universities and flailing indiscriminately with staves and pipes. It has probably been the most violent student movement in the world.

Here is a part of my diary entry for Christmas Eve, 1968. The aftermath of 1960 lasted through the decade and indeed is with us yet. Members of this and that Maoist faction still get clubbed to death.

"I wrote a few letters . . . and in midafternoon went down to [Sophia] again, to seek again to have a look at the damage. This time Father Roggendorf and I were allowed to make a leisurely inspection.

"What we saw can only be described as disgusting, and makes the students of the movement seem subhuman. Litter everywhere, bottles and dirty dishes and dirty bedding and magazines and toilet paper, and the stench of urine mixed with the far pleasanter smell of tear gas. And here and there the remains of fires, where they burned furniture to keep themselves warm. Subhuman—but there is the other side. They stayed on through it all, the cold and the darkness, and the fear too, for factional fighting seems to have gone all the while. . . . Warned, apparently, by the good gentlemen of our free press, the leaders had all fled before the police arrived and only underlings were still in occupancy.

"They apparently spent much of their time scribbling on walls. Why, unless they expected to be driven out and wished to make plain their hatred? Hatred, particularly of foreign priests. The xenophobia is very ugly. . . .

"I presently began to feel ill, both because of the sordidness of it all and because of the hopelessness implicit in it. . . .

"I did not come away with a very grand impression of the sort of English that Sophia teaches its students. In all the invective against the priests I did not once see the word 'priest' spelled correctly.

"Japanese Red Guards do not seem to share the puritanism of their Chinese fellows. Pornography liberally sprinkled through the graffiti, and the cheapest sort of weekly magazines everywhere."

Early in April I report that the university has reopened. "The ordinary students, at the opening ceremony, were ready for the helmeted forces, and subdued them by the simple device of stripping off their helmets. A perfectly brilliant device, say I."

I liked Palo Alto far better in 1966 than I had liked it in 1962. I liked Amherst Street and my friends up and down it, and I liked its pussycats. The family next door to the Kilmartins had a cat named Joshuena. It had been Joshua before its gender became clear. Farther up the hill, for Amherst Street lies along a slope, was a cat named Entropy. Entropy was perfection, a black beauty.

The departure of the Sansoms had made a difference, but I had grown wise enough not to expect constant entertainment in Palo Alto, as I expected it in Tokyo. It always took a while to get used to Palo Alto after a summer in Tokyo, but I no longer had high expectations with regard to fun and frolic. I knew that I would soon fall back into Palo Alto rhythms.

I did not know, at the beginning of that academic year, that I would be leaving Stanford at the end of it. March 8, 1965, was the day on which Sir George Sansom died. I remember it for another event, which was to change my future. On that day my colleague Bob Brower received an offer (a "feeler," as academic jargon has it) from the University of Michigan in Ann Arbor. His initial impulse was to decline. He knew Ann Arbor well, having been at the Army Japanese Language School there and having, after the war, done his graduate work there. He had no wish to go back. Even less eager was his elderly companion, Laura Gray. Though a native of Pennsylvania, she had spent most of her life in suburban Detroit, which may be held to include Ann Arbor. It was in Ann Arbor that she and Bob met.

If he had merely said no to the people in Ann Arbor, that would have been that. I myself had no great desire to go to the Midwest, though I would probably have accepted almost any offer on the Atlantic coast. If I ever knew why he did not merely say no, I have now forgotten. What he did do was ask whether I would consider going to Ann Arbor with him. I too could merely have said no, but what I did say was that I would not mind going and having a look at the place.

Brower reported my response to Ann Arbor, whence came the reply that I too would be welcome if I chose to go. When, almost a year and a half later, we found ourselves on the Ann Arbor faculty, the convention was to refer to the two of us as "the package deal," in imitation of the dean of the liberal arts college, a rough-hewn fellow whose origins were in the labor movement. I recorded in my diary at some point during the Michigan years that he sat behind me at a musical performance and that his mode of expressing himself made me think of a Jersey City barkeep. A colleague on the Chinese side of the department once asked us, at one of the receptions which marked our debut in Ann Arbor, whether it did not weary us to be constantly introduced as Tweedledum and Tweedledee.

We paid our visit to Ann Arbor early in 1966, on our way to an academic conference in Puerto Rico. I say in my diary entries for mid-January: "Ann Arbor, to one used to the San Francisco Peninsula, has a most traditional look, large frame houses, somewhat like Brattle Street in Cambridge [the Massachusetts one]. It is a city of elms, more beautiful bare, perhaps, than leafed—like fountains against the sky. But, alas, we will not have them with us much longer. Already the blight is upon them, and American know-how does not know how to stop it.

"Another slightly tempting feature to be noted: the possibility, absent at Stanford, of taking a little stroll downtown.

"Well, already I waver, if slightly. But what a nuisance to move—and Palo Alto from a distance does have its points. One would not leave it without a sigh. . . .

"The burning of one's dry, chilled, and then centrally heated skin feels exactly like Colorado."

Of Detroit I say: "[It] is not as ugly as I would have expected, or as dirty—and on the other hand it has no life. There was scarcely anyone on the downtown streets, and you are in and out of downtown in what seems no more than half a mile. . . . Detroit does not come to seem like the sort of city one could learn to love. . . . I have not learned to love San Francisco, and how then can it be in the case of Detroit?"

Back in Palo Alto after Puerto Rico, we informed the chairman of the department, Patrick Hanan, a New Zealander and a student of Chinese literature, of the joint offer from Michigan. "It brought out a hitherto unseen side of his character, a cold, blue steeliness. I told him I would like to talk to him over the weekend. 'There is nothing to talk about,' he snapped."

On February 4 I record that my mind is made up: I will stay at Stanford. Then on February 7 things changed utterly. Both of us, Brower and I, received notes from Hanan which seemed to us insulting. We told him all the same of our decision to stay at Stanford. Nastiness rose to new heights. I went home with a sick headache and had a couple of stout drinks of bourbon. In midafternoon Brower appeared. He said that he had been fired. "So where did that leave me? I had not been fired, I suppose, but after the incidents of the day I could scarcely sit around awaiting a similar summons. We took the precaution of calling Ann Arbor to learn whether we were still wanted. We got Ward [Robert Ward, a political scientist], who told us that we were. Then I called Hanan and made my speech. . . .

"I really do not know what happened. Was I fired? If so, why? The only sane answer I can think of is that Pat is willing to let Japanese slide, and will use the money to build up Chinese. . . . Whether I am the victim or the villain of the piece I will probably never know. . . . Marian Hays's first remark, when told the news, was: 'Well, the two of you certainly do seem to be married, don't you.'"

Marian is a classmate of my sister's whom I saw frequently during the Stanford years, and still see when I pass through California. She lives a bit farther south on the Peninsula. I thought and think the remark a most canny one. I solemnly certify that nothing of a sexual nature ever passed between Brower and me, and I do not think that Marian meant to suggest anything of the sort. Yet at the beginning of the upheaval was his reluctance to go to Ann Arbor alone, and my dithering answer to his suggestion that I join him.

Al Kilmartin's reaction, most appropriate for a military person, was: "You got caught in crossfire."

I now think, though without great confidence, that something of the sort did happen. The quarrel was between Brower and Hanan, and I was incidental. Donald Shively, Hanan's predecessor as head of the department, and a very witty fellow, said: "You have to give Pat credit for one thing: he gets rid of the dead wood." There was very persuasive evidence later that he did not want to get rid of me but did want to get rid of Brower. After I was settled in Michigan, I was asked to go back to Stanford. I did not consider the possibility. I liked Ann Arbor better than Palo Alto, and, even as Tweedledee, I was well treated there. The important point is that I doubt very much that Brower had such an offer. Had he had one, Laura Gray would have raised a great stir, for she longed intensely to go back.

Hanan was not friendly during the crucial days at Stanford (and neither was anyone else on the faculty), but I am inclined to think that Brower was not entirely truthful. It is not easy to "fire" a tenured professor from an American university, and nothing as fluffy as an offer from another university will suffice. Maybe the real culprit was those two strong shots of bourbon. I was not thinking well.

I may seem to make too much of my departure from Stanford; but to be at the center of forces which one cannot identify is a strange and disturbing experience.

The spring and summer were restless. I went out to Honolulu for the spring vacation. Honolulu had become for me in California what Seoul was for me in Tokyo, an alternative to the principal place when the latter became excessively irksome. Late in June I departed Palo Alto. Mark Mancall, a professor of Chinese history, had invited me to drive with him to Mexico City via Los Angeles and El Paso. I drove half the distance, I am proud to say, and had no brush with any creature, biped or quadruped. I think I have not had such an intense and extended spell of driving since. Several of the Mexican colonial towns along the way quite delighted me. In one of them, alas, my dear friend Maggy Burrows of the bayside weekends was to drink herself to death. I think the summer of 1966 was the only one during which I did not have to go to the ward office in Tokyo and get myself an alien-registration certificate. I was not there long enough, since the Stanford academic year ended late and the Michigan one began early.

After an elaborate dinner given by Kodansha "I found myself with Nobuki [then the director of Kodansha International] at the Rat Mort, said to be the most popular bar in Tokyo—the most fashionable, at any rate. Probably it is among the most expensive too. . . . Beside me was a pretty young thing introduced as the model for Kawabata's 'One Arm.' I find it hard to see how anyone could be the model for such a work, but that is the fact as I had it from the good Nobuki."

"One Arm" is a story which I have translated. It is fantasy (obviously) about a man who passes a night with an arm lent him by a young woman. Since the woman never appears, it is difficult to see how she could have had a model.

"The evening with Kawabata. He thinks that only Natsume Sōseki among Meiji novelists has any chance of surviving this century; that the idea of writing 'One Arm' came to him one year upon seeing girls' arms exposed for the first time in the spring; that he deleted the age of the hero because it seemed incongruous, the one concrete detail in the story. And many other things I am sure. One ought to come provided with a tape recorder.

"Leaving him at Tokyo Station, I proceeded to Ueno for a nightcap, at the New Orleans, where I found myself engaged in the silliest argument there could be. One of the bartenders asserted that Japanese have firmer erections than Americans. I was most heated in defending the virility of my kind. I think it was the soupy music and not wounded patriotism that really got me. I must go back and apologize.

"The traffic in front of the palace was a real tangle. . . . And will you guess the reason? There has today been, said the driver, a crackdown on traffic violations. Now I call that one real slick way to solve the traffic problem."

Late in August, after stops in California and Colorado, I arrived in the quiet of Ann Arbor.

SEVEN

LIFE ON THE MIDDLE BORDER

IN THE AMERICAN MIND, the expressions "Midwest" and "Middle West" are generally pejorative. They signify the ultimate in the provincial. They may not be identical with "Bible Belt," but they are not far from it.

I prefer "Middle Border," which conveys a better sense of history. It is not much used now; a sense of the country's history is weakening all over the country.

The Middle Border was the original western border of the newly independent republic. It lay generally along the Mississippi River and separated the lands ceded by King George from the French lands farther west. The new republic did not border on Spanish lands in the West until it acquired the French lands. I like to think myself in the dwindling minority that still knows what it means. The chief difficulty is that Michigan, in addition to being in the St. Lawrence basin, is not near the Mississippi. From Ann Arbor you have to cross most of Michigan, all of Wisconsin, and at least one of the lakes to get to it. Almost immediately I liked it better than California. My part of Colorado did not join the United States until the annexation of Texas. So it lay a good distance past the Middle Border, not far from half the distance to the Golden West. Yet I felt at home along my vaguely defined Middle Border as I had not in California.

A few entries from my diary for September 1966 may help convey a sense of how it was.

"Perhaps the chief glimpse of pleasure during the day . . . came from the recollection of the waitress we had at the Flaming Pit last, the dumbest little blonde with the sweetest eyes, the flattest midwestern accent, enormously pleased, it would seem, with her ignorance of every item on the menu. Americans are *not* all alike. You would find no such specimens, I think, among precocious, self-assured California young ladyhood. That's why people wish again they was in Michigan."

"The lady-keeper of my safety-deposit box, where, in the morning, I deposited my deposit certificates, has a most fetching name, Milda Whipple. Done what to a whipple? The kind of name that comes to me in my dreams."

"And what will I dream of tonight? Last night I was evicted from my house in Tokyo by a faint mist of rain that came right through the ceiling. Why should I be homeless in my sleep when I feel so much more at home here . . . than in California? Maybe it is the cumulative homelessness, building up since I left Tokyo. The word 'home' has sounded so strange, so remote from reality, since 1962."

"The way to Birmingham, through green, rolling, wooded land much as last Saturday, but even heavier with the autumn. The colors have deepened considerably in this one week. The pumpkins lie in the fields, awaiting Halloween and Thanksgiving. This is a land of nostalgia, even for one who grew up in a very different sort of land—as California, more similar to Colorado on the surface, is not. For this is the land of the mythical American, of blueberries and bare feet and pumpkin pies and sumacs."

The landscapes are certainly very different. Michigan is much lusher and greener. There are no pumpkins or sumacs in Colorado, leastways none in my part of it. I could take walks through the countryside around Ann Arbor as I could not in and near Palo Alto. I loved the azure dots of chicory. I do not think I ever saw chicory in Colorado. He who had a try at climbing a golden California hill was immediately turned into a porcupine by all the burrs and barbs from the golden grasses. One afternoon Joshuena and I went for an ill-advised walk in the then undeveloped hills above Amherst Street. I spent most of the evening getting her back into a condition in which I thought she could go home with some dignity.

It was not the landscape of Michigan that made me feel at home there. So it had to be the culture. Michigan was attached firmly to the culture of the Eastern Seaboard, whence it came. The first northern-European settlers in California went by wagon or ship past vast empty expanses to do their settling, and after they had done it they seemed to have trouble reestablishing contact with their place of origin. The first northern settlers in Colorado (as distinguished from wandering French trappers) came a few years later than those in California, pushed the frontier ahead of them, and did not cross empty spaces.

People ask which of my American universities—Stanford, Michigan, or Columbia—I liked best. The frequency of the question makes me think it must be of some interest. They seem always to expect my choice to be either the Harvard of the West, the first of three, or Columbia. They evince surprise when I reply with my university from the Middle Border. They look sternly at me, as if I had just made a cheap attempt at attracting attention.

But it is an honest answer. I was happier at Michigan than at either of the other two. I had such good students. I had some good ones at the other universities too, but it will already be apparent that I had some poor ones. At Michigan, at least among the graduate students, I had no really poor ones. I more than once gave every student in a graduate seminar an A. The registrar's office never objected. It seemed civilized enough to grant that there could be good reasons for such grades.

I have said that I was well treated at Michigan, but of course this has to do only with matters in which I was the passive party, the recipient. We of the faculty got on well at Michigan as at neither of the other two. I do not doubt that there were factions, but I never found myself clearly and actively involved in factional feuding. One of the annual observances was a quarrel with the China specialists over the division of government money. They argued, rightly, that China was a larger and more varied country with a longer and richer history. We replied, also rightly, that the Japan side had the better students. The hassle always ended in a most civilized manner, by dividing the money evenly between the two. Probably all of us knew from the outset that this would happen, but it was rather fun to shout at one another for a while.

Charles Hucker, the chairman of the Asian Language and Literature Department, which offered only Chinese and Japanese (Columbia was the only one of my three universities that offered all three of the major East Asian languages), was a sinologist, and an amusing fellow. Sometimes his humor was unintentional. "Yesterday afternoon, just as the office was about to close, Charles Hucker put a cheerful head in at the door. 'What are you doing over the weekend?' he asked. 'Not a thing,' said I, expectantly. 'Well, have a good time,' said he, looking a bit confused." It happened to be Thanksgiving weekend.

He reached his finest height at a faculty meeting one afternoon. His subject was a graduate student, a Chinese battle-axe who was threatening to take us to court. He urged that we maintain a united front. "We don't want any chinks in our armor," he said, and looked very surprised when we all laughed.

Midway through my Michigan years came my rudest imposition upon his kindness. I had an offer from another university. He did not want me to go. He had been instrumental in arranging the "package deal" that brought Bob Brower and me to Ann Arbor, and was proud of the achievement, which he wished to be as permanent as anything is in this world. I said that I would stay at Michigan if I would be allowed to teach only one semester. He said that he could not answer without consulting the administration, but he would see what he could do.

He did well. So from the academic year 1971 and 1972 I taught only fall semesters. I was very grateful to be in Tokyo in the spring of 1972, for it was then that two people very dear to me died, Hirabayashi Taiko and Kawabata Yasunari.

I had successfully engaged in academic blackmail. The conditions have to be right for this sort of thing to succeed. The chief condition is that the person making demands upon his old university must be prepared to leave. I was. At about the same time a Japanese friend on the university staff made a similar attempt at blackmail when he was not really prepared to leave. He found presently that the University was not prepared to accept his demands, and he *had* to leave. Much embarrassed, he told everyone he was going to Hawaii (it was also Hawaii that had invited me) because he did not want his children to suffer from race prejudice. This was nonsense. There was not the slightest chance that the children would be victims of prejudice in Ann Arbor. The incident is worth mentioning because those who attempt academic blackmail should know all about the game they have chosen to play, and because racism is blamed for many things that are not its fault.

My main reason for being happy to stay in Ann Arbor was that I felt at home there. Home was the huge central basin of North America. The Great Lakes are a part of it, and so, though many miles away, are the headwaters of the Platte.

I quickly learned that Ann Arbor was not a place people passed through. San Francisco had been, and New York was to be. People passed through both of them on their way to and from all manner of places, and stopped for a few nights, and were stimulating. Only people who had business at the university came to Ann Arbor. So Ann Arbor had about it somewhat the look and feel of a backwater. This does not sound like much to recommend it, but in a way it was. I liked having visitors such as Kawabata Yasunari and Muramatsu Takeshi in San Francisco; and, on the other hand, in Ann Arbor there were fewer distractions from what one might consider one's important work.

Then there were the visiting professors, mostly from Japan. They were uniformly interesting and amusing. With one of them, Tanaka Kunio, I shared a birthday. We had birthday parties together.

"He talked of many things, but in sum they came down to a single thing, sex. He told us of his experience as a writer of advice to the lovelorn for the Kansai *Yomiuri.* This lady used to hate doing it with her husband, and now just loves it, only he has come to dislike doing it with her. What is your solution, dear Dr. Tanaka? Kill him and find someone else, he says he said, though I doubt if he really did. Most of the letters, he says further, are pranks. And, with most graphic gestures, he told us of the love life of the praying mantis, and he told us of a disappointment in Chicago: he went into a place that advertised itself as having no cover and no minimum, expecting it to be topless *and* bottomless."

Another Michigan kindness was letting me bring my accumulation of Stanford sabbatical time with me. The custom is to have a year without academic duties after having served six years with them. Because I had brought four years with me I became eligible for a sabbatical my third year at Michigan, the academic year of 1968 and 1969.

I was rather surprised at the readiness with which Michigan accepted this arrangement, and had no way of knowing when it was made what a fortunate arrangement it was. It had me in Tokyo in the autumn of 1968, and present for the great literary event of the season. I sometimes have pangs of guilt about the way I behaved when next a sabbatical year came round. I was an ingrate. The regulation was that after a sabbatical year a professor had to spend a year on duty before moving on. Towards the end of my next sabbatical, news came of the sudden death of Ivan Morris, the eminent translator of Japanese and writer on Japan. I was invited to teach one of his classes. I was not pleased. To accept would have meant commuting to New York, and the only way to do so would have been by air, and I have a strong aversion to air travel. But that was not all. I thought it very presumptuous of Columbia. I said no.

I was fairly certain, however, that I would be invited to succeed Morris, in a full and regular capacity. When this happened I hurried off, without having worked my way through the requisite year at Michigan. There were complex reckonings, to be sure, having to do with the fact that I had taught only one semester. Yet it was fairly clear that I was violating Michigan regulations. If anyone there noticed, no one said so. The Middle Border is in many ways a very civil place.

I was not actually in Japan when the great event occurred. I was having one of my times in Korea.

"October 18 [1968]. Mr. Kawabata won the Nobel Prize! Kwak and I got back to Kwangju [a city in southwestern Korea to become famous for bloody anti-government riots], to the inn of night before last, to find there a message that I was to call Tokyo. I was of course much alarmed. Had my house burned down? Had my father died? And how could they in Tokyo have known at what obscure inn in Kwangju I was staying? But a call to the American Cultural Center revealed the truth. Resourceful Japanese journalism had learned my whereabouts and wished to have my comments on the happy news. Moments later a *Mainichi* reporter and a *Chosun Ilbo* reporter were at the inn to interview me. They had flown down from Seoul expressly for that purpose. Evidently Japan is in a great stir. This is the news of the year; I am, for the Japanese journalist, the most newsworthy object in Korea at the moment. . . . I think what a pity that I had to choose this moment to be away from Japan—and again I think it is better this way. No point in getting drunk on reflected glory."

Even before this smashing climax the day had been a lovely one. The autumn weather was perfect, and Kwak, an old friend from the American embassy in Seoul, and I had climbed the highest mountain in South Korea. It had been a sensuously lovely day, and it had had in it a delicious sense of danger. We went half the distance up the mountain by jeep. The road was extravagantly bad. More than once the jeep had to back up in order to round a corner, and we would not have survived the fall either to the front or to the rear. There are almost no Siberian tigers left in the Korean wild, but one was said to roam the mountain. Alas, we did not sight it. "Kurye to Kwangju to Seoul—each step takes you from nothing to something. Kwak calls Korea 'the Republic of Seoul.'"

I spent several more days in Korea. They were "littered with newspaper reporters." So it was too in Tokyo upon my return, and so it had been, apparently, since the announcement of the award. A man came around from a big weekly magazine at midnight to interview me. "The very first notice of the event, said the Saitōs, was a call from Mr. Kawabata himself, wishing to offer me his thanks. There came a complete deluge of telephone calls from the press. It may have been a bit of a trial for the Saitōs, though I think they in some ways enjoyed it. Certainly the children did. I seem to be almost as important in their eyes as Nagashima."

After my departure for Stanford I always had a Japanese family in my house. When I was in Tokyo we managed all of us to live in the little place, cheek by jowl. When I was away, the family of the moment watched the place for me. The Saitōs were the last in a rapid turnover of occupants. It was the rapidity of the turnover that was shortly to persuade me to give the place up. I would have thought that I offered such attractive conditions, no rent and scarcely any duties, that almost any family in Tokyo, notoriously high in its rents and poor in its accommodations, would have leaped at them; but of course every family wanted a place of its own.

Nagashima was the great idol of Japanese baseball. Now, thirty years later, he still is. All these decades he has been among the banes of my existence. I am suspicious of everyone and everything that everyone else likes.

Late in October I saw Kawabata for the first time after the great event. Mrs. Kawabata was with him, and several of the pretty young women who always orbited around him. "We had dinner at one of the many restaurants in the Okura Hotel, then went to a go-go place in Akasaka name of Little Caesar or something of the sort, where for a time we had our eyes and ears knocked out. Mr. Kawabata seemed quite captivated. Such an object of congratulation as he was—he spent all his time shaking hands and giving autographs. . . . I think it rather nice of the Japanese to make an obscure—I mean difficult, not inconspicuous—novelist into such a hero.

"For me the event of the evening was this: Mr. Kawabata invited me to go to Stockholm with him. If he does not change his mind I will certainly go—can't remember when I last met a king. Plenty of queens, but no king." Kawabata wrote a charming article about the evening. "So now I will be in the collected works of Kawabata Yasunari. My little finger clings precariously to immortality."

The rest of the Tokyo season, down to our departure for Stockholm early in December, was all felicitation. Kawabata, and other good and influential friends such as Tateno Nobuyuki, saw to it that I was near the center of things. Kawabata told the press that half the prize should go to me. This was more than kind of him, but it is probably true that without my translations he would not have been a candidate for the prize. I had at that point translated two of his masterpieces, both of them in Strauss's Program. There were translations into other European languages, most though not all of them retranslations from English, but mine were the first. I suppose those weeks in Scandinavia brought my nearest approach to the life of the celebrity and jet-setter.

Excerpts from two days late in November should give some suggestion of how it was.

"Thence to the Swedish Embassy, to be at the reception for Kawabata. There was a fearful traffic jam all the way from the Mantetsu Building [South Manchurian Railways Building, then an annex to the American Embassy]. We asked a policeman why, and he said he had no idea, it had just all of a sudden happened. Well, it turned out that everyone was going to the Swedish Embassy. That is the sort of reception it was. Just everyone was there, the prime minister and Prince and Princess Takamatsu and U. Alexis [Johnson, Reischauer's successor as ambassador] and all the rest of us. The Swedish ambassador made a nice speech to which Mr. Kawabata replied thanks very much, and I had a chat with the prime minister, who said that my Japanese was better than his, and I had my picture taken with Prince Takamatsu and U. Alexis. And I learned . . . Mr. Kawabata has not yet begun his acceptance speech. I suppose I will have to take my typewriter to Europe."

"Down to the Press Club in late afternoon, to be interviewed by a very pleasant Swede, who represents what he says is the largest morning newspaper in Scandinavia. The Swedish ambassador seems to have told him in advance that Mr. Kawabata was likely to win, though the smart money in Stockholm was on Mishima to the end—which fact would explain why the *Mainichi* had him closeted. Or would it, really—he is too clever to allow himself to be closeted under such circumstances. No one in Sweden, I learned, has much respect for the Royal Academy. 'They have made too many mistakes.'

"The Kawabata thing [a reception organized by the Japan PEN] at the New Otani was gigantic and sumptuous, but for me most of it was torture. I had to make a speech in Japanese, after such speakers as the prime minister and the Swedish ambassador and Niwa Fumio [a famous novelist]. I guess I did all right. People snickered at the right places, and I hope I made the right number of mistakes. . . . Mr. Kawabata, in response to all this, said almost nothing. That is the sort of thing only he can do gracefully."

The prime minister was Satō Eisaku, who, to the virtually unanimous derision of his countrymen, received the Nobel Peace Prize in 1974. He is remembered more for corruption than for peacemaking, although peace with Korea and the return of Okinawa were both accomplished during his administration.

Through it all ran apprehension, having to do with what I here call "the acceptance speech," although "commemorative lecture" would come closer to indicating its nature. It is the lecture Nobel laureates in literature deliver before the Swedish Academy and (in Kawabata's case) a number of elderly ladies. The arrangement was that I would translate it and deliver it in English, and that Kawabata would read in Japanese the quotations from old Japanese literature.

"I begin to feel panicky again—tomorrow comes the departure for Stockholm. Part of the Nobel speech was delivered in the morning, and it is . . . full of recondite titles and quotations and names. And, alas, I do not think it very good, for it is highly impressionistic, and also highly fragmented. . . .

"Well, it will have to wait until I get to Copenhagen. I hope the Japanese embassy in Copenhagen has a spare typewriter and a good reference librarian.

"I wish that panic had the effect of making me go madly to work. It has the effect of paralyzing me."

Haneda airport was bedlam on the evening of December 3. For me the most touching of senders-off were Mrs. Tanizaki and her sister, Mrs. Watanabe. I go on suspecting that had he lived a bit longer Tanizaki would have been on his way to Stockholm that night (or some night near-by). "I wonder if Mr. T. would have been as generous as Mr. K. has been. I'll bet he would have that speech written."

Mishima was also at the airport, "and said he is not angry at me any more." I had made him angry by certain patronizing remarks about his immaturity in which I suggested that if he waited patiently like a good little man he too would win a Nobel one day. It is always and everywhere a mistake to make remarks one would as soon not have get back to the subject, and it is especially so in Japan, where they always do get back. More to the point: who was I to be patronizing towards a man so far more eminent than I? I was, in any event, very glad to learn that he was not mad at me any more.

Kawabata sat across the aisle from me on the flight to Copenhagen. He looked as if he were dead. "I almost wonder if I ought to go over and feel his pulse. Remarkable man—I can think of no one else who could leave me with an impossible speech to translate at the end of a trip around the world and not make me positively hate, hate, hate him."

I worked on the speech in both Japanese embassies, that in Copenhagen and that in Stockholm. Both embassies were most obliging, and the Copenhagen one found me a consultant, Fujiyoshi Jikai, a professor in a Buddhist university in Kyoto, who was that year lecturing in Copenhagen. I record in my diary that he radiated repose and erudition, and pulled me from the pits of despair. So I worked on such of the lecture as Mr. Kawabata provided me, and went on having a not very high opinion of it. "There are good moments, but there are moments of near nonsense, and then there are starts that lead nowhere, as when we are told how Mr. Kawabata fainted at Akutagawa's funeral. And it must be summarized for the press, we are told, and how can anyone summarize anything so fragmented and episodic?"

There was a press conference in Copenhagen. It was rather nasty. The very first questioner asked Kawabata's views of a remark by Irving Wallace, who thought that Nobel literary prizes should be discontinued when they were awarded to writers unknown in their own countries. Some malicious Japanese may have told Mr. Wallace that Kawabata was unknown in Japan. It is not at all unlikely. Many a Japanese thought that, if the award was to go to a Japanese, it should go to someone more robustly committed to the world of ideas, by which was generally meant either French or German ones.

"And what did Mr. Kawabata think? His answer I thought very good: we will have to wait thirty or fifty years to see whether the award was appropriate." He was in great good spirits afterwards. I record in my diary that I thought that he had expressed his thoughts honestly, and was glad. I interpreted for the conference, and, though I was not aware of any howlers, am seldom pleased with my performance as an interpreter.

And so to Stockholm, where the excitement continued. I surprised myself by taking an immediate liking to Stockholm. "As we came out of the ambassador's residence, the moon was actually shining. The air was cold and dry, as in Colorado—in Copenhagen the cold has a nagging quality. Here it is clean and straightforward."

On the day following there was, again, a press conference, and again I interpreted. It was more austere than the one in Copenhagen, and for me it was a big embarrassment, one of two items in the Nobel medley that I wish could be expunged from the record. I botched the very first question, and this is beyond comprehension, since I had been warned by the pleasant and efficient young Swedish diplomat assigned as Kawabata's factotum that it would be asked. It was asked, and of course Kawabata answered it. How did he propose to spend the prize money? I became aware, from the following questions, that something had gone wrong, but felt helpless to correct it, largely because I was not sure what had gone wrong. I could only hope that it would be allowed to sink without a ripple. Of course it was not. It was the top headline in the newspapers the next morning.

I knew how Kawabata had answered the question, but I had said something else. He had said that he wanted to buy something, perhaps a work of art, to remember Stockholm by. I had said that he wanted to give Stockholm something to remember him by. What to do? "The Japanese embassy wavered between forgetting about the whole thing and issuing a denial, Mr. Kawabata was in favor of forgetting about the whole thing—and Japanese journalism, at my elbow, insisted that something be done. Had it not been for the alertness of Japanese journalism, probably nothing at all would have happened—such of the world as had noticed . . . would have forgotten. . . .

"And so then it was time to go to lunch with their excellencies the members of the Swedish Academy. . . . In the circumstances it seemed about the last thing in the world I wanted to do; but it turned out to be delightful. Such a dear bunch of old gentlemen, such a pleasant medieval basement of a restaurant. . . .

"I felt much better after this event than before, but not for long. Back at the hotel young Mr. Kawabata had the tape of the press conference, and there can be little doubt about it, I misled the press. So, after an hour or so more of fussing, we telephoned a denial [of the Kawabata answer to that first question] to the press, placing the blame for the misunderstanding precisely where it belongs, upon me. With that, let us hope, the energetic Japanese press is appeased, and let us hope further that no one will even notice. . . .

"The phone has not rung all evening, and perhaps we may assume that the gentlemen of the press are at rest. What a hell they must make of the lives of really important people."

The jury for the Nobel Prize in Literature—it is different with other Nobel Prizes—is the Swedish Academy, a small body of illustrious Swedish persons of letters elected for life. In one of our last conversations I learned that Kawabata hated reporters. There was no hint of such an aversion during our time together in Scandinavia.

The unfortunate incident was not forgotten. It was unrealistic to hope that it ever would be in a country as self-conscious and as worried about its image as Japan. Even now, thirty years later, I come upon references to it, and doubtless I will continue to do so until I shuffle off this mortal coil.

Two days later came the award ceremonies. The introduction offered to the king and the assembly by a member of the Swedish Academy was disappointing. I had spent quite a few hours during the preceding weeks seeking to convince the Japanese that silly exoticism had not been the reason for the award—that a very good writer had been recognized as a very good writer.

"It does seem to have been a superficial, sentimental sort of exoticism that got the prize. . . . Burblings about the quiet beauty of Kyoto, the quiet beauty of Japanese women. . . . The academician even managed to get in a dig or so at the Americans—Japanese going back after the Occupation to erstwhile off-limits precincts, to see whether the barbarians had cut down those old trees. How I would have loved to show him what happened to those old trees in front of the British Embassy at the hands of Governor Azuma. The translator into Japanese, whoever he is, and he should be remembered, managed to edit out the more objectionable passages—as well as the mistakes. . . .

"It will be seen that I am down on the Swedes—who have made so much of me. It is really very disappointing to see that Mr. Kawabata might as well be writing J.A.L. advertising copy."

The next day the Kawabatas and I went to the palace and had a king to show us around.

"I had a leisurely breakfast and had leisurely scanned the paper, in which Mr. Kawabata got all the headlines . . . and was about to settle down, to what I still had before me of the rewriting of the speech, when I remembered that we had an appointment with the king. So I scraped off a few whiskers and dashed downstairs, sure that I had missed my only chance to meet a king. But I need not have worried. Mr. Kawabata was late and Mrs. Kawabata was yet later, and we kept the king waiting fifteen minutes or so.

"He is, as the Honorable Agatha [Evelyn Waugh's Agatha Runcible] would say, a dear old boy, and it was a lovely morning. He showed us his Chinese collection. It contains very beautiful specimens, and Mr. Kawabata did exactly as he should have done, praised the good and damned the bad, and His Majesty beamed at each correct response, clearly holding the same view as to the good and the bad. . . . The king gave us a full hour, despite the fact that a chamberlain was nervously urging him on to his next appointment, and for another hour we wandered around the king's private chambers on our own. There are family photographs all over the place and what looked to me to be amateur paintings; but try though one will to make a palace a home, it does not work. They who live in palaces must feel homeless.

"The evening was a dreary thing. 'We still have tomorrow,' said Mr. Kawabata cheerily, setting off to have dinner with His Majesty, and leaving me with the merest driblet more of the manuscript. . . .

"I translated the driblet and then went down to the bar, where I learned that I was not the only unhappy one. The gentlemen of the press are very angry at not having been provided with copies of the lecture, are inclined to think that they have been sent on a bit of a goose chase. When I left them, at about midnight, they were in congress assembled waiting to accost him on his return from the palace. I must say that he deserved it, at this point. But I must add that the behavior of the gentlemen of the press seems curious too. If they are going to act so in concert, making quite sure that no one gets a jump on anyone, then why could one reporter not do as well as the dozen or so we have with us?

"Walking the streets of Stockholm, one sees evidence of the isolation and provincialism of the Swedes. In Copenhagen virtually every automobile bears the DK emblem indicating that it has been or is going abroad. In Stockholm the corresponding S is rare."

The lecture was delivered at the Academy, a lovely building from the time of its founder, Gustave III. My diary entry for the day is long, but substantial enough that I will beg leave to quote most of it. "The morning and early afternoon of this, the day of the second great event, were utterly mad. Mr. Kawabata did not finish the lecture until noon, and even afterwards kept coming in with deletions and revisions. I quite threw a tantrum when the last page was brought to me, for it is made up largely of a long and incomprehensible quotation from an obscure Kamakura text having to do with Saigyō's poetic theories. The last third or so of the manuscript never got to the embassy for typing, and I did not know until ten minutes or so before we left for the academy that the first two-thirds would be back from the embassy. Then there were the gentlemen of the press, justly grieved, but somehow making it seem that this was all my fault, that I should have wrung it out of him earlier. They were after him until three in the morning, and finally were given the first ten pages of the Japanese draft, a step which went against the arrangements made with the Nobel Foundation, but about which I quite refused to worry.

"Just before we left for the Swedish Academy Mr. Kawabata decided to delete considerable portions of the lecture. It would have been nice if he had done so before they were translated, but it was a step in the right direction all the same, because the passages in question, such as the discussion of Dazai's suicide, were among the more pointless. . . .

"A most remarkable way to work, and everyone tells me that it is Mr. Kawabata's usual way. It would really seem to be true, as he has told us, that he is able to work only in the last extremity, so to speak, when he has given up hope. The great mystery is how he began writing in the first place. When he was young and not famous, there cannot have been people doing what I was apparently expected to do, wrench manuscripts from him.

"When it was all over, which is to say when we were on our way, late as usual, to the academy, he was as sweet and apologetic as he could possibly be. He slipped me an envelope with a small *orei* [return of a favor], he said. Back in the hotel I found that it contained, dear me, a five-hundred-dollar bill, the first, I think, that I have ever laid an eyeball on. I will of course return it, and ask for a one-dollar bill to frame in memory of the occasion.

"One result of the last-minute revisions is that I am the only person in possession of the final revision of two or three pages. Bet I could make a heap off of them. Of course I won't. I will frame them, and let my heirs make a heap off of them.

"The lecture was in due course delivered, mostly by me, before an audience mostly of old ladies. Usual for Nobel lectures, said Mr. Falkman [the young Swedish diplomat referred to earlier as Kawabata's factotum]. . . . Mr. Falkman is an extremely intelligent man, and, to my considerable surprise, he liked the lecture. He liked its formlessness, its freedom from sentimentality (due, let it be recorded, to my maternal care), its refusal to explain itself. So be it. I am sure that most of the old ladies disliked it because it came from my mouth and not that of the master. For my part, this has perhaps been the first occasion on which I have not had an uncomfortable feeling that I might be intruding myself unnecessarily.

"A huge reception at the Japanese embassy in the evening. Unpleasantness over the copyright, which I stayed out of as much as possible. It does seem that we went against the wishes of the Nobel Foundation. I felt very sorry for Mr. Maeda, the sweet man who is counsellor of the embassy. The steely Swedes of the foundation—how very Prussian they are—had him completely rattled, and of course the fault lay entirely with Mr. Kawabata and his dilatory ways."

On the next day, Friday the thirteenth, we had lunch at the Stockholm Opera House with the editor-in-chief of Bonniers, the most important Swedish publisher and also Kawabata's publisher. "The sun had come out and streamed through the southern windows, making the place seem like an orangerie, and Lucia of All Sweden came to greet us—she is a robust blonde, said to be a swimming champion—and I was happy." Lucia presides over the light festival at the dark time of the year, doubtless a pagan relic. Numbers of Lucias came into our several rooms at the Royal Hotel in the dead of night, their uniformly blonde hair crowned with a blaze of candles. There were photographers too. Photographs of me did not make the papers, but photographs of the Kawabatas, sitting up in bed and looking bemused, were everywhere.

I learned much about Nobel Prizery. I learned that Bonniers knew a full day in advance of the announcement that Kawabata would get the prize. "It all seems to be, as with guessing who will be the new pope, a matter of knowing who the chief candidates are and then guessing from the passage of time what is happening in the sacred precincts." In this instance it was judged that a deadlock between two European candidates had developed, an outsider was coming to the fore, and this person, or so Bonniers thought, could be no one but Kawabata. This is not wholly in accord with the views of the Swedish reporter who had interviewed me in Tokyo. He said that the bets were on Mishima. What is fairly clear, however, is that the cognoscenti do not wait for the announcement.

The next day I spent in Uppsala with Olaf Ledin, seeing how Linnaeus had lived and sipping what was called mead, but I suspect was really sweetened beer. Olaf is a Swedish japanologist teaching in Copenhagen. He gave me a vivid glimpse of how it is when spring comes to the north country. Once, in a commuting train between Uppsala and Stockholm, he said, everyone suddenly looked up, as if upon a signal. It was the first morning since autumn on which they could see the sun.

The next day we all got ready to depart. I looked in on the Kawabata suite a couple of times and found it utter chaos. I indicated doubts that they could be ready in time. I should have seen their house in Kamakura, Mrs. Kawabata replied, on the night before we left Japan. "I said to Mr. Kawabata that it must be nice to be alone again with the Mrs. He replied that it was about the last thing he wanted."

In Copenhagen I spent several days with the Woodburys, resting and recovering from a cold. Wendell had been with the Reischauer embassy in Tokyo and was now in the Copenhagen embassy. I arrived back in Tokyo on the nineteenth. "I suppose we must have been in the air some fifteen hours. I slept through most of them. I kept having pleasant dreams of Professor Fujiyoshi. When you come upon someone as placid and composed as he, you think there must really be something in Zen."

The return was far quieter than the departure. I was by myself, the Kawabatas having proceeded on further travels through Europe. It had been an exciting time. I am strongly inclined to think of it as the best time in my relations with the Japanese. It was the time when I felt nearest to thinking I belonged and mattered. To say that it has been downhill all the way since would be to simplify unconscionably. Yet the road traveled does sometimes have that look about it. The decade of the sixties was perhaps the most exciting of them all, and certainly nothing has been quite like it since.

I have yet to mention the other matter (besides the botched press conference) that I wish people would forget about. It is the title of the Nobel lecture. In Japanese it is a peculiar title, *Utsukushii Nihon no Watakushi.* The peculiarity is concentrated in a single syllable, the genitive particle *no.* What it says literally is: "I of Beautiful Japan," though conceivably it could convey "Beautiful I of Japan." The second possibility can be rejected as ludicrous, but the other is surely a very crabbed and unnatural title in English. When, a short time later, the Japanese National Railways used the title as the slogan for a big tourist campaign, they changed the *no* to *to.* This makes it perfectly clear and manageable: "Beautiful Japan and I." It is not, however, the Kawabata title.

At the airport on the evening we departed for Copenhagen, Nicholas Ingleton (the Australian editor who objected to all the pinuses in my translation of *House of the Sleeping Beauties*) suggested the title the lecture has ever since borne, "Japan, the Beautiful, and Myself." "That is what it will be," said I, much relieved at not having something too utterly uncouth. Having said it, I did not look back.

All through the decades since it has been called a mistranslation. Indeed it might well be exactly that if I had ever thought of it as a translation. I have not. I have thought of it as a prudent adaptation, even as is *House of the Sleeping Beauties.* Some of the criticism has been downright metaphysical. The very formlessness of the lecture seems to demand system-building. Recently, without explanation, I received an offprint which looked to me like Russian. Indeed it did prove to be. A person who knows Russian gave me a summary. A lady in Moscow reproved me for misconstruing that mischievous syllable, and said that it must be even so with all us Anglo-Saxon types and our dualistic stance towards nature. There may be something in it. All I can think of by way of contrition is to say again that I have never considered the English title a translation at all.

In the Japanese media, of course, the lecture was made much of. "An extravagant article by Etō Jun [the famous critic—he it was whom Fukuda Tsuneari thought to have flipped sides too easily during the 1960 disturbances] in the evening *Asahi* a couple of days ago, in which he sees the Kawabata lecture as a great challenge to the West, a flinging down of the gauntlet. It seems that the rejection of history must have had us of the West, . . . dedicated as we are to history, shaking in our boots. I cannot imagine that the elderly ladies whom he addressed in Stockholm thought of it as other than very pretty, if they thought of it at all. And won't Mr. Kawabata be surprised to learn that he had a purpose so serious? What might he not have done had he proceeded in a more orderly manner?

"The lecture might have ranked high in the body of Etō Jun's work had it been written by Etō Jun, but to me it still seems not very good Kawabata."

To its credit, however, must be set down the fact that it earned lots of money, for Mr. Kawabata and for me. A paperback containing both the original and the translation was something of a bestseller. Generous in this thing as in most things, he let me have half the royalties.

Shortly after my return to Tokyo, I received, through a suitable emissary, the news that my most recent family, the Saitōs, were going to move out on me. Few private matters of importance in Japan can be undertaken without the aid of an emissary who takes on responsibilities somewhat like those of a godparent. It is his (emissaries in my experience have always been men) responsibility to see that the transaction proceeds in an upright manner.

For all the worthy aspects of the practice, I have sometimes wished that we the principals could sit down and talk things through; but of course I am a foreigner, from the adversarial West. The Saitōs chose my friend the photographer Sakaguchi, who was presently to fall victim to the automobile. They had bought themselves a condominium beyond the Tama River in Kanagawa Prefecture and would be moving into it in the summer or autumn.

Their behavior was impeccable, but they badly upset the tranquility of my life. The turnover of "families" had become too rapid. The time had come for me to close the house during my absences, or to move into an apartment that would be secure even when unoccupied. Only the latter seemed practical. Even in peaceful, secure Tokyo, unoccupied houses were always being occupied by uninvited guests and vandalized, and sometimes burned down.

I had little trouble finding a new place, in Hongō, the eastern half of Bunkyō Ku. People in the rich southern and western parts of the city may sniff at the name, but I am rather proud of it. To me it suggests threadbare gentility. Hongō means, for most people, Tokyo University, the snootiest educational institution in the land. The Yushima part of Bunkyō Ku, where I moved in 1969, has been my Tokyo residence ever since.

Occasionally, when kept awake by the fire engines in which the neighborhood abounds, I have regretted coming to Yushima, but not frequently, or for long. It is convenient, it has a history, it sits on a hill above Shinobazu Pond, one of the prettiest places in the city and the most famous place for viewing lotus blossoms in full summer. And it abounds in Iwasakis as well as fire engines. Iwasaki is the family name of the founder of the Mitsubishi enterprises. A nineteenth century Iwasaki mansion is across the street and visible from my windows in winter, when leaves do not interfere, and it is an Important Cultural Property. Not many people in Tokyo can look from their windows at an Important Cultural Property. One day I ran into *the* Mr. Iwasaki on his way down the hill to practice his swing at a driving range, and learned why there are so many of them. None are related to him, but when they say that they are of the Yushima Iwasakis, people think they are.

Disposing of my old residence did prove to be troublesome. The process was full of surprises, to remind me that I was in the Mysterious Orient, which perhaps I was beginning to take for granted. The obvious person to sell to was the landowner. The first surprise was learning that the elderly lady who had been collecting rent all these years, a decade and a half of them, did not own the land. It belonged to a man whose imposing if somewhat vulgar house I had noticed on evening walks. My best source of information was the barber whom I patronized, out on the main street. Oh yes, did I not know, he said, when I made inquiry in this regard. She was long ago the landowner's mistress. He was surprised that the owner should still permit her such liberties, she being the hag I knew, he (whom I did not know) still being plump and youthful. Why he permitted the liberties I never learned.

Then I went to said owner, a man named Kanda, accompanied by an appropriate emissary (the real-estate dealer through whom I had bought my house). How much did I want, asked Kanda. Well, said I, the house was thirty or forty years old and could not be worth much. Not the house, "you fool," his tone of voice added. The land. But, said I, the land was his. How was I to charge anything for it? This produced much the most important surprise. I learned that, having occupied the land for some fifteen years, I had certain rights which could be converted to money. How much did I want?

I felt as if I were where, through much of my boyhood, I had longed to be, back in the Middle Ages. Not having dreamed that such rights existed, I had no notion what they were worth. I asked my emissary what he thought. He said that at this point he was out of his depth. I doubt that this was true, but thought it rather admirable of him to say so. I should, he said, get myself a lawyer. I already had one, Mr. Asami, a friend of my Australian friends the Robinsons. I had had his help in getting the house.

The emissary now withdrew, and we began discussions with Kanda the landowner, He was an unpleasant man. Having so little notion of what the rights I suddenly found myself sitting on were worth, I would probably have accepted whatever he offered. But I presently found myself in court. The chief reason was that he was so obnoxious. He kept telling me that rich Americans ought not to be squeezing large amounts of money from impoverished Japanese.

It was a thing many Japanese said in those days, and it always annoyed me beyond description. There may have been some justice in it thirty and forty years ago, but it is still said occasionally today. ("Ours is a poor country, you must not ask more of us than we are capable of giving.") In the Kanda case there was no justification even all those decades ago. Anyone who owned that much Tokyo land was many times richer than I. Even the land on which his imposing house sat was enough to make him thus. So it was off to court with Mr. Asami one morning late in July.

"I went around to Mr. Asami's office in midmorning and the two of us, after reviewing our papers and our stories, then went around to the Tokyo District Court, or a certain part of it, in a corner of Hibiya Park. A shabby, stifling place. . . . The villainous Kanda and his lawyer were a half hour late in arriving, and the judge and his clerk, both in shirtsleeves were yet later. There followed a most casual looking into the facts, such as how much rent I have been paying. . . . I said almost nothing, and Mr. Asami little more, and Kanda talked and talked, to the obvious annoyance of the judge, who, however, continued to smile. Finally he offered the pleasing but I thought rather surprisingly frank view that the judgment was likely to be nearer my proposal than Kanda's. Still Kanda showed no disposition to do what was obviously being suggested, settle out of court. . . ." It was in a *kan-i saiban,* a summary court, I was informed, that this was happening. I had no further days in court.

I had already, on a windy April day, moved out of my house in Koishikawa. "The house rocked in the wind, as if waving me farewell, or as if trying to toss me out a few hours early. I could not decide which of the similes was the more appropriate." I moved into a hotel near Shiba Park, once the grounds of the more southerly of the two mortuary temples for Tokugawa shoguns. It was there that I saw the moon-landing. This was exactly a week before my day in court. "As Armstrong came down the ladder and put a toe gingerly on the ground, I could only think of the night in my childhood when my father got out of the car to open a gate and disappeared, having stepped into a hole. I am sure that if Armstrong had disappeared I would have laughed as uncontrollably as I did then."

Because the hotel was unable to let me have a room for the whole summer, I spent a fortnight or so in the northern Ryukyu Islands with my friend Fukuda Hiroshi, or Hirokazu, an artist in a traditional genre, the woodcut print.

My father died in August. I returned to Colorado for his funeral, and went on to Ann Arbor. My cousin Mary Clarke had come upon some old newspapers that much interested me, "the *Castle Rock News,* or the *Douglas*

County News, I forget which, from the 1870s. They showed that Castle Rock in those days, though it probably had a population of no more than a couple of hundred, was more of a town, a gathering place, than it is today. It had two hotels, and the guest lists, dutifully published, show that people came from such places as Bear Creek (my great grandfather, George Ratcliff) and Lake Gulch (George Doepke) and spent the night in town. Now, of course, only tourists on their way to California and behind schedule would spend an isolated night there. . . . And I learned what a lovable and universally loved man my great grandfather was. The letters to the editor suggest strongly that he was a penny pincher, a loudmouth, and perhaps a bit of a cheat."

Bear Creek is in the western or English part of the county, Lake Gulch in the eastern or German. Lake Gulch Creek flows into Cherry Creek, which in those years devastated Denver from time to time, giving Douglas County feelings of great power.

On November 5 came a call from Lawyer Asami telling me that the court had reached a decision. Not surprisingly, since the judge knew more about the matter than anyone else, it was as he had said it would be, nearer what I had asked than what "the villainous Kanda" was willing to pay. "It would have been nice, of course, if Kanda had offered me a decent price from the outset; but I do not enormously regret the time and expense I have been to. He gained nothing from it, while I gained insights into the Japanese property system."

What I learned chiefly, of course, is the major role old customs have in modern law. In a sense I knew it all along, because I do not tire of saying what a profoundly conservative people the Japanese are; but it was a world I had had little opportunity to explore. I thought that when next we met I would thank him, Kanda, with perhaps a touch of a sneer in my voice and manner, but I never saw him again. The house of which I had grown so fond was torn down some years later, and the land became a parking lot. The house of the barber who was my chief source of neighborhood gossip has suffered the same fate.

I was again in Colorado, on family business in the coldest part of the winter, and again I found it interesting and moving. I spent an afternoon at the Great Western Stock Show in Denver. "The sheep dogs were marvelous, and there were evidences of connoisseurship all around me, ladies and small girls able to guess to a split second how well the cowboys had performed. . . . The West has become a tradition, with standards and subtle differences, and one approves of such things. . . .

"Back out to Castle Rock as the evening was in the sky, and Pikes Peak stood guarding the somber plains. There it was watching over them when the wagon trains came in, and there it will be when we turn back eastward across the plains once more, having used up all the water. Along the Platte River is a line of cottonwoods indifferent to all the urbanity around it. Indifference—the mark of the things that will last."

In the spring I was in Europe again, for an academic conference in a villa on Lake Como. I spent several magical days driving through Tuscany with the Murfins, once of Yokohama and Sicily and now of Genoa, and driving around Jutland with the Woodburys, still of Copenhagen, and then flew to Tokyo, to occupy my new apartment.

Within a span of little more than a half dozen years, the three most important Japanese writers I have known all died. It need not surprise us that Tokyo has since seemed a less interesting place.

Of the three deaths, no one has ever suggested that Tanizaki killed himself unless, like drinking oneself to death, eating oneself to death can be considered an oblique form of suicide. The other two deaths are generally held to be suicides. Technically Mishima Yukio was murdered, although he clearly wished the last incident in his life to end in his death. He went through the motions of disposing of himself in the honorable (to many of us it seems merely gruesome) warrior fashion, by cutting his entrails open. He was beheaded by a young follower before the ritual could be completed, however. Old friends of Kawabata held to the end that his death was accidental. I know of no one who still thinks so, now that all the old friends have in their turn gone away. Mrs. Kawabata's initial reaction was utter confusion, but now she too is of the view that he died by his own hand.

Suicide has been common among modern Japanese writers. At least a dozen prominent ones have killed themselves or are averred to have done so. Sometimes, as in the cases just mentioned, there is an element of doubt, but that the incidence is uncommonly high seems beyond doubting. Suicide has always been frequent among the young of Japan. Most of the literary suicides, however, have been of the middle years and beyond. Numerous explanations are possible. Perhaps the agony of being alive is the best explanation. It is present among all sorts of people everywhere, but perhaps it is more acute in a country where change has been too rapid and complicated.

It is also true that Japanese have from time to time felt a mass urge towards martyrdom, and that they take a casual view of distinctions between life and death. The dead are next door, and look in from time to time. None of this offers adequate explanation for the fact that the most imaginative of people should in so many cases come so quickly to the conclusion that they have no other recourse. If the phenomenon must be put down as one of the mysteries, it is not the only one in modern Japan. Why the nation allowed itself to be led into a suicidal war is probably a deeper and more important mystery.

Some of the suicides could be predicted. I myself thought that Mishima would one day kill himself, and that if he did not his whole career would be a lie. I did not predict the form that his suicide would take—it was as much of a surprise to me as it was to everyone else, including his family; but I was not surprised that it came to pass.

I was very surprised in the Kawabata instance. I have spoken of the massive repose I sensed in Professor Fujiyoshi, the Kyoto gentleman who was of such great assistance in translating the Nobel lecture. I sensed something similar in Kawabata. "I have never experienced pains and sorrows of the Western kind. I have not once seen in Japan emptiness and decay of the Western kind." This is from a beautiful and justly famous essay called "Sadness," written in 1947.

And this is from a Kawabata essay written a dozen years earlier: "I believe the Oriental classics, and particularly the Buddhist scriptures, to be the greatest of the world's literature. I respect them not for their religious teachings but for their literary fantasies. For fifteen years now I have had in mind the plot for a story to be called 'Song of the East.' I have thought that I would like it to be my swan song [this expression is a literal translation]. I will sing the classic Eastern fantasy after my fashion. I may die without having written it, but I wish to have it known that I wanted to write it. I have been baptized in and have tried my hand at imitating modern Western literature; but, at heart Oriental, I have not once lost my direction these fifteen years. I have thus far told no one of this fact. It has been the happy secret formula of the house of Kawabata." This is the voice of profound resignation, not that of self-destruction. Of course resignation can lead to suicide as the final fulfillment; but I sensed nothing of the sort in Kawabata. I sensed only quiet endurance.

With Mishima it was very different. I had long predicted that he would kill himself. Here is part of a diary entry from late 1967. In a newspaper advertisement "Kōbunsha tells us that Mishima has put his hand to what I take to be the editing of the *Hagakure.* Why, he asks himself in the ad, did he do it when he has mountains of other work to do? Because, he answers, he could not bear to let anyone else have *his Hagakure.* It meant so much to him in the unenlightened days after the war, when it was banned. Really, if the man is telling us the truth these days, he is one day going to have to commit suicide, or admit that he has not been true to himself."

Hagakure, from the early eighteenth century, is a sacred text, so to speak, of *bushidō* "the way of the warrior." Probably the most famous statement is: "Bushidō is the discovery of death."

Mishima's death occurred on November 25, 1970 (November 24 on the eastern side of the date line), some two years after the Nobel excitement. Kawabata's occurred a year and a half later. There has been a considerable tendency, in the chitchat one hears in literary bars, to find a relationship between the two events. That Mishima was deeply disappointed at not getting the prize himself seems beyond doubting. It is also true that Kawabata was greatly affected by Mishima's death. The two were close. At the beginning of his career Mishima looked to Kawabata as patron and protector. Whether in either case the emotion was strong enough to lead to suicide is highly doubtful. I may say all the same that I sensed a different Mishima after the prize. He seemed to withdraw into himself and into Japan. Earlier he had been among the better instances of Japanese cosmopolitanism. He was a bit of a dandy, and not at all a Japanese sort of dandy.

I was in Washington on November 25, giving a lecture at the State Department. The lecture, not that it matters, was on terrorism. My qualifications to talk on the subject derived from my observations of the Japanese student movement. The news of Mishima's death, which had occurred by Eastern Standard Time in the middle of the preceding night, was in the morning newspapers of both Washington and New York.

I had several calls from newspaper reporters. They are very clever at tracking a person down even when he is away from home. It was a chance to crack the big time and I failed. None of them quoted me. I did not have high hopes, even while they were interviewing me, that I would succeed.

The trouble was that I was unable to come up with quotable one-liners. I kept adding qualifications. This was most surely the case, I would say, but it is not all that simple, and we must also remember that . . . and so on and so on. I reminded myself a little of Henry James. But I was being honest. Mishima was a very complicated man, and this final act of his life did not lend itself to less than complicated explanation. And there was much that I did not understand and still am not sure I understand. And certain subjects seemed taboo. More than one reporter told me that the subject of Mishima's homosexuality was not one he could do much with. It seemed to me a very important topic, one without which an approach to complete explanation was not possible. Aphorisms were called for, and I was incapable of producing them.

My first thoughts as I recorded them in my diary make the problem abundantly clear.

"The thing of the day was Mishima's suicide. I had the news from the *Washington Post* as I was waiting for the shuttle bus to take me across the river to the Foreign Service Institute, there to deliver the talk, on the Japanese Left. It seemed silly, as we went across the Potomac, not to be talking about the Japanese Right, but then, I said to myself, they move by the same romantic rules, and the chief difference between them is that the Right has a courage and a firmness of purpose which the Left lacks, and why this should be I for one do not know, and so why talk about that, why not talk about the Left.

"I suppose my initial reaction—no, about my fourth—my first was of course shock—my second, I hate to say it, but honesty dictates, was a kind of relief, for he *has* weighed upon me, made me feel so chronically that I have let other people do what I ought to be doing myself—and my third, after some contemplation, was *naruhodo* [an all-purpose word for which the best rendition in this instance might be "of course"], it has been there all along, and haven't I said so myself, that he must commit suicide if he is not to be accused of plain dishonesty—and then my fourth, after I was over at the institute, was of how little moment are Japanese except for their quaintness and eccentricity. No one over there seemed to be more than mildly puzzled or amused.... And then, after a bit more contemplation, yet another thought: that the suicide succeeded, for it will be remembered, and who but Mishima could have made both the *Times* and the *Post*, and the front page, no less a page, of the *Evening Star.*

"It is not often that the newspaper reporters are after me, and when it does happen I have a way of being in retreat somewhere.... They asked whether I looked upon this with fear and horror, as evidence of a revival of Japanese nationalism, and that too was easy enough to answer.

Goodness no, dear me, dear boy, said I—I should think the very opposite. Anyone who wishes to see a revival of Japanese militarism and thinks there is the slightest possibility—any such person would have behaved, surely, very differently. . . .

"So I answered, easily enough; but it was merely an easy answer, for I knew the next question, and any honest attempt to answer it would give the lie to the preceding one. What were his motives? Why did he do it? . . . I cannot believe that an extreme kind of romanticism, which may have had to do with the completion of what he was always calling his 'life's work' and emotional exhaustion and a feeling that this was the time, did not have a great deal to do with it, and this, of course, as the reporters kept trying to get me to say, leads to a suspicion of posing and self-dramatization.

"And . . . there is . . . the sexuality. It is all there in 'Patriotism' [a late story made into a movie, with Mishima himself in the lead], the bliss of dying in and with beautiful youth, blood with warm blood. One can imagine that Mishima, in the last stages of his life, brought himself to a sort of ecstasy, in the knowledge that his favorites in the Tate no Kai were prepared to go the whole distance with him."

I seem to be assuming that everyone will remember the memorable events with which Mishima's life ended. It is not necessarily so. A brief description is called for. On that November morning Mishima and several members of his Tate no Kai (Shield Society), a para-military band of young men who marched about in "Chocolate Soldier" uniforms, occupied the office of the commanding general of an important army (more properly, Ground Self Defense Force, because Japan is not allowed to have an army) barracks at Ichigaya, beside the western arc of what had been the outer moat to Edo Castle. It was the building, since torn down, in which the Class-A war crimes trials, of General Tōjō and his fellows, had been held, just after the war.

Upon Mishima's demand, the soldiers of the Self Defense Force were mustered. He harangued them. The time had come to rise and put the nation to rights. Recordings tell us that their clear reaction was a mixture of amusement and contempt. He went back into the general's office, performed ritual suicide, and was beheaded by the young man designated for the task. The young man himself was then beheaded. The general, tied to his chair, could do nothing but watch the gory scene. Though it is hard to think of him as in any way responsible, it brought his military career to an end.

Almost thirty years have passed. I would not reject any of my original thoughts, though the second one, about how "he weighed upon me," puzzles me. I think the reference must be to translating his work. He had been after me to translate the final tetralogy, the final installment of which bears the date of his death.

I would, I think, rearrange them, however. Mishima was a performer, constantly making himself over, and always at work making his life a theatrical production. I think this of first importance in explaining the circumstances of his death. He planned the details of the last act brilliantly, to make sure that it would be noticed and he would be remembered.

He was too intelligent a man to believe that the soldiers at Ichigaya would rise at his exhortation and rebel. He was also too discerning not to recognize the essential silliness of his Tate no Kai. The uniforms (provided at Mishima's expense, of course) were silly, their comportment was silly, everything about them was silly.

He had always been something of a nationalist, not inconsistent with the cosmopolitanism remarked on above, and towards the end of his life his nationalism ran to extremes. He continued to be something of a European dandy and to entertain foreign guests in European surroundings, even as he urged the monarch to be a genuine theocrat. Some would say that the latter at least was part of a complex and self-conscious act. I doubt it. He said that he continued to believe in the divinity of the emperor, a notion rejected by the emperor himself shortly after the war, and proclaimed himself among the emperor's worshippers. This too may seem difficult to reconcile with his very high intelligence, but in it I sense deep seriousness. He trained with the army (the Self Defense Force), and he said that he found the experience deeply satisfying.

At this point, I think, though some would disagree, and some do not mention the matter at all, his sexuality must come into the discussion.

I did not myself think him a good-looking man, but he seems to have been rather in love with himself. He was fond of being photographed in the nude or near-nude. Probably the most famous photograph has him as St. Sebastian under the rain of Roman arrows. In *Confession of a Mask,* an early work that is indeed a confession, and is more straightforward than most of his work, he described the intensely erotic effect a picture of the saint had upon him.

If the nationalism and the emperor worship and the soldiering and the Tate no Kai are seen as manifestations of a longing for a society of young men bound by something like love, then they may produce a shudder, but they are not to be smiled at.

He had a horror of old age. This of course is not hard to understand in terms of the narcissism and the longing to be in a world of young fighters. I predicted that he would kill himself when he turned fifty. He did it four years and a few weeks sooner.

I received far fewer written messages from Mishima than from Tanizaki and Kawabata. I think the reasons may be that I did not admire his work as I admired theirs, and he knew it. I am not good at concealing my likes and dislikes, and I did not think it would be possible to deceive so astute a man. He occasionally wrote in English. His English was not impeccable, but it showed flair. "I love to see you soon and talk about our mutual mountainous frustrations." This is dated May 31, 1970, less than half a year before his death. There is little of substance in his cards and notes. Mostly they are about appointments. We generally met in Ginza, and, without careful instructions, one cannot be sure of turning up at the right place in Ginza.

I had many an interesting conversation with him, including one early in July 1970. "The evening with Mishima Yukio. What an interesting person he is, and I cannot think why I once thought him wanting in humor. He has a richly sardonic sense of humor and is a very good mimic, with several fine routines, among them a liberal housewife from the western suburbs discussing the educational value of the writings of Mishima Yukio.

"And here are some of the subjects upon which he had interesting things to say:

"The police. He thinks they are responsible for violent feuding among leftist student factions. They plant inflammatory rumors.

"The government. He had hoped that the rioting last year and into this would stir serious thought of constitutional reform; but the rioters proved too feeble a challenge, and the situation is hopeless. We must live with that awful Peace Constitution.

"The literary world. It is corrupt. When you serve on the juries that award the literary prizes, you realize that the jurors make the awards to their friends for all the wrong reasons—and fundamentally by way of serving their own interests. (But after all new people *do* sometimes get recognition—so the corruption cannot be absolute.)

"Limited warfare. We will always lose a limited war, in which we cannot make use of 'the people' as the other side can; and so we should work to do away with the weapons that make all-out war impossible.

"His own writing. He worked hardest on the trial scenes of *Runaway Horses,* to make sure he was right about prewar court procedures. (This seemed to me to demonstrate that he is a very conservative kind of novelist—not that I had not already discerned that fact behind all the sparkling modishness.) He thinks of ending his tetralogy by having Honda, a very old man, visit Satoko in Nara, where she denies having known such a man. I told him I liked the idea, though I did not quite know what it meant. That life is a dream? He allowed that he did not know either."

This is in fact the way the tetralogy ends. Honda is the only character present through the four volumes. Satoko, the aristocratic girl who is the heroine of the first volume, becomes a Buddhist nun at the end of it. In the paragraph about the "Peace Constitution," the postwar constitution, most famously outlawing arms, is suggested yet another reason for the final act in the drama of his life: desperation. He really does seem to have given up hope for changing Japan when the big confrontation supposed to come in 1970 did not. The security treaty with the United States, a bilateral one signed in 1951 at the same time as the multilateral peace treaty, could have expired in 1970. Revision in 1960 was the occasion for the disturbances that so upset me as to make me decide I wanted to live no longer in Japan. Something similar was predicted for 1970, but not much happened except that the two governments agreed on automatic extension of the treaty conditional on the return of Okinawa to Japan. This was accomplished two years later.

On a June evening in 1968 he came very close to telling me of plans for that last act. It will be seen that I did not grasp the significance. I cannot be sure whether or not the details were already forming in his mind.

"The evening with Mishima Yukio, at a Ginza restaurant. . . . Initially we were alone, and he talked of his hatred of democracy and his fellow men of letters, of violence and suicide, the conjunction of which he considers to be the essence of what is Japanese, and in his fascination with which, I think he is being honest, as he is not in many things, including most of his fiction up to 'Patriotism.' Of the recent troubles in America he said in effect: splendid, splendid, a sign that America is not dead. England and Sweden are dead. Just you wait—we are going to have plenty of assassinations in Japan. He means to do something dramatic before he is fifty, and he clearly does not mean something literary. Just what was not made clear; but his belief in the efficacy of violence would seem to be very deep. And very Japanese. The calm of Japan at almost the speed of sound [a reference to an advertisement Japan Air Lines kept running]. . . .

"He said at one point that he wanted to accomplish at least as much as Nakano Seigō did. What he means, once again, I do not really know. But he is up to something, and at least he is interesting, as not many of them are. He treats his hangers on [of whom two were present] as a Kōda Rohan *oyabun* would, and he is ostentatiously proud of his masculinity. That there is something homosexual about this need scarcely be pointed out."

Oyabun, literally "father surrogates," were bosses among such sorts as gamblers, gangsters, and construction workers. Kōda Rohan, 1867–1947, excelled at depicting the moral and ethical system by which they were governed.

Nakano Seigō (1886–1943) was a maverick journalist and politician who greatly admired Hitler and Mussolini. After plotting unsuccessfully for the overthrow of the wartime Tōjō cabinet, he was briefly imprisoned. He killed himself after his release. One may say that Mishima quite outdid his mentor.

The next case is that of Kawabata Yasunari.

Kawabata was found dead on the evening of April 16, 1972, in a studio he kept in Zushi, the next town down the coast of the Miura Peninsula from Kamakura, where he lived. The gas for heating the bath was turned on, but not lighted. These circumstances very strongly suggest suicide. My diary informs me that at the time I assumed suicide. I have since come to harbor doubts, and I still harbor them, for at least two reasons.

The strongest is that I do not want it to be suicide, and I grasp at excuses for other explanations. I did not mind in the least in the case of Mishima, because a suicidal impulse runs through much of his work and thought, and his suicide, if we may call it that, was carefully planned. This was not true of Kawabata. I am happier with his memory thinking that he did not kill himself.

I plunge through such narrow escape hatches as I come upon. The widest of them is that some of his oldest friends agreed with me, while they were still in this world. Much the same thing had happened before, they said, and it had been accidental. It is true that the very first of them to arrive on the scene said that he saw the face of someone who was happy to die.

To me this does not seem the same thing, however, as saying that he wished to destroy himself.

The second is that when I last saw him, a month and a half before his death, I thought that he was a dying man. Here is a part of my diary entry for March 4, "In the evening, at Ueno, there was a large gathering in honor of Hasegawa Izumi and his huge Ogai work. There were large numbers of speeches, through most of which the room rocked with conversation. I was among the victims, though I was treated better than most. The decibel count dropped noticeably when I began, said Val Viglielmo, who was also among the victims. Professor Hisamatsu was there, looking very hearty for his years. Mr. Kawabata was there, looking dreadful, as if the flicker were about to go out."

The guest of honor was an eminent critic and scholar of Mori Ogai (1862–1922). Professor Hisamatsu, among my benefactors at Tokyo University, has been mentioned above. Valdo Viglielmo of the University of Hawaii is a student of modern Japanese literature and an old friend.

If indeed it was suicide, then my explanation for it remains very much as it was at the time. "The question everyone is asking, of course, is why he did it. Some say it was because of illness, some because of the Nobel Prize [which kept him too busy to do his real work], some because of Mishima. To me the most likely explanation is that he was very tired and could not sleep.

"But probably, in the final analysis, the only thing one can say is: 'I don't understand it. I just don't understand it.'"

The words in the single quotation marks are Mrs. Kawabata's. She repeated them over and over again on the night of the death. I would add only that if it was suicide, I feel strongly that it was impulsive. Mishima planned his death carefully, towards the most dramatic possible effect. Kawabata, I think, planned his not at all. This is perhaps another reason for thinking it might have been in some sense accidental. He may not have known what he was doing.

The night of the sixteenth, a Sunday, and the days following were as completely dominated by the media as the days of the Nobel excitement had been. Most of my friends had the news by television. Subtitles were imposed on whatever program was in progress.

The following are excerpts from my diary entry for April 18, the first entry after the event. "It was when I came back up the hill, at about eleven, that I had my first news. The telephone was ringing as I came in.

It was a *Sankei* reporter. Needless to say, the shock was considerable. Mishima had given us plenty of inklings; Kawabata, as far as I was aware, gave us not a one. . . .

"I was on the telephone until one in the morning, and reporters have been after me all the hours since. . . . In the initial agitation I said yes to everything I was asked to write, and afterwards I had trouble remembering what all the things might be. In any event they have occupied all my spare hours since, and destroyed a good part of my sleep as well.

"On Sunday night I got no sleep at all. Among the journalists who called was Miss Ibuki [of Chūō Kōron]. She had a car, she said, and was going down to Kamakura, and she suggested that it would be a good idea if I were to go to Kamakura too. So she came by for me, and we were in Kamakura at two in the morning. The lane leading into the Kawabata house was jammed, and there must have been a hundred automobiles parked out on the main Hase street. The flashing of bulbs and thrusting of microphones was horrendous, and the television cameras were so bright that it was next to impossible to avoid the mud puddles.

"Within the gates all was quiet. Numbers of people had gathered . . . and discussion of the funeral arrangements was in progress. When first I offered incense there was a towel over the face. When, an hour or more later, I was invited to say farewell, the towel had been taken away. The face was calm, there seemed no discoloration. I would be tempted to say that he looked as if he were asleep but for the fact that I never saw him asleep, and that the absence of those extraordinary eyes made the face very different."

Another little trick of memory is to be observed here. I had, as I have indicated above, seen him asleep, on the airplane to Copenhagen in 1968. When asleep he had looked as if he were dead, and, dead, he looked as if he were asleep.

On Monday night, the seventeenth, "sleepless since Sunday morning, down to Kamakura again, again with Miss Ibuki, this time to attend the wake.

"The wake, at which vast numbers of celebrated persons were, most naturally, present, was very different from the Tanizaki wake. That was almost fun. This was hushed and stiff, with everyone keeping to himself. There were Buddhist services. The Buddhism of our day is not very elegant. The priests, though from one of the grander Buddhist centers, . . . seemed rustic and uncouth. And oh the photographers. If reporters are unpleasant fellows, photographers are worse, refusing even to dress as a sad and solemn occasion demands, and looking as if they were recent graduates of extortionist gangs."

Although I do not mention her in my diary, I have a vivid recollection from that night of a person who was particularly withdrawn, Mishima's widow. We were most of us out in the garden from which we could hear the services in the open house. She hid in the underbrush. I do not think that there was anything affected about this. She had had enough of photographers and reporters.

On April 20 there is a mildly interesting summation of it all. "Yesterday evening and again this evening I went down the hill for a bedtime drink. . . . People recognize me, uniformly saying that they have seen me on television. I appeared on television for perhaps ten minutes, and my picture has been in I know not how many newspapers and magazines, sometimes very conspicuously."

A fortnight later, early in May, there are further observations on the Kawabata death. "I have thought I have understood, these last few days, why aging people commit suicide in the spring, and I have thought too that I have come to understand more of Mr. Kawabata's suicide. Below my window all is life. The *keyaki [Zelkovia serrata]* over beyond the Iwasaki house are, with the wind riffling through them, a wonderfully fresh spring green. Over in the second lot to the south of me, where recently the tearing down of a house fascinated me, the putting up of a house has been equally interesting. The way in which the carpenters seem to go each his own way, with no consultation and no cooperation and yet a house emerges, is very interesting indeed, but above all it is a scene of great vitality. I have thought how nice it would be to find one's purpose in squatting half naked in the spring sun and banging nails into a roof.

"And that is the thing: to feel life all around you, and to feel none in yourself. At least I have my *Genji* to go back to. [I was at the time engaged in translating *The Tale of Genji.]* I swear that tomorrow I will go back to it. Apparently, to judge from a letter Harold Strauss recently had from him, Mr. Kawabata did not have that much. He had kept his royalties in the United States, expecting to go there again, but in the letter, written perhaps two or three weeks before his suicide, he asked to have them sent to Japan, because, he said, he was too tired to think of going abroad again, and indeed too tired to think that he would ever do more writing.

"I have said that I think I understand the suicide better, but what it comes down to is that my original view, spontaneous and so I suppose instinctive, finds support. An aged gentleman was very tired and longed for sleep. There was an interesting article in the *Asahi* this morning on the relationship, indirect, between sleeping medicine and suicide. Sleeping medicine can lead to addiction and change of personality, and presently to desperation. Might it be that the stuff, no longer strong enough to put him to sleep, contributed to the diminution of his powers? I am glad that my addiction is to alcohol—which *does* put me to sleep."

I have three dozen letters from Kawabata. The earliest which I can precisely date is from 1953. Another may possibly be older. It is dated June 1, but no year is indicated. This is commonly the case with letters in Japanese. I do not know why. Perhaps it has to do with the Japanese national agony we keep hearing about. They are torn between East and West, and it may be that they are torn between the cumbersome old system and the much easier new or Western system, associated, alas, with a foreign god. The lunar calendar prevailed until 1873.

The 1953 letter is about the Dazai translations I did for *Encounter.* The other is about my translation of Kawabata's own *The Izu Dancer,* which I had either translated or was thinking of translating. Specifically, it concerns the ages of the principal characters. This is an important matter, in which, once again, the conflicting pulls of East and West figure. The question is: how old are the principal characters? What could be simpler, comes the response. If the author tells us, believe him. If he does not, forget about it. The trouble is that he does, but does not say whether he is calculating by the old system or the new. Under the old system the count was of the number of years in which a person had lived, so that if the person was born on New Year's Eve the count was two the following day. The new system is as in the West, the count of full years, birthday to birthday.

The count was the old one, he assured me, and so I should take one or two years, depending on birthdays, from the age given. He did not himself know when the dancer's birthday was, although there was an actual model. I was glad that he did not suggest that I write to her and find out. I happily subtracted a year from the sixteen which the hero thought her to be. The matter is not insignificant. At the outset he is strongly drawn to her sexually, and presently he discovers that she has not yet reached puberty. I was glad to have Kawabata to ask, but would probably have deducted the year anyway. She is at a delicate stage, and fifteen makes the mistake more probable than sixteen.

About two-thirds of the letters are written with the traditional brush on Japanese paper, the remainder in pen on Western manuscript paper. Kawabata was an accomplished and famous calligrapher, and such persons make a thing of illegibility. I do not know why, since it is far less important with their Chinese mentors. In any case most of my Kawabata letters are beautiful to look at but impractical. They do not succeed immediately in their initial purpose, to communicate. I was able, with time, to read all of them unassisted, with a single exception.

For that one I consulted an expert, and not even he was able to make out everything. It is the most interesting of the three dozen, not so much because of the contents as because of the appearance and the time. The date is March 5, 1971. Addressed to Ann Arbor, it is the first communication I had from him after Mishima's death. The writing is highly disordered, and it is hard to think the disorder intentional. The ink—it is written with brush—is frequently blotted. Even the address on the envelope is obscure. Ann Arbor is not specified, though Michigan and its university are. He does not see his way, he says, to recovering from the sorrow of Mishima's death. "We have lost a novelist and an important critic." The writing tells more than the words do about the shock of Mishima's death.

I find only three letters from him during the three and a half years between the Nobel Prize and his death. The last, written only two months and a few days before his own death, and about a month before our last meeting, is altogether less disordered. It speaks of the weather and my translation of *The Master of Go,* which came out that year. There is no mention of Mishima. I have no doubt that he was in great distress when he wrote the 1971 letter. That he had much recovered in the year following seems equally clear. I am inclined to doubt, therefore, that the Mishima death was crucial in his own decision to die, if there was such a decision.

I may have made it seem that the deaths of Tanizaki and Kawabata cut great holes in my life and made Tokyo much less of a pleasure then it had been. I missed them, certainly, Kawabata more than Tanizaki, because he was more accessible and I saw more of him. The other death that spring of 1972, however, Hirabayashi Taiko's, made more of a difference. I would not have gone to either of the two men if I needed help, except maybe with literary things, such as copyrights. I would have gone to her, however, even as I would have gone to some of my American wartime friends, such as Owen Zurhellen. She too was a wartime friend, the war being that of the fifties, with the intellies. I still miss her, as I have never, really, missed either of the two men. I can still hear her voice, even as I can still hear that of her happy mynah bird.

Back in Ann Arbor, the work for which I was paid was of course teaching. The Michigan years were my happiest ones as a teacher, because of the students. As for the university, it was a college in the original sense of the word, a gathering of like-minded people. Stanford and Palo Alto were a scattering; Columbia was dwarfed by New York City.

The work for which I was not paid was translation, and far and away my largest translation was of *The Tale of Genji.* I did presently get an advance from Knopf, and royalties in the years since have amounted to a sum that would have seen me through the years at which I was at work on the translation. I did not have them at the time, however. Initially it was a labor of love. Japanese are always surprised at my answer to a frequently asked question, what Japanese writer is the most widely read in the English-speaking world. Murasaki Shikibu, I reply. This is the author (a lady, not that I think it matters much) of the *Genji.* She lived a thousand years ago. I speak from only my own experience. The *Genji* translation has brought me more money than all my other translations combined.

I first heard of the *Genji* before the war, during my years at the University of Colorado. It came to pass that in the dormitory room next door to me was Matthew Huxley, the son of Aldous. I may have heard of the latter, but I had never read anything by him. So I started reading such things. In *After Many a Summer* I came upon a reference to the *Genji.* I found a copy of it in our (as a Harvard student in the language school put it) adequate little library. This was of course the Arthur Waley translation—the library had scarcely anything in Japanese. I took it out, noting that not many people had taken it out earlier and that it was very long; and I took it back.

It was not until during the war, when I had become deeply involved with Japan, that I read it, again in the Waley translation. I found it a most wonderful work, dating from a time when scarcely anything was being written in Europe, and scarcely any prose fiction had been written anywhere. I could think of no work in English literature (it may be remembered that I was an English major) that had such frequent and delicate references to nature, and nothing down to Shakespeare that had such vivid characters—and Shakespeare did not write prose fiction. It may be that I would have found something of the sort in Chaucer, who lived almost half a millennium later than Murasaki, but I did not do well with Chaucer.

My first considerable work of translation was from slightly earlier in the Heian Period than the *Genji*. When I was doing the earlier work I may have thought vaguely that the only brave and honorable thing would be to have a go at the supreme masterpiece. The thought was, however, most inchoate. For one thing, it is a long and very difficult work, full of passages that people pretend to understand—but no one really does, completely. For another thing, there was the Waley. I had and continue to have great admiration for it. I seek to make this clear in the introduction to my translation. There would be no point in following in his shadow if one did not hope to emerge from it, and this seemed a daunting task indeed. One of the most perceptive comments, and quite probably the most discouraging, during my years at work on the translation, came from Donald Keene. "I would rather do the sixteenth translation than the second."

I am not aware that I ever resolved to do the whole translation. I sidled into it. I began doing bits of it during my Stanford years. Having puzzled out passages I meant to go through with students, I thought it a waste not to set a translation down on paper. The time spent in doing so would be paltry compared to that spent on puzzling. I did so. They were from the last chapters, held by most Japanese specialists to be the best. I agreed at the time. I am no longer sure that I do. I now think I like the chapters before Genji's (Genji is the appellation, a family name, by which the hero is known) disappearance from the scene better than those that follow; but then it is quite possible to recognize one work as the great masterpiece of its kind and like another work better. I like the Mozart masses better, though I accept the claim that Bach and Beethoven masses are the supreme masterpieces.

Early in my Michigan years I gave a lecture called "A Decade for the *Genji*." It was not to announce my resolve to do a translation. It was to ask my audience whether that seemed like a good idea. About a decade is what it took. The translation was finished early in 1975. Not the whole of the decade went into the translation. I translated quite a bit of Kawabata and Mishima's last novel in the course of the putative decade.

I thought to do only the last ten chapters, isolated and reasonably independent following the sudden disappearance of Genji from the scene. I announce the completion of them in my diary on March 30, 1971. I say on April Fool's Day that they are "in the hands of the gods now, which is to say, Harold Strauss and the postal authorities."

I had gone to Strauss for advice. I did not expect him to be interested in the manuscript. He had told me that Knopf did not publish translations of classics. I wanted advice on what other publisher I might most hopefully make inquiry of. Strauss, like others among us, did not speak and behave with complete consistency. In addition to giving me his position on translations of classics, he had recently rejected Ivan Morris's translation of what the Japanese consider the other prose masterpiece of their Heian Period, *The Pillow Book.* One does not reprove inconsistency when the results are so benevolent. One looks upon it as lovably human.

Strauss's reply to my query was: "Well, now. A new translation of the *Genji* is another matter." He did not, however, like the idea of publishing the last chapters first. I must do the whole thing. So once again, I suppose it may be said, I had my mind made up for me. As in other similar instances, I am grateful.

"A letter came from Harold Strauss," says my diary entry for April 3, 1972. "He is having a contract drawn up. My deadline is to be the first of July, nineteen hundred and seventy-five. I think I can make it, provided I have not by then ruined my liver."

I did make it, with months to spare. I mailed the finished translation in January 1975. It was published, two very handsome volumes, almost eleven hundred pages, the following year. My favorite anecdote in that regard is a little exchange with my friend Dick Rabinowitz, an American lawyer who used to practice in Tokyo.

"How much does it cost, Ed?"

"Twenty-five dollars."

"That's terrible."

"Think of it as seven thousand yen."

"That's nothing."

Which tells us much about the workings of exchanges. The dollar buys more than its exchange equivalent in yen. Exchange rates are concerned with the demand for currencies and not their purchasing power. This is why this Japanese person or that bank is said to be the richest or largest in the world, and really is not. It is because monetary worth is calculated according to exchange rates, generally in dollar terms.

The reviews were on the whole friendly. I liked the English ones best, not because they were friendlier, but because they seemed more intelligent. The American ones sometimes got things wrong. "Casanova, Don Juan, the Earl of Rochester, Humbert Humbert, and Hugh Hefner's Playboy fantasy life pale by comparison" with Genji and his affairs. This is from the *New York Times.* Genji was not remarkably promiscuous by the standards of a polygamous society, and if we are to accept Leporello's count in *Don Giovanni,* and there seems no compelling reason not to, he was a very inactive sort of philanderer by comparison with Don Juan.

I liked C. P. Snow's review best. It appeared in the *Financial Times.* The judgment that my translation is the nearer of the two to the original "the rest of us will have to take on trust. But one is entitled to say that if there is a gain in fidelity there is no loss at all in literary effect." I had expected English reviewers to be a bit on the prod, defending the Waley translation. I detected nothing of the sort.

It should be clear from chapter 4 above that my rambles among the intellies have not been completely safe from assault. There has been some pettiness in the reception of my translations, but on the whole it has been friendly. The unfriendliness has been annoying, no worse. People send lists of mistakes in my translations, and I do not doubt that other translators have been similarly favored. Critics who should know better write niggling reviews and give niggling lectures. They will skim through a translation in search of place names, for instance, and, finding that not all those of the original are present in the translation, triumphantly proclaim the translation a bad one. I frankly confess that the temptation to cut names that will mean nothing to the reader is sometimes irresistible.

The most annoying element in these insignificant endeavors is the implication that Japanese literature has been worse treated by translators than foreign literatures translated into Japanese. I am very confident that if anyone would take the trouble it could be demonstrated that the incidence of mistakes in translation into Japanese is far higher than in translation out of it. But who will take the trouble? Not I, certainly.

On the whole my translations have been received gratefully, and for this I am most grateful.

EIGHT

CLOSING THE CIRCLE

AND WHAT DOES IT SIGNIFY, this closing of the circle?

It refers to the fact that the Chinese ordered the succession of years in sexagenary cycles, or circles, of sixty years each. So too, in greater or lesser degree, did the peoples who fell within the Chinese cultural sphere, including the Japanese. For this huge part of the human race, the century is a new-fangled concept, introduced to be in harmony with people from far away who happened to be more advanced economically a hundred years or so ago. The word *kanreki* signifies the sixtieth birthday and the beginning of a new circle.

I had my *kanreki* in Palo Alto on February 11, 1981. My life has been gradually less interesting since the departure of the eminent writers I knew. A certain loss of interest is to be detected. There is less to write about.

I have lived through the whole of one Chinese cycle. Not everyone can say this, for the beginning and end of a cycle can come midway through a lifetime. I was born near the beginning of a cycle, and my sixtieth birthday came near the end of that cycle. The Chinese sexagenary system begins in 2697 B.C. So my cycle was the seventy-eighth, which began in 1924 and ended in 1983. I was three years old in the course of the year in which it began, and sixty-three in the course of that in which it ended. I used to wonder whether it was by intent that George Orwell gave his masterpiece the date of the first year in a Chinese sexagenary cycle. Inquiry seems to establish that it was not. In my case, the dislocation was only three years. My sister and a favorite cousin, Elizabeth Boyer, already mentioned, both born in 1924, had it perfect. It seems a pity that neither had a *kanreki* celebration.

Ivan Morris, a leading student and translator of Japanese literature, and at the time a professor at Columbia, died suddenly in Italy in the summer of 1976. Our relations were somewhat strained in his last years, but he had been a good friend, and I generally stayed in his very beautiful apartment on Riverside Drive on visits to New York.

During the last decade of his life, a certain coolness grew up between us. Some years before his death, when he was head of the East Asian Department at Columbia, there was an interesting development. Donald Keene decided that he wished to teach only one semester a year. He asked if I would be willing to come to Columbia as a tenured professor and alternate with him, I to take the autumn semester, and he the spring semester. I was delighted. Ever since *my* year there just after the war, I had thought of Columbia as my university, and then there was the prospect, most exciting (and to me not in the least frightening), of living in New York. I accepted with alacrity.

Then Morris decided that he himself wished to alternate with Keene. Perhaps because of his important administrative position, his wish prevailed. I thought, and still think, that I was treated shabbily. As if by way of compensation, Morris suggested that I come to Columbia as an untenured professor. This doubled and tripled the feelings of having been put upon.

I was in Tokyo when news of his death came. I was in close enough touch with the people in the department at Columbia, and especially with Keene, who was also in Tokyo, to have some sense that I would be invited to replace him. In September, when I was back in Colorado, a telephone call came from Columbia. Would I take over one of Morris's courses for the fall term?

Perhaps it was small of me, but again I was insulted. "Were I to do so," I say in my diary for September 3, "I would have to be in New York one day a week all semester. It seems rather wonderful that Columbia should have enough confidence and prestige to think of such a thing. I doubt that the thought would have come to us in provincial, humble Michigan. I said no, of course."

In 1975 I received the Order of the Rising Sun. It was only a Third Class decoration. Donald Keene had received the same Third Class decoration some time earlier. His was later raised to Second Class. First Class is reserved for people like Reischauer. I have never been raised from Third Class. After receiving the decoration, I went off to Honolulu for some weeks. I had at the time an apartment in Honolulu, a rented one, the second floor of my friend Jack Kerr's little house, a remodeled stable, in Makiki Heights, one of the most beautiful parts of Honolulu. People sometimes said that, given the very modest rent, it was the best rental in the state of Hawaii. I was inclined to agree.

While I was in residence there, plans proceeded for a congratulatory gathering in Tokyo. It occurred on October 8, in a Tokyo hotel.

Here is a part of my diary entry for the evening: "The speeches . . . were uniformly sweet and kind. I liked Mrs. Tanizaki's best. She said that I was like [Tanizaki] in that I translated Murasaki Shikibu, was a true son of Edo, and liked cats. Miss Muramatsu and Saeki were both very witty, and the former remarked . . . on my having declined the emperor's invitation . . . and so now everyone knows, and that is very nice." Muramatsu Hideko and Saeki Shōichi were the joint masters of ceremony.

The details of how I stood the emperor up are these. Towards the end of my stay in Honolulu there came an invitation to a dinner in Washington honoring the Shōwa emperor and empress, on their only visit to the United States. To accept would, I thought, have meant changing the plans for the Tokyo celebration. Bitter though the regrets were, I thought that I had only one choice. When I returned to Tokyo I learned that the date of the celebration had been changed. This of course added to the bitterness. I could have attended both affairs.

At some time during the academic year of 1976 and 1977, I was invited to go permanently to Columbia. Although my dealings with Columbia in recent years had somewhat diminished my affection, I was eager to go. I told people that I did not want especially to go to Columbia, and certainly was not happy to leave Michigan. It was to New York, rather, that I wanted to go. The remark suffers from a certain glibness, but there is much truth in it.

Michigan, once more, was very kind. It did everything it could think of to make me stay, and asked frequently if there was anything that had been overlooked. We finally hit upon a compromise. I would go to New York for a trial year. If my decision was that I wished to stay, I could then resign from the Michigan faculty. So it was arranged.

And because it was so arranged, I once again had my mind made up for me. Not long after my arrival in New York I had a call from Marjorie Petring, secretary of the East Asian Languages and Cultures Department at Michigan. She wished to know my decision, she said, because if I was going to stay at Columbia, she must quickly get down to the business of finding a successor at Michigan. So, scarcely thinking, I told her to do so at her earliest convenience. A strong and efficient secretary, she had in effect canceled the commitments undertaken by her chairman and dean. I was grateful. When I am going through a time of indecision, I like having my mind made up for me.

In such diary entries as I have from the autumn, my first at Columbia, the words "inefficient" and "unfriendly" occur with much frequency. They characterize Columbia. In the entry for December 30, I say: "I remarked upon the fact that I do not yet feel, really feel, at home here in New York. 'It is *for* people who do not feel at home,' said Herschel. 'I have never felt at home myself, and that is one of the reasons why I like it.'" Herschel Webb was a historian of Japan who died suddenly one Sunday during my years at Columbia. Though not at all well organized, he was an intelligent and amusing fellow.

I was not wholly honest in the remark that brought on Herschel's bon mot. I meant not New York but Columbia, and probably could not bring myself to say so to someone whose whole academic career had been at Columbia. Only a fool would deny that New York has its defects, but I have loved it ever since my first visit, in the course of my first visit to the Atlantic seaboard, when I went to Washington to be interviewed for admission to the Japanese Language School. During my New York years I was frequently heard to say that I had an ideal arrangement. I taught there only one semester, and so I was free to spend as much of the rest of the year as I chose in Tokyo. So, I would say, I was commuting between the two most interesting cities in the world. I grant that this is no better than arguable. Many would say that Paris, London, Rome, and so forth, have among them a city or two of more interest than either New York or Tokyo. So perhaps I exaggerated. It is, all the same, how I felt.

Columbia was another matter. Disorganized and unfriendly it did indeed seem. In both regards Michigan was much its superior. The gracelessness of the early invitations to teach there had led to the beginnings of a suspicion that, all these years, I had thought of Columbia as *my* university because of dear old Mr. Tsunoda, who was then in his grave more than a dozen years. I did not, however, regret having moved to New York. If Columbia were to find grounds for dismissing me and Ann Arbor were willing to take me back I would go, and not unhappily. This was unlikely to happen, however, and I had no thought of resigning.

The quotation from the wit and wisdom of Herschel Webb is followed by a soliloquy that refers again to the Chinese circle or cycle. There are two lesser cycles in it, one of a dozen years, and one of ten. The years of the dozen are designated by the creatures, real and mythical, of the Chinese zodiac. Thus the year of my birth, 1921, was what I like to call the Year of the Chicken, though others prefer Cockerel, or Chanticleer, or something. (There is not the smallest touch of male chauvinism in Year of the Chicken.) It chanced to be the case that 1978, when I would have to get myself moved to New York, was the Year of the Horse.

"An interesting thought came to me a little while ago. The Year of the Horse seems to be, for me, moving year. Next year, as I believe is well known to all readers of this document, I must get myself moved from Ann Arbor to this New York. In 1966, I moved from Palo Alto to Ann Arbor. In 1954, I am fairly sure, I moved into my Hayashi-chō house, the only one I have ever owned. In 1942, the move was perhaps more spiritual than physical: I left English behind and began my pursuit of Japanese. But in 1930, my first Year of the Horse, I doubt that much of anything at all happened, save that I moved into that cheery south room in Castle Rock Grade School." The south room, which I think I have not mentioned, had much the best view of autumn colors. Colorado may not have much foliage, but what it has is fine in the autumn.

During my first term at Columbia I used Donald Keene's apartment, for he was away, high up by Harlem on Riverside Drive. Early the following year, before I went out to Tokyo, I got myself moved from Ann Arbor, and while I was about it got myself a different place in New York. It was farther down on the drive, just below the main Columbia gate. Upon his return to New York, Keene moved into the same apartment. He still has it. Ours was a Box and Cox arrangement. The two of us were never together in New York for more than a few days a year.

It must be said that Columbia was not in every respect disorganized and unfriendly. It did very well by me in the matter of housing. The apartment which Keene and I shared was a fine one. It was spacious, with a turn-of-the-century dignity and a beautiful view—out over Riverside Drive and the Hudson, and on to the New Jersey Palisades. There have been some attempts along the New Jersey shore to disfigure the Hudson, but it remains a very beautiful river.

When my possessions, including what excuse I have for an art collection, arrived from Ann Arbor, I was devastated. Nothing was damaged. The truck driver was a Maine Yankee in whom I had complete confidence, and he proved worthy of it. My best-loved Korean vase was missing, however. The collection is almost entirely ceramics and almost entirely Korean and Chinese. In this regard I have preferred the continent to Japan. I once mentioned my fondness for Korean things to a famous Tokyo art dealer. "But Korean things are so sad," he said. "They look up at you and say if you won't be nice to me no one will." I knew what he meant, and was reminded of my cat, Hanako. Of her more later. The vase was white ware of the Yi Period, decorated in cobalt with a bird madly singing in a tree. It had already had a curious career when it came to my attention, and what had happened to it in its earlier couple of centuries is beyond my knowing.

My good Honolulu friend Jack Kerr had bought it in Japan before the war. He gave it to the Honolulu Academy of Arts in memory of Sir George Sansom, of whom he was as fond as I. The academy "deacquisitioned" it. I thought then and I think still that there was malice in the decision of the director to do so. He and Jack were not on good terms.

Jack was able to find who had bought it. The person was a Chinese. Jack went to him and asked if he would sell it back. He was very civilized. He said he would sell it back at the price he had paid for it. Jack was in dire straits at the time, and did not have the money. So he asked me to buy it. I did, and it entered my modest collection, and quickly became one of my favorite pieces. I was willing to let Jack have it back. He said that he would think about it when enough money to repay what I had paid came his way. Either it never did, or he forgot. So it went with me to Ann Arbor, and then in 1977 or 1978 it disappeared.

So that was that, for a number of years. They included my New York years and several of my Honolulu years. I did not easily reconcile myself to the loss. Indeed I am not sure that I ever did completely. "And where, if ever, will I find my Korean nightingale?" I ask in my diary on February 10, 1978. "I try not to think about it, but sometimes the yearning is so intense that I feel sure I am about to come upon it, just over there."

Then one Honolulu day there came a call from an old Korean friend, Choo-won Suh (actually she is a naturalized American), who works in the university library in Ann Arbor. In process of moving she had found it in her garage.

This came as a huge relief, in more than one way. I was delighted, of course, to know where the dear bird was, and I was relieved of dark suspicions. I had given myself a big farewell party, scores of guests, just before I left Ann Arbor to go out to Tokyo and then to New York. It was winter, and the hall outside my door was a mountain of overcoats. I thought that someone had put the bird in the mountain and then, upon departing, concealed it in his or her overcoat. So one of my friends had to be the culprit. This was a painful thought—though I tried to take comfort in the further thought that whoever had taken it would be kind to it. Now I knew that this had not happened.

Choo-won had no notion how it got to her garage. I have a persuasive theory. I took it there and then forgot that I had done so. I left other things with her, and I can well have separated it from them, giving special treatment to a special object. That sort of thing is usually a bad idea, because I forget. At any rate, there it was. Choo Won did not want to put it in the hands of the post office or other shipping agencies. It had suffered enough tribulations already. So, if I did not mind waiting, a Honolulu boy on her staff would be going home for Christmas holidays and she could have him carry it. He did, and it was without question my best Christmas present that year.

When I am gone it will return to the Honolulu Academy and round out a circle in its own career. The academy assures me that it is a worthy addition to the Korean collection, as indeed it is, and will not be deacquisitioned again. The fact that it is a better piece than some of the ones now on display strengthens my suspicion that there was malice in the heart of the director who deacquisitioned it. I think the story of my Korean nightingale a somewhat wondrous one.

When I had finished the *Genji* translation, I started on a novel, an eccentric sort of novel. It is an epistolary novel, and the form is not much in vogue these days. The correspondents are three in number: a young Japanese woman who works for a big trading company and is central, an American newspaperman on whom she has a crush, and an American university professor, a woman, whom she thinks a comrade in arms. The battle is for women's rights, although the American woman is by no means completely committed to the cause. The principal setting is Tokyo. A secondary one is Kyoto.

I finished it early in my New York years. I set about finding a publisher. I thought that, after all we had been through together, Knopf would be understanding of its eccentricities. This did not prove to be the case. The editor to whom I sent it found it facetious and rejected it out of hand. I myself thought it pretty humorous, and could only stamp my little foot and say that one person's humor is another person's facetiousness.

He also found the characterization flat. I thought it rather subtle, and could point out a number of Knopf novels in which it was much flatter. This of course was to no avail. I was no more successful with other publishers. A New York agent told me that it was original, amusing, and unpublishable. I wrote back that if a book can be all three things simultaneously, then American publishing does not look very good. I got no answer. I finally had it published in England, at my expense.

The title, *Very Few People Come This Way,* is from Edward Lear, and anyone familiar with Lear can see his influence everywhere, and that of Lewis Carroll as well. Indeed I think of it as in the nonsense tradition. There is good nonsense writing and there is bad, and the good, as in Lear and Carroll, has its own mad reasons. I thought that people would see what I was up to, even without explanation, and I offered none.

A few did, many did not. Even the unfriendly editor at Knopf liked the "poems," intentionally bad ones, with which it is dotted, but he disdained reading the whole work in a similar vein. There was a very disappointing response from James Laughlin, a scholar of poetry and himself a poet. He wondered why I had translated what must have been beautiful originals into such dreadful doggerel. I had thought no one could conceivably believe that there were originals, and that everyone would see that the doggerel had a certain nonsensical point.

Enough of that. I go on thinking the work rather good, certainly much better than many things that find publishers, but there is little point in arguing. It is satire, and the media these days have little place for satire, and it is in very intimate juxtaposition with Japan, a place not many people feel much intimacy towards.

I produced three other novels during my New York years, and have found publishers for none of them. Clearly I do not have the touch, though once again I may state it as my conviction that far worse things have been published.

I have done no long translation since *The Tale of Genji,* and think I probably never will do another. The modern Japanese writers I would like to translate are the ones I have already translated, especially Kawabata and Tanizaki. I think I got the best pickings in both cases, and, in any event, the greatest Japanese writer is neither of them but rather Murasaki Shikibu. After her great work anything would be anticlimax. Everything, furthermore, would be easier, and translation, as I have noted, quickly becomes a bore when it is easy. Struggling with a difficult text may not be fun, exactly, but it is absorbing. Many a modern work is difficult because sloppily written, but that is quite a different matter. Murasaki is difficult because her language is remote and because she left so much unsaid. She left so much to the reader. Many find this exasperating, but I find it most generous of her.

Japan is not alone these days in being without giants. Many another country is that way. I think myself that the last American giants were Harry Truman, Dean Acheson, and George Marshall. A sharp-tongued and very intelligent Japanese lady politician recently described the three candidates for the premiership as a mediocrity, a trooper, and an oddball. This caught the matter rather well. So too is the world of letters, without giants. The last universally recognized one was probably Tanizaki. I may find the literary world rather lonely without giants, but there is little I can do except decline to do much of anything. Thirty years ago I found literary gatherings exciting. I no longer do. There are a great many speeches not worth listening to. Nor do I find anything that seems worth the trouble, and it is trouble even when easy and boring, to translate.

What has brought this condition upon us? I blame television for many of the evils of the world, and I am inclined to believe that it is largely responsible for this one too. It is with writers as with the ladies of the night. For the latter it is far easier to be a bar girl than a geisha of the old highly honed sort. For a young person with a flair for words, it is easier to become a television "talent" (the English word is used), and the measure in which the performer has real talent is of little concern. And people do not read as they once did. A printed page is not as much fun to look at, perhaps, as a lush television image.

There is no point in lamenting this state of affairs, and it is by no means an exclusively Japanese one. The fact is that they who once, with justification, called the Japanese a nation of readers can no longer do so. And literary giants tend to be sensitive creatures requiring an audience.

I also produced some nonfiction during my New York years, but it takes us beyond the rounding of the circle. I wrote a two-volume cultural history of Tokyo from 1868, when it became Tokyo, down to the completion of the second volume, after I had moved from New York to Honolulu. The first, *Low City, High City,* the title deriving from the plebeian flatlands and the moneyed highlands of the city, was published in 1983, two years after the circle was rounded. The second, *Tokyo Rising,* the title this time referring to the recovery of the city from utter ruin, after the earthquake of 1923 and again after the fire bombings of 1945, was published in 1990.

Knopf, which had a higher regard for my nonfiction than for my fiction, published both of them. The first volume ends with the earthquake; the second comes down to what was the present at the time of writing. Both received friendly reviews. The *New Yorker* said that the second was "popularization of a very high order." This seemed to me perhaps somewhat faint praise. I suspect that the reviewer was told by a New York specialist or two that it was popularization.

The time has come to explain why the remark of the Tokyo dealer about Korean art reminded me of my cat. I bought a cat, a female Siamese, in June 1978. I know exactly when it was, because I was on my way back from the Torigoe Festival, just south of Asakusa in Tokyo, when I espied her. The Torigoe is my favorite among the "summer festivals" of Tokyo, many of which are in what most of us would call spring. The famous ones, like the Sanja in Asakusa proper, have become sights for sightseers. They are cordoned off by the police and crowds come from afar to see. The Torigoe still has a communal quality to it, and it can be somewhat violent. More than once I have been trampled underfoot, though I have escaped without injury. Once I found myself flattened in a vat of water lilies. I love it.

I was on my way home from the Torigoe when I passed a pet shop. In a cage on the sidewalk in front of it was a litter of Siamese kittens. There is an expression, "St. Luke's pig," referring to the inevitable runt in a litter of piglets. She was St. Luke's kitten. She looked up at me and spoke to me, and the effect was exactly that of a Korean work of art on the art dealer. She seemed to be saying that if I was not nice to her no one would be. I was sure that she was right. I was sure that if I did not buy her she would soon be put to death. I debated the matter for an evening, and the next day went back and bought her. Probably because she was so unpromising a kitten she did not cost much. Veterinary bills were to come to many times the initial outlay.

She was very thin and weak, and I did not expect her to last long under my care; and she lasted seventeen years, a long life, I am told, for a Siamese, not a long-lived species. When, presently, the pedigree papers came I learned that she was born on March 3, the Girls' Festival, or Doll Festival, a lovely day, I think, for a female kitten to be born. If she had lived two days longer, she would have died on May 5, Boys' Day. This would have given her, I think, a richly symbolic life. I named her Hanako, after my favorite member of the Japanese royal family.

She was a moody, ill-tempered, somewhat violent little creature, not really very lovable. Yet I was very fond of her. She was pronounced in her dislikes. She disliked women. She was an indoor cat, but on days when the cleaning woman came I tried to take her out walking, on a leash, to make things easier for the cleaning woman. She dragged her paws every step of the way, until she saw a policeman, when she sprang to the offensive. She also disliked policemen. I would be hard put to say how she recognized policemen, but she did. Others of her dislikes were less well defined. One day an editor came calling. He left with a bloody nose, administered by Hanako.

A big event in Hanako's life, probably her nearest approach to celebritydom, although I doubt that she remembered it for very long, occurred on May 16, 1980. A monthly magazine called *Engekikai, The World of the Theater,* learned of her existence and her name, and pointed out that the Kabuki actor Nakamura Utaemon had a dog by the same name. Might we arrange a meeting between them? I was happy to oblige, and Utaemon, probably the most highly regarded of living Kabuki actors, offered no objection. He lives way down at the southern limit of the city. I took Hanako by taxi, and the meeting occurred.

"Hanako was very nervous all the way," I say in my diary, "but after we arrived she behaved beautifully, and I think that the meeting was a great success. . . . Utaemon was, as of course everything I knew about him would have led me to expect, every bit as beautifully behaved as Hanako."

Pictures and a descriptive article appeared in the next issue of *Engekikai.* The best picture, Utaemon and the two beasts and I, sits on a shelf in my parlor. The dog looks very interested in Hanako, she looks suspicious. I am not sure what sort of dog it was (or is, if it yet survives, which does not seem likely), but it seems to be a small terrier, perhaps a Yorkshire. I do not doubt that, like Hanako, it had pedigree papers. I cannot imagine Utaemon having a lesser sort of dog.

I had a dinner engagement on the evening of May 3, 1995, a holiday, the anniversary of the promulgation of the present constitution. Hanako was grievously wasted and refused to eat, and I knew that the end was near. As I stepped out the door to keep the engagement. I heard a clattering from the room in which I had left her. I went back in. She had climbed from her basket and upset the bowl of water beside it. I dried her and put her back in the basket, and she was gone.

And that is the story of my Hanako.

In a diary entry late in June, 1978, I mention a meeting with my old friend Fukuda Tsuneari, the intellectual I admired most among them all. "It will soon be a quarter of a century since he wrote his famous article on the pacifists. It has gone by in a hurry, that quarter of a century, and seen the fairly complete dispersion of the pacifists from the center of the stage."

But something new was coming along. Back in 1959 I had been advised by a very wise Japanese, Takeyama Michio, that the great wave of the "progressive" was receding. I came only gradually, with time, to see that this was true. As early as 1967, when I accepted the receding of the tide as fact and thought that happy days lay ahead, I was informed of this new something, by another very wise Japanese, and only afterwards, and again gradually, came to accept it as a genuine threat. It need not surprise us that wise Japanese have a better sense for such things than I do. Yet I am sorry that it is so. I am made to feel obtuse.

The second of the two was Fukuda. I will quote the whole of the message on his New Year card for 1967, pausing only to say that it is a very Japanese card and a very handsome one, a pattern of fans and waves in dark blue on a white ground, the paper finished to resemble woven fabric. Rare among the cards and letters I had from him, it is in English.

"Now, I am afraid the way of ours, the liberals', might be narrowed between the left & the right hereafter in Japan. Anyway, I have just finished the last volume of *my* Shakespeare, which will be published next February. If you have any interest in Japanese version of Shakespeare, that is a poetry-robbed poetry, I will send them to you."

I like the expression "poetry-robbed poetry." I think it probably means something like "poetry robbed of poetry," with deprecatory reference to his own translations. I suspect that he wrote in English because he did not want to use a misleading Japanese translation of "liberals." He meant the word in the nineteenth-century British sense, indicating tolerance and magnanimity.

I did not at the outset understand very clearly what he was talking about. I now think it was the rise of nationalism among nonviolent conservatives. The phenomenon itself and my awareness of it have been so gradual that they must inexorably and untidily slop over well beyond the date of the closing of my circle, which I have set as the conclusion to this narrative. So be it. The phenomenon is important, whatever my awareness of it may amount to. I now think that it is what Fukuda had in mind when he spoke, almost obsessively, albeit cryptically, of the need for Japanese and American intellectuals to get together.

There has always been a fringe of radical conservatism, worthy successor to the militarists and violent reactionaries of the two decades before 1945. Fukuda may have been, by the standards of the progressives, a "conservative-reactionary," a favorite catch-all of theirs, but he was in every respect a moderate. The radically reactionary conservative fringe did not much matter back in the days of Fukuda's famous polemic against the peace movement. Mostly it was an embarrassment. At almost any hour of the day and sometimes night, its sound trucks were inescapable at the Sukiyabashi crossing in downtown Tokyo. They were inescapable mostly because of the amplified harangues they sent forth. For me the fact that they always flew American flags was a big embarrassment. The police seemed to think that nothing could be done about the matter. Usually when the police do nothing it is because that is what they want to do. I suspect that they rather enjoyed our discomfiture. I did not wish such allies, but I had them.

The new conservatism is very different. It is essentially the conservatism that in an earlier day opposed the progressives. In a very vague and rough way, it is the conservatism of the Republicans in the United States. And, if it is to be taken at its word, it dislikes America every bit as much as the progressives did.

But I do not wish to call the entity "America." It is the West, and Western ideas. Back in the progressive days, when I sallied forth on a minor skirmish with the progressives, I was called "an American agent," and, when some anonymous columnist or other wished to deliver a particularly telling blow, "an agent of the C.I.A." Now people like me are called cultural imperialists. To the charge I have two answers, not wholly consistent with each other. One is that it is not very significant, since I have small chance indeed of ever putting together an empire. The other is: yes, I am. I think the Western ideals of tolerance and the nearest approach possible to equal rights are the best ones the human race has yet come up with. If supporting them means being a cultural imperialist, well, then, of course I am one. A recent remark by the last British governor of Hong Kong delights me: "I have often noted that the greatest beneficiary of the patriarchal family was, not surprisingly, the patriarch."

The anti-Western elements visible in recent Japanese conservatism are, it scarcely needs to be said, all tied up in a knot with its nationalism. This is unrealistic, not because it can never be made the basis of national policy, but because it reveals such an unrealistic view of the world. This is clearest in talk of the origins of the war.

It has become their common belief that the United States trapped Japan into going to war. I would say that this is a perpetuation of the Great Satan view of history so popular among the progressives. Again the United States is that creature.

What is the truth? It is very hard to say, but it is certainly not as simple as this view holds it to be. The events of the autumn of 1941 are complicated indeed, and I would not pretend to a specialized knowledge of them. The view of the new nationalists, however, seems patently false. They say that Japan reluctantly concluded early in December that war was inevitable. They blame the decision on the Hull Note of November 26. The note was an ultimatum, and ultimatums are by their nature communications which are unacceptable to their recipients. The United States had concluded that war was inevitable. So, it seems, had Japan, for by early December a fleet was already several days out at sea from the Kurile Islands on its way to Hawaii. The events leading up to the Hull Note receive little attention. This is gross oversimplification, whether or not it is dishonest. As with the progressivism of a half century earlier, the United States is made out to be altogether too clever and effective in its pursuit of evil. I sometimes ask nationalist acquaintances whether there is not an occasional speck of evil which the United States overlooks. It is a kind of irony that is not very successful with the Japanese.

The fact that in December, 1941, Japan was already at war with a very large part of the world is not hard for the nationalists to explain. It was a good war, they say. It was fought for purposes of liberating Asia from European and American imperialism. It was silly of the world to think that something must be done to help China. China was in the hands of its ablest and most dedicated helper.

It is arguable, certainly, that the Japanese invasion of the continent speeded up the end of European and American colonialism. The British and Americans would probably have gone away fairly soon anyway. The continental Europeans might have tried to hold on. So it is arguable. This is very different from saying, however, that, the purpose of Japanese expansion was anticolonial.

It may seem like a huge change. The progressives who seemed a half century ago to be sweeping everything before them have largely fallen silent. The Socialist Party, their chief institutional support, has collapsed, essentially under the weight of its useless, outmoded intellectual baggage. The conservatives have come to the fore. One element of continuity runs through it all, however: wooly thinking, and an uncertain grasp of reality. The nationalists of this day are every bit as wooly as were the internationalists of that day. For they were internationalists of a hare-brained sort. Their theme song was the Internationale.

Of the new nationalism one pleasing thing can be said: It brings feelings of release. The things it advocates are none of my business. This could not be said of the things the progressives advocated. If the nationalists want us to go home, fine, say I. Let us go home. If they wish us to stay but to be less of a burden on poor, long-suffering Okinawa, that is fine too. Let them find us places elsewhere in Japan. This would be virtually impossible, so strong is the not-in-my-backyard sentiment the whole country over. But that is their problem. Forty and fifty years ago I felt that I had to stand up and argue, if not fight. I do not any more. If we do go home, it will be what the Japanese want, and that will be nice. I will, to be sure, feel a little sorry for the Koreans, who will be scared stiff. It is quite possible that they will face no direct challenge from even a nationalistic nation to the east, but they may be forgiven for feeling that they face war on two fronts, and that help lies far away.

If the new nationalism brings this measure of consolation, it has not on the whole made life easier. Forty and fifty years ago the lines were clearly drawn. There was the enemy, including the dominant faction at the PEN during the Koestler affair, and there were friends, including the people—Hirabayashi, Takeyama, Fukuda, Hayashi—for whom I have indicated such great respect. Now the enemy lurks everywhere, in the office of every big company, on the staff of every news agency. It may be that "enemy" is too strong a term. "Vague hostility" might be better. It is everywhere, however.

Life should have been made easier, on the ideological front, by the collapse of the Soviet Union and the end of the Cold War. It has not. The conservatives are riddled with the new nationalism, and they are all we have. For this we may continue to curse the old progressives. They ruined the Socialist Party, which should be the opposition. Now all we have on that side of the spectrum is the Communists, who will never be voted into power.

I sometimes think that a communist government might be rather fun, provided it were to swear most solemnly that it will go away when it is told to. It would be better than a conservative government, at the very least, at tempering the arrogance of the bureaucracy.

By way of emphasizing the complexities of life under the new order, I might say that some of my best friends are conservative nationalists, and we have amusing and interesting conversations, quite without animus. This was not the case with the progressives of old. I hated them, and, when they paid any attention to me, they hated me. A discussion with one of the new conservatives never comes any closer to agreement than did one with the old progressives (see my views above on Ambassador Reischauer and his interrupted dialogue with the Left), but it is more amiable. By virtue of that fact, it is more difficult.

I continued to pay visits to Colorado during my New York years, generally in the winter and summer, on my way to and from Tokyo. One February I was kept in New York longer than usual and flew directly to San Francisco. I would not have dreamed that a flight between Kennedy Airport and San Francisco International Airport would take me almost exactly over my birthplace, but it did.

"The plane was but scantily occupied, and I could move about as fancy and the wish to peer down upon something took me. From the left side, the south side, of course, Douglas County was clearly on view. . . . I could see Castle Rock, and even Dugway. A bleak, frozen expanse of tundra Douglas County appeared to be, this February afternoon. Not a fit place for man or beast."

Dugway was a hill we had to ascend on the way from the village to the house in which I was born. It could be frightening, especially during winter. One winter, for better traction, I believe, or maybe it had something to do with the fuel supply, my father drove up it backwards, and the way was a dangerously winding one at the best of times. An automobile occasionally went over, but no one, I think, was ever killed. In the valley below was the best stand in the regions round of that loveliest of wild flowers, the Rocky Mountain columbine, the state flower of Colorado.

Occasionally my sister and I—my brother had no part in such doings—went out in search of what are called I think roots, although, except for Mexican ones, roots in Colorado are rather shallow.

"We went for a walk in the morning, she [my sister] and I. Bill Hier [her husband] took us up to the north flank of the limestone mesa south of the upper house [the house in which I was born—the Hiers lived in the lower house], and we climbed it, and crossed the dry top, and descended the other side, where he met us for exploration of Douglas County antiquities. . . .

"The antiquities consisted of a stone corral with a stone fence running up the mesa. I remember having come upon it in the course of my boyhood wanderings, but she discovered it for the first time last winter. Where the corral is protected by oak scrub, the stone walls, without benefit of mortar, must be very much as when they were put up, upwards of a century ago. [This entry is from August 1980.] I doubt that I much let my eye dwell upon it when I was a boy, though I did notice with interest. They are rather beautiful, and they must be about the earliest Western artifacts remaining in this Douglas County. What do you do when you have something of the sort on your hands? Let the world know, and risk plundering, which is what would come, in this land of rugged individualism? Or keep quiet? The latter course is certainly the easiest. But if it is taken perhaps no one will ever know except us few how hard they worked, the early German settlers."

This last statement is a bit of an exaggeration. Remnants of stone fences run all across the pastures in the eastern or German half of the county. I knew, however, of no better preserved remnant of an early farmyard. Another relic, ancient as ancient goes in those parts, is to be found on my sister's property, the boarded-over cabin said to be the birthplace of the earliest child of European descent born in the county. She was legendary, known to all of us as Mrs. Sam Smith. I am not sure I ever met her.

I told myself when I moved to New York that I would stay no longer than a decade. This had to do not with dislike for New York but with an awareness of its perils. I gave two reasons for wishing to take early retirement and leave the place: I did not want to live in New York when I was no longer able to run for my life; and I did not want to die in St. Luke's Hospital. There was jocular intent in both, but there was also truth in both. New York is not a good place for old people, and St. Luke's, just to the east of Columbia and the hospital where beneficiaries of its health insurance are expected to go, is grim. I could have left Columbia at any time, but by "early" I meant retirement at the age of sixty-five. In fact I lived in New York for eight years and a season, more or less.

I had plenty of time to decide where to go next. My list shortened to three places: Vancouver, San Francisco, and Honolulu. To go to Vancouver would have meant emigrating, and the Canadians were not in those days welcoming immigrants with open arms. I made inquiry at the Canadian embassy in Tokyo, and was received by those friendliest of people with a certain coolness. I went on being suspicious of San Francisco, which I had never really liked as well as everyone else seemed to like it. So it was Honolulu, which I had loved during the war and ever after, down to that point.

I will not say much of Honolulu, save that life there has been pleasant and not very exciting, and that, like many a cultural outpost, it takes itself too seriously. It contains the East-West Center, and thinks of itself as exactly that, the center of a huge entity known as the Pacific Rim. For someone going between New York or Los Angeles and Tokyo or Seoul or Peking, however, it is a detour. One starts fretting over local issues, such as sovereignty for indigenous Hawaiians. It is like fretting over the inadequacies of the baggage system at Denver International Airport. If I have any regrets over moving to Honolulu, it is because I do not like it as well now that I live there as when I did not live there. This might have also been true of Vancouver, however. Of San Francisco I set out with no hugely high regard.

I was honored with two celebrations for closing my circle. The first, slightly ahead of time, was held at a Chinese restaurant in New York and was organized by two good friends of Chinese ancestry on the Columbia faculty, Loretta Pan and Mary Hue. When I have characterized Columbia as unfriendly, I have referred to a general atmosphere and an institutional presence, and have not wished to suggest that everyone there was unfriendly.

The second, on the precise date of the rounding of the circle, February 11, 1981, was in Palo Alto, and had all the trimmings. I was all dressed up in red. I was an infant setting forth on a second infancy, which expression should not be taken for the same thing as "second childhood." Maribel Kilmartin, the hostess that most memorable evening, had found the trimmings in Berkeley.

"I helped Maribel clean up, and then, on foot, went shopping for her at the bottom of the terrace. Being there at the bottom, I went yet farther, down California Avenue to the [Southern Pacific] tracks. The spring flowers were lovely and the air was soft. . . .

"In the evening was my *kanreki* party, and a fine old party it was, too. About fifty people assembled, and Bill McCullough [once a colleague at Stanford, then at Berkeley, and now deceased] gave a splendid toast, warm and erudite, informing people of the nature of the *kanreki,* and of my works. Maribel had acquired a *chanchanko* [a red jacket] which I wore through most of the evening, and one of those silly pancake caps, which I wore intermittently, chiefly to have my picture taken. I kept thinking: people do not bore me here. . . . The interests of many of them are nearer mine, of course, but the matter is more general, having to do with a certain broadness of vision. . . . And people do not complain. Everyone was most friendly and felicitatory, and I got numbers of presents, such as a dear little frog from Pony [Pomona Mitchell, an old Palo Alto friend, whose divorced husband was a San Francisco magnate]. It was, I say, a fine old party, almost . . . enough to make a person wish to be sixty."

INDEX